ACADEMIC

FREEDOM

IN THE AGE OF

THE UNIVERSITY

BY WALTER P. METZGER

COLUMBIA UNIVERSITY PRESS

NEW YORK

Academic Freedom in the Age of the College, by Richard Hofstadter, and *Academic Freedom in the Age of the University,* by Walter P. Metzger, were originally published in one volume entitled *The Development of Academic Freedom in the United States,* by Richard Hofstadter and Walter P. Metzger.

PREFACE

ACADEMIC FREEDOM has become one of the central issues of our time. It has been our aim in this volume to write an account of the problem of academic freedom in American colleges and universities from the founding of the first college to the recent past. While we have tried to provide historical perspective on the current struggle over intellectual freedom in higher education, we have tried also to avoid the pitfall of interpreting the past solely from the standpoint of present issues and current anxieties. Ours is an analytical history, not a full-throated polemic for academic freedom. We have no desire to conceal an ineluctable prejudice on behalf of freedom of thought, and we hope and expect that this inquiry will be a history, not an autopsy. Our commitment to freedom has no doubt affected in many ways our treatment of the problem, but our foremost intention has been to shed new light on the history of the academic man and the complex circumstances under which he has done his work, in the faith that an enlargement of understanding will in the end be an enlargement of freedom.

One of our earliest decisions in planning this work was to make it more than a running account of "cases." To write only about the outstanding violations of freedom would be to treat the story of academic freedom as though it were nothing but the story of academic suppression. The cases are, in a sense, the pathology of the problem. The distortions that would arise from dealing with them alone are comparable to those that would be found in a history of the labor movement telling only of strikes, a history of science telling only of the encroachments of theology, or a history of political democracy devoted only to its defeats. It is, of course, an important part of our concern to learn what forces in society have ranged themselves against the freedom of teaching and research and what successes they have scored; but we have also been interested to know what freedom has meant to successive generations of academic men, to what extent they have achieved it, and what factors in academic life itself, as well as in American culture at large, have created and sustained it.

We consider it as much a part of our task to explain why freedom exists as to explain why it has been limited.

Cases, moreover, serve only as guides to the nature of the problem; they do not exhaust its meaning. To ask what it was that men wanted to be free about, why the freedoms they claimed were considered by other men to be improper or dangerous, what arguments were employed on both sides, and where the power lay to settle the issues is to pass from the academic institutions to the community that supported them, set their goals, and (in America at least) governed them. Such questions have led us to try to tell our story against the background of the religious, intellectual, and political issues that gave to academic controversies their special urgency and broad social significance. They have taken us not only into the discussion of such matters as the development of the American form of academic government and the professional organization of academic men, but also into the educational policies of religious denominations, the history of theological controversies, the rise of Darwinism in American thought, and the relations between men of business and men of learning.

Broad as our scope has been, we have not dealt with every aspect of the theme. We have discussed primarily the freedom of faculty members and have dealt with the issue of freedom for students only at those points where the two have converged. In our minds the history of student freedoms and student discipline is a matter of comparable importance, but it is a large and in many respects a separate question that deserves a treatise of its own. We have also confined ourselves to college and university education. Those who are interested in the history of freedom of teaching in schools below college grade will be enlightened by Howard K. Beale's two earlier volumes, *A History of Freedom of Teaching in American Schools* (1941) and *Are American Teachers Free?* (1936). Finally, we have brought our story to a close without treating, except by occasional reference, the current crisis in academic freedom; but this is analyzed in the companion volume sponsored by the American Academic Freedom Project, Professor Robert M. MacIver's *Academic Freedom in Our Time*.

There is a sharp difference between the main concern of Part One, which deals with the American college down to the period just after the Civil War, and that of Part Two, which deals with the modern American university. Part One deals with an age overshadowed by religious and theological questions, Part Two with an age preoccupied with science and social problems. Part One begins with an introductory chapter touching upon some phases of the history of intellectual freedom in the universities of Western Europe up to the time of the Reformation. No reader should imagine that this chapter presumes to be even an abbreviated history of intellectual freedom in the universities of Europe—several volumes would be necessary to accomplish that task—but it seemed desirable to touch upon this background in order to bring the long history of this issue, and the various forms it has taken, to the attention of readers who might be excessively preoccupied with recent events and American conditions. Moreover, while it was clear that whatever we might write on the subject of academic freedom before the Reformation would be more than ordinarily incomplete and inadequate, we did not want to indulge ourselves in the provincialism of beginning our story as though the problem originated with the founding of Harvard College in 1636.

The rest of Part One deals with what might be called the prehistory of academic freedom in our own country. It treats of a period when colleges were under denominational control and there were hardly any universities worthy of the name. In the denominational colleges the problem of academic freedom as we now understand it was hardly posed, for the sponsors of such colleges, on the whole, did not intend that they should be to any significant degree intellectually free, and the men who taught in them had for the most part only the slenderest aspirations toward intellectual freedom. Our inquiry into the severe limitations upon freedom in the old colleges should not be taken as a total indictment of their services to their students and the community or as a denial of their right to exist. But in the pre-Civil War era the denominational colleges not only accorded an inadequate measure of freedom to those who taught and studied in them, but their friends and sponsors were disposed to choke, sabotage, and destroy such attempts as were made to establish larger and more capacious institutions supporting advanced scholarship and providing the conditions of university freedom. Despite these limitations, collegiate education before the Civil War had its own merits and on occasion its significant controversies and gestures toward academic freedom; the period was also one of educational agitation when most advanced thinkers presaged the coming era of university development.

Since religious commitments and sectarian aspirations did so much to create the restrictive atmosphere of the old college and to cramp the early work of the rising university, religious leaders figure in an exceptionally prominent way among the opponents of intellectual freedom in the first half of our story. We hope that no reader will infer from this a commitment to aggressive secularism on the part of the authors. While there are still circumstances under which religious interests can restrict the free expression to which the secular mind is entitled, we are also aware that there is now some likelihood that here or there the unconsciously secularist bias of our formally "religious" but too often spiritually hollow society will impinge upon the full development of the genuinely religious student or scholar. Nor have we forgotten that some of the same religious denominations that a hundred years ago were culpable for their indifference or opposition to intellectual freedom have in recent years produced some of its most impassioned and powerful spokesmen.

With the coming of the modern university, the theme of Part Two, the entire situation was transformed within the life span of a single generation. The university, not the college, became the model institution. While in the ante-bellum period the very existence of the entrenched denominational colleges limited or checked the emergent universities, in the later period the development of universities reshaped in some measure all but the most backward colleges. The emergence of the university was nothing less than an educational revolution in the United States. Research took a place along with teaching as a major function. The methods and concepts of science displaced the authority of religion. The academic profession took on, for the first time in a full measure, the character, aspirations, and standards of a learned profession. Within the university, the growth of resources, the proliferation of activities, the assemblage of large faculties gave impetus to bureaucratization—to tenure rules, formal procedures of promotion and dismissal, the delegation of authority. A self-conscious and well-formulated rationale for academic freedom appeared, framed in terms to fit the new realities of academic life. Aspirations for intellectual freedom that had been expressed in the denominational era only by pioneers or rebels in the colleges were now understood and endorsed by powerful figures of the educational world. While freedom in the modern university was, as it always has been, only imperfectly realized in practice, those who would oppose and limit freedom were now for the first time in our history put upon the moral and intellectual defensive. It may put some of our current difficulties into perspective to realize that the academic freedom which is now under fire is not an ancient prerogative but an acquisition of relatively recent date.

It is impossible to acknowledge by name all the scholars—almost three score of them—who have given freely of their time by reading drafts, offering criticism, catching errors, and providing us with access to materials, but our sincere gratitude goes out to them. Without their help this study would have been far less adequate. We are indebted above all to Louis M. Rabinowitz, who conceived the American Academic Freedom Project and brought to it not only ample resources but the close interest of a generous heart and mind. We are grateful for our association with Robert M. MacIver, the director of the American Academic Freedom Project, whose advice and criticism have been of value on many occasions, and who has consistently shown a quality that must be recommended to administrators of academic research projects—a wise and cordial regard for individuality and independence. Finally, without the help of our research assistants, Francis Wilson Smith, Joseph Katz, and Juan Linz, this work would have taken far longer and would have rested on a much less sufficient base of information.

A word on the nature of our collaboration. Although each author has assumed full and final responsibility for a part of the text—Hofstadter for Part One, Metzger for Part Two—the interpretive structure of this volume and all the major problems that have arisen have been objects of frequent discussion, as the text has been of mutual criticism. Thus, except for the fact that it contains no collaborative prose, this has been in every sense a collaborative enterprise. On most of the broad issues the authors have found themselves—not always at the beginning but usually at the end of discussion—in substantial agreement on the meaning of the facts. If there are still marginal inconsistencies in interpretation or in tone, they remain in the text not through an oversight but as a consequence of our resolve not to try to submerge individual differences for the sake of an unnecessary uniformity.

RICHARD HOFSTADTER

WALTER P. METZGER

Columbia University
in the City of New York
April, 1955

Note: The Preface of this volume is reproduced here exactly as it appeared in Hofstadter and Metzger, *The Development of Academic Freedom in the United States,* of which "Part One" is now *Academic Freedom in the Age of the College,* by Richard Hofstadter, and "Part Two" is *Academic Freedom in the Age of the University,* by Walter P. Metzger.

CONTENTS

ACADEMIC FREEDOM

IN THE AGE OF THE UNIVERSITY

I: THE OLD REGIME AND THE
EDUCATIONAL REVOLUTION

Between the years 1865 and 1890 a revolution in American higher education took place. Ideas that had been debated in pre-Civil War journals—the elective system, graduate instruction, scientific courses—became educational realities. New mansions of learning, more imposing than any the nation had seen, were built at Cornell, Johns Hopkins, Clark, Stanford, and Chicago; new towers were added to Harvard, Columbia, Yale, and Princeton, to Wisconsin, Michigan, and Illinois. Along with the establishment of new institutions and the renovation of old went the adoption of new academic goals. To criticize and augment as well as to disseminate the tradition-at-hand became an established function—a great departure for a system that had aimed primarily at cultural conservation. To serve the whole community in its vast variety of needs became a creditable aspiration—an important innovation for a system that had served mainly the limited needs of the learned professions. The institutional setting, the educational objective, and the meaning and status of academic freedom are, as we have seen, intimately connected. Inevitably, therefore, during this quarter-century, the problem of academic freedom was as drastically revised as its context.[1]

Every revolution is born in an old regime, and every old regime, while it clings to exalted ideals, is undermined by prosaic events. This was true of the university revolution and of the old regime from which it sprang, the denominational college. Founded by evangelical fervor, the denominational college allied Christian piety and humanistic study against the skeptical rationalism of the Enlightenment. A center of culture on crude frontiers, it endeavored to endow a haphazard society

---

[1] To point out that the connection between the institutional setting and the ideal of academic freedom has not been adequately studied for this period is to call attention once more to the vast untilled areas in the historiography of this subject. The work that comes closest to filling the gap is Howard K. Beale's *A History of Freedom of Teaching in American Schools* (New York, 1941).

with religious truths and values. Taking it all in all, the denominational institution was not by any means unsuccessful in these difficult undertakings. But like all other old regimes, the denominational college in the period between 1800 and 1860 faced two commonplace problems with which it could not cope—the problem of internal disorder and the problem of financial insolvency. In attempting to resolve these problems, it developed practices and devices that only weakened its authority and cohesion. The need to check constant student disorder led to the growth of faculty (as opposed to trustee) control over discipline and instruction. The effort to offset mounting deficits resulted in the organization of alumni into collegiate philanthropic associations. By a paradoxical turn that was not without parallel or precedent, the remedies proved harmful to the regime which they were intended to fortify. The first remedy, by diffusing responsibility, in time destroyed the college's unitary purpose. The other, by summoning secular support, in time weakened its religious aspirations. And neither completely solved the basic problems which were, in the last analysis, symptoms of the college's failure to answer the needs of society. The story of academic freedom under the old regime can be plotted in terms of these paramount ideals, these unresolvable problems, and these self-defeating remedies.

THE EDUCATIONAL IDEALS OF THE OLD REGIME

The American college in the first half of the nineteenth century was centered in tradition. It looked to antiquity for the tools of thought, to Christianity for the by-laws of living; it supplied furniture and discipline for the mind, but constrained intellectual adventure. Like most institutions anchored to tradition, the ante-bellum college [2] was also paternalistic and authoritarian. In honoring the past and depreciating the pres-

---

[2] We use "ante-bellum" to denote all the colleges in the period between 1800 and 1860; "denominational" to denote all except the state universities.

[3] Whatever concessions were made in the curricula to modern languages, modern sciences and modern history, disdain for the interests and achievements of the present was deeply characteristic of this philosophy. Noah Porter wrote: "We hold the opinion very earnestly that upon the retention and successful regulation of classical study more than upon any single feature of the college economy hangs the question for this country whether we shall continue as a people to respect and honor what is noble in the past or shall give ourselves up to the unsteady and often mistaken guidance of the unreflecting and uninstructed present." *The American Colleges and the American Public* (New Haven, 1870), p. 273.

ent,[3] it drew the doubtful conclusion that age best imparts its wisdom when youth surrenders its style. Students took prescribed courses and recited their lessons by rote; professors acted like schoolmasters, drillmasters, and prisonkeeps. The dreary assumptions of American pedagogy in this period were hardly touched by the romantic mood of transcendentalism, or by the democratic faith of Jacksonianism. Despite the triumph of the ideal of perfectibility in the outer world of affairs, the academy lived in the inexorable presence of Sin, which only mental exertion and piety were presumed to temper or expiate. "Man is born free and is everywhere in chains," and its gentler Emersonian equivalent, "Whoso would be a man, must be a nonconformist," were never the cardinal mottoes of these colleges. The theory of collegiate education was perfected by Yale and Princeton—Phoenicias of the educational world—and was disseminated in their academic colonies through their graduate sons. Whether one reads the *Yale Report* of 1828 or Noah Porter's *The American Colleges and the American Public* (published in 1870), one encounters a consistent spirit and argument: the preceptive importance of religion, the disciplinary advantage of the classics, and above all, the waywardness and immaturity of youth that called for precepts and discipline.[4]

This triad of assumptions—traditionalism as an educational goal, "stamping in" as a pedagogical method, the contumacy of youth as a major expectation—effectively stifled the desire for academic freedom in the ante-bellum colleges. First of all, the emphasis on traditional subject matter and mechanical drill discouraged comment from the professor's rostrum on the burning issues of the day. To this there was one exception: the course on moral philosophy, which had replaced moral theology as the science of conduct at the end of the eighteenth cen-

[4] "Original Papers in Relation to a Course of Liberal Education," *American Journal of Science and Arts,* XV (January, 1829), 297–351; Porter, *American Colleges,* p. 98 and *passim.* The former was establishing policy, the latter desperately defending it; hence the differences in overtone and emphasis. The first report was not so concerned about the fate of religion in the colleges, resting in the assurance that it was secure; Porter, writing after Darwin, was apprehensive.

There is a great body of literature on these two important educational papers. A concise statement and analysis covering the *Yale Report* from the progressive point of view can be found in R. Freeman Butts, *The College Charts Its Course: Historical Conceptions and Current Proposals* (New York, 1939), pp. 118–25. A point of view more sympathetic to conservatism may be found in the section on Noah Porter in George W. Pierson's history of Yale, *Yale College: An Educational History, 1871–1921* (New Haven, 1952), pp. 57 ff.

tury.[5] This course—and its later offshoots, constitutional history,[6] political philosophy,[7] and political economy [8]—dealt with some of the problems of active life, particularly when they were taught by the college president.[9] But moral philosophy was a dessert for seniors, to be taken only after the less appetizing studies of Greek verbs, syllogistic logic, and English grammar; and it was the ingenious or conscience-driven tutor who could insinuate living problems while drilling in the *Graeca Majora*. More than this, the college with rigid standards for student piety also had rigid conventions for professorial propriety. While the colleges were custodians of student morals, professors had to be exemplars of good behavior. As long as students lived under parental rules, professors had to dwell close to or in the colleges in order to be able to enforce them.[10] Despotism limits the despot: the other aspect of parental power is the burden of parental responsibility. Freedom, aca-

[5] L. L. Bernard and J. S. Bernard, "A Century of Progress in the Social Sciences," *Social Forces*, XI (May, 1933), 488–505.

[6] The publication of the various national and state constitutional documents fostered the development of this subject after 1825. Treatises on law and government gradually increased in number to accommodate the growing number of courses in constitutional law and constitutional history.

[7] The two outstanding works in the field of political philosophy were Francis Lieber's *Political Ethics* (1838) and Frederick Grimke's *Nature and Tendency in Free Institutions* (1848).

[8] Chairs in this subject were established at Columbia College in 1817 and soon afterward at the College of South Carolina, Dickinson College, and William and Mary. It was taught by such prominent men as John McVickar of Columbia College, Thomas Cooper of the College of South Carolina, Henry Vethake of Dickinson (later of the University of Pennsylvania), Thomas R. Dew of William and Mary, and George Tucker of the University of Virginia. Such issues as the tariff, money, currency, and banks were touched on.

[9] Gladys Bryson, "The Comparable Interests of the Old Moral Philosophy and the Modern Social Sciences," *Social Forces*, XI (October, 1932), 19–27; George P. Schmidt, *The Old Time College President* (New York, 1930), pp. 108–45.

[10] That the residential requirement rankled is seen in Edward Everett's unhappiness over his forced seclusion at Cambridge. After his sojourn in Germany, he dearly wished to stay in the more congenial and intellectually stimulating atmosphere of Boston and to go to Cambridge only for his classes. Ticknor, as a very special dispensation, had won that privilege. But in 1822 the Overseers of Harvard, voting on Everett's application, decided that "it would be highly detrimental to the interests of the University to depart from the ancient usage of requiring the constant residence of those professors, whose offices, from the nature of them, are essentially connected with the necessary studies of the undergraduates." Everett remained at Harvard, chafing at this restriction, until his election to Congress ended his connection with the college. Paul Revere Frothingham, *Edward Everett: Orator and Statesman* (Boston, 1925), pp. 72–75. Undoubtedly the majority of American professors would have considered Cambridge the epitome of sophistication compared with the isolated hamlets in which their own colleges were situated.

demic or otherwise, requires a private sphere where prescriptive codes do not apply, and the discipline of the ante-bellum college was the eternal foe of privacy.

The temper of this age was factious and zealous: public issues like those of Republicanism vs. Federalism, abolitionism vs. slavery, free trade vs. protectionism, were fraught with an almost religious emotion. It is thus the more remarkable that academic cases in this period were rarely joined over questions of intramural utterance. When, for example, Professor Benjamin Hedrick of North Carolina was dismissed in 1856 for supporting Fremont, he was not accused of having aired his views in class; [11] Francis Bowen, rejected by the Harvard Board of Overseers, presumably for articles favoring the compromise of 1850 and opposing Magyar independence, was not charged with the crime of trying to convince his students.[12] To be sure, the colloquies of the classroom are almost as scantily recorded as the dialogue of the confessional, whereas a speech or published essay is in the public ear or eye. Nevertheless, one gets the impression that the teacher *qua* teacher was far less willing to engage in controversy than the teacher *qua* citizen, and that this was in part related to the colleges' educational norms. The contentious Thomas Cooper of South Carolina College, a firebrand of anticlericalism, repeatedly swore that he had not in any way tried to influence the religious opinions of his students.[13] President Robert Hamilton Bishop of Miami University, while fighting within the councils of the Presbyterian church against the institution of slavery, tolerated but would not join the antislavery society on campus.[14] The Amherst faculty, opposed to abolition but favoring the settlement of Negroes in Africa, felt it "inexpedient" to allow students to organize either abolitionist or colonization societies.[15] Francis Lieber, privately a staunch opponent of slavery,

[11] Kemp P. Battle, *History of the University of North Carolina, 1789–1909* (2 vols.; Raleigh, 1912), I, 654–59. See also Clement Eaton, *Freedom of Thought in the Old South* (New York, 1951), p. 203.

[12] Samuel Eliot Morison, "Francis Bowen, An Early Test of Academic Freedom in Massachusetts," *Proceedings of the Massachusetts Historical Society*, LXVI (February, 1936), 507–11.

[13] Dumas Malone, *The Public Life of Thomas Cooper, 1783–1839* (New Haven, 1926), p. 338.

[14] James H. Rodabaugh, "Miami University, Calvinism and the Anti-Slavery Movement," *Ohio State Archaeological and Historical Quarterly*, XLVIII (1939), 66–73.

[15] Claude M. Fuess, *Amherst, the Story of a New England College* (Boston, 1935), pp. 110–11.

granted in a letter to Calhoun that he had no right "to use my chair for propagandism of specific and personal views." [16]

How closely connected were professorial and student freedoms was demonstrated by one academic-freedom case in this period. In 1833 an antislavery society was formed at Lane Theological Seminary in Cincinnati by students and a number of the faculty. The board of trustees, composed of solid businessmen and some clergymen, banned this society, stating that "education must be completed before the young are fitted to engage in the collisions of active life." This was a standard reaction of trustees to student initiative in the realm of ideas: what made the statement inappropriate, however, was the fact that the "young" in this case happened to be rather old—thirty of these seminarians were over the age of twenty-six. Nor were they of mood or mind to accept the stricture of the trustees. "Free discussion, being a duty," they announced, "is consequently a right, and as such, is inherent and inalienable. It is *our* right. It *was* before we entered Lane Seminary; privileges we might and did relinquish; advantages we might and did receive. But this *right* the institution 'could neither give nor take away.' " After firing this broadside, the students removed in a body to Oberlin, where they won the concession that their faculty (which included a professor who had been dismissed from Lane) would supervise them without interference from the trustees.[17] Unfortunately, this case was altogether atypical. Elsewhere students were more likely to rebel against the food served in Commons than against the repression of freedom of speech. A mass boycott of this kind, reminiscent of the medieval universities, was never to be repeated. And the moral that it taught—that *Lehrfreiheit* and *Lernfreiheit* were closely related—was not one that the parent-professors of the college would quickly learn or wish to apply.

In short, the current assumptions of educational psychology stymied free discussion in the classroom and discouraged bold intellectual excursions. On the one hand, since the college student was regarded as morally deficient or immature, the college teacher had to render a firm decision on all the normative issues he raised. The weight of this responsi-

[16] Joseph Dorfman and Rexford G. Tugwell, "Francis Lieber: German Scholar in America," *Columbia University Quarterly*, XXX (1938), 169. Also, Frank Freidel, *Francis Lieber: Nineteenth Century Liberal* (Baton Rouge, 1947), pp. 115–43.

[17] Robert S. Fletcher, *A History of Oberlin College* (Oberlin, Ohio, 1943), I, 150–78.

bility kept the instructor from venturing very far from received and safe opinions. On the other hand, the college student was also regarded as intellectually innocent and impressionable—an assumption that had a close if paradoxical affinity to the supposition that he was totally depraved. Great care had to be taken lest, by some irreverent remark, he be misguided by his teachers and led astray. The college in America could not be a market place of ideas so long as it regarded its students as both gullible and perverse. For the conclusion is inescapable: if students are both iron and clay, it is wasteful or it is rash to treat them to controversy.

SCIENCE UNDER THE OLD REGIME

We have touched upon the demand for academic freedom in the area of classroom instruction; we have now to see that the demand for academic freedom was just as slight in the area of research. In this area, however, another set of inhibitions operated, as can be seen when we consider the status of scientific studies in the ante-bellum colleges.

It has already been pointed out that the curriculum of the American colleges had never been closed against the sciences, despite the dominance of classical subjects and the ruling interest in religion.[18] That religion and science could coexist within Protestantism had been demonstrated as early as 1642, when President Dunster of Harvard made provision for a course in astronomy, and it was reaffirmed by the increasingly large place assumed by physics, chemistry, and geography in the Harvard curriculum of the next century and a half.[19] It is true that the intense scientific interests of the Enlightenment, as reflected in the curricula of the University of Pennsylvania and King's College, were not sustained in the era of religious reaction. Yet even in the early nineteenth century, mineralogy, chemistry, geology, botany, and zoology made their way into many courses of study;[20] "natural philosophy" and "natural history" were taught in the most orthodox centers;[21] Amherst and Union pioneered in offering

[18] See Chap. IV.
[19] Theodore Hornberger, *Scientific Thought in the American Colleges, 1638–1800* (Austin, Texas, 1945).
[20] Louis Franklin Snow, *The College Curriculum in the United States* (New York, 1907).
[21] For an example of the potpourri of subjects covered in the typical natural philosophy course, see James Renwick's text, *Outlines of Natural Philosophy* (New York, 1826). At Columbia Renwick taught mechanics, ballistics, hydrostatics, climatology, meteorology, electricity, optics, and astronomy—all in a half-year

parallel courses in science and classics; [22] Timothy Dwight, champion of Christianity against all that smacked of heresy, put Benjamin Silliman, Sr., in the chair of chemistry at Yale.[23] After 1840, scientific courses began to be differentiated and considerable specialization was allowed. By no means, then, was the college curriculum of the early nineteenth century as archaic and as rigid as later reformers thought it had been, nor was science as under-represented as its votaries usually claimed.

But the significant fact is that, with exceptions made for a few unusual institutions and men, the addition of scientific studies to the curriculum did not bring about a free flowering of scientific research. Instruction was didactic and catechetical, or else demonstrations were used merely to cause wonder or to amuse.[24] Scientific speculation was diverted either to natural theology, where the conceptual framework was given, or to survey, classification, and invention, where the conceptual content was slight. Science, in short, was integrated into the disciplinary and conservational goals of the college, and if there was gain in knowledge organized and seen whole, there was no gain in intellectual friction.

Three factors blighted the courage and imagination of college science in the ante-bellum period. First, and least important, was the emphasis on utility and practicality which was general at that time. In the eighteenth century the "promotion of useful knowledge" had not been by any means

---

sequence. For the subjects covered in natural history, see W. and M. Smallwood's discussion of William Dandridge Peck's "Lectures on Natural History" in *Natural History and the American Mind* (New York, 1941), pp. 302 ff. Peck lectured on botany, ornithology, ichthyology, and entomology at Harvard.

[22] George P. Schmidt, "Intellectual Crosscurrents in American Colleges," *American Historical Review*, XLII (October, 1936), 46–67. Fuess, *Amherst*, p. 99.

[23] Charles E. Cuningham, *Timothy Dwight, 1752–1817* (New York, 1942), pp. 198 ff.

[24] This is exemplified by the retarded development of laboratory techniques in teaching and research. Russell H. Chittenden summarizes the state of experimentalism in the colleges in the year 1845: "The study of the physical and natural sciences in the United States, at this date, was exceedingly simple and very elementary in character. It was confined to undergraduates, for graduate students were practically unknown at that period, and was limited to textbook work, supplemented by lectures and some demonstrations. Laboratories, as we know them today, did not exist and consequently there were no opportunities for the pursuit of scientific studies by the method which alone will give satisfactory results. . . . Indeed it is probably not far from the truth to state that some, and perhaps many, of the professors of science in the early years of their appointment had never done experimental work." *History of the Sheffield Scientific School of Yale University, 1896–1922* (2 vols.; New Haven, 1928), I, 25–26. See also John F. Fulton, "Science in American Universities, with Particular Reference to Harvard and Yale," *Bulletin of the History of Medicine*, XX (July, 1946), 97–110.

the sole justification for scientific studies. In the pansophist ideal of the American Philosophical Society, in the encyclopedic interests of men like Benjamin Rush, David Rittenhouse, and Benjamin Franklin, in the speculative materialism of Cadwallader Colden, Joseph Priestley, and Thomas Cooper, one finds an interest in nature as law side by side with an interest in science as technique.[25] It was only after 1830 that a truly rigorous practicality was demanded. The Jacksonian transformation of American society—the decline of aristocratic standards, the liberation of entrepreneurial energies, the conquest of the open continent, the growth of a new business class—made profits and efficiency, the foes of intellectual curiosity, predominant social values.[26] It was then that charities and benefactions went primarily toward the useful sciences: toward hospitals rather than medical laboratories, toward engineering rather than basic physics. It was then that government subsidies favored the more exploitable sciences—geological surveys were preferred to studies of geological theory; engineering at the Military Academy was subsidized, rather than science at the National Institution for the Promotion of Science.[27]

Up to a point, the ante-bellum colleges were able to resist these utili-

[25] The practical interests of the Enlightenment have been overemphasized. A genuine concern with theory and basic research was there, overlaid perhaps by the optimistic faith that all truths had ultimate and important applications. See I. Bernard Cohen, "How Practical Was Benjamin Franklin's Science?" *Pennsylvania Magazine of History and Biography*, LXIX (October, 1945), 284–93; Richard H. Shryock, "American Indifference to Basic Science during the Nineteenth Century," *Archives Internationales d'Histoire des Sciences*, V (1948), 50–65; Harold A. Larrabee, "Naturalism in America," in *Naturalism and the Human Spirit* (New York, 1944), pp. 331–38; Richard H. Shryock, "Factors Affecting Medical Research in the United States, 1800–1900," *Bulletin of the Chicago Society of Medical History*, V (July, 1943), 7.

[26] Not until about 1900 did the implications of basic research for technology become more apparent to business leaders. Bernal's sharp antithesis between science as a contemplative art and science as an instrumental art, and his dictum that "the history of science shows that both the drive which led to scientific discoveries and the means by which those discoveries were made were material needs and material instruments," underplays the importance of abstract thought in both the motivation and application of science. J. D. Bernal, *The Social Function of Science* (London, 1939), p. 6.

[27] The interest of the states in subsidizing surveys was almost entirely given to prospecting and the opening up of exploitative possibilities, rather than in the discovery of guiding principles. See Charles S. Sydnor, "State Geological Surveys in the Old South," in David Kelley Jackson, ed., *American Studies in Honor of William Kenneth Boyd* (Durham, N.C., 1940), pp. 86–109. Exceptions should be noted: Lardner Vanuxem's stratigraphical correlations (South Carolina) and William Barton Rogers's study of the formation of the Appalachian chain (Virginia). See George P. Merrill, *The First One Hundred Years of American Geology* (New Haven, 1924).

tarian pressures. They had too much of the Aristotelian contempt for common industrial pursuits to turn themselves into schools of applied science.[28] In some of the Eastern colleges engineering courses were added, but Harvard's example of applying a gift for a school of engineering toward a school of general science (1847),[29] and the widespread retention of the term "natural philosophy" in the titles of scientific professorships,[30] are indications of the genteel aversion to technology that persisted throughout this period.

But the colleges did succumb to practicality in their preference for scientific teaching over scientific research. Just as the clinical demands on the medical doctor retarded original research in that profession, so the pedagogical and monitorial demands on the college scientist withered his interest in investigation. Required to live in a world of "dorms" and early-morning chapel, the college scientist was far removed from the professional climate of the scientific societies. Since academic honors hinged on his work as a teacher, he lacked the energy and time for that systematic investigation which, rather than occasional observation, is the method of scientific research. Indeed the idea had a certain currency among college officials that research was positively harmful to effective teaching. As late as 1857, a committee of the Columbia College Board of Trustees pointed to the fact that three professors "wrote books" as a possible cause of the low state of the college.[31] It cannot, of course, be contended that the Princeton of Joseph Henry, Albert B. Dod, and Stephen Alexander, the Yale of Silliman, Olmsted, and Dana, the Harvard of Agassiz and Gray, were antipathetic to research. Yet even these institutions, which after 1840 forged far ahead of all others in America in the study of the physical and natural sciences, invariably placed teaching first. In 1869, Charles W. Eliot, the new president of Harvard, declared that his institution did not possess, "with the single exception of the endowment of the Observatory

[28] Madge E. Pickard, "Government and Science in the United States: Historical Background," *Journal of the History of Medicine*, I (April, 1946), 254.

[29] Samuel E. Morison, *Three Centuries of Harvard* (Cambridge, Mass., 1936), pp. 279–80.

[30] Thus Silliman was professor of chemistry and natural philosophy and Denison Olmsted was professor of natural philosophy and astronomy at Yale; Gurdon Saltonstall was professor of mathematics and natural philosophy at Alabama (1831–33); in 1837 F. A. P. Barnard occupied a chair of "mathematics, natural philosophy and astronomy" at the same institution; Hitchcock at Amherst was professor of natural theology and geology. See Howard Mumford Jones, *Ideas in America* (Cambridge, Mass., 1944), p. 283n.

[31] Frederick Paul Keppel, *Columbia* (New York, 1914), p. 7.

. . . a single fund primarily intended to secure to men of learning the leisure and means to prosecute original researches," and that "the prime business of American professors in this generation must be regular and assiduous class teaching." [32] The dictum was not to be obeyed—a new era of college and university science was about to begin—but the priority Eliot gave to teaching reflected prevailing conditions.

More important than the practical bent of college science in limiting its range of speculation was the doctrinal moralism of the colleges. We use this phrase as a caption for the discussion of two assumptions which, if not often explicitly acknowledged, were seldom in this period controverted.

The first assumption was that character was a function of belief. "To say a man is an Infidel," wrote Timothy Dwight the elder, "is understood of course as a declaration that he is plainly an immoral man." [33] The logic was St. Paul's essentially: anyone who was "faithless" in religion was, beyond doubt and by definition, "faith-less" in all other affairs. That this assumption is still maintained in certain secular universities of our own day becomes readily apparent if one substitutes the word "disloyal" for the word "faithless." In both cases it is assumed that a man who believes certain things cannot be fit for his office: the premises force the conclusion, and the disparities that actually exist between a man's belief and his behavior are not taken into account. This assumption, however, had even greater force and wider appeal in the ante-bellum period (where a paternal interest in morals was combined with a vital concern for creed) than it has today. Then it was applied to professorial appointments in such a way as to exclude religious nonconformists, even where open religious tests were impolitic or forbidden. Timothy Dwight barred from the Yale Medical School one of the leading medical practitioners of the time, Dr. Nathan Smith, until the latter recanted his doubts of the truth of divine revelation. [34] The Presbyterians in Virginia kept Thomas Cooper out of the state university by attacking the chronic intemperance which they thought could safely be inferred from his resolute religious skepticism. [35] In short, where belief is the main clue to character, creed can become a

---

[32] Charles W. Eliot, "Inaugural Address," in *Educational Reform: Essays and Addresses* (New York, 1898), p. 27.

[33] Timothy Dwight, *The Duty of Americans at the Present Crisis* (New Haven, 1798).

[34] Cuningham, *Timothy Dwight*, pp. 216–19.

[35] Malone, *Public Life of Thomas Cooper*, pp. 240–41.

test for employment, not on the mean ground of sectarianism, but rather on the high ground of righteousness.

More particularly damaging to the interests of science was the second tenet of doctrinal moralism, the assumption that an idea was warranted and verified by proof of its moral advantages. This kind of moral pragmatism thoroughly imbued the thinking of scientists in the ante-bellum colleges. It was seen in the attitude of Benjamin Silliman, Sr., the so-called "Nestor of American science," when he took exception to the theories of James Woodhouse, a pioneer American chemist. Silliman thought Woodhouse's theories were incorrect because they could have impious and harmful consequences. Particularly did he object to the "levity and ridicule" with which Woodhouse treated "the idea that the visitations of the yellow fever might be visitations of God for the sins of the people." Woodhouse should not have forgotten that "physical causes [of disease] may be the moral agents of the Almighty." [36] In reviewing Robert Chambers's *Vestiges of the Natural History of Creation,* an adumbration of the theory of evolution, Professor Albert B. Dod, the Princeton mathematician, wrote "we trust it would be deemed an ample refutation of any system to show clearly that it was atheistic in its essential character." [37] Again, the tendency to subject ideas to the test of their moral results can be discerned in many quarters today. The language of invective has somewhat changed—now the refutation is deemed ample if a system can be called "socialistic," "communistic," "globalistic," or "subversive." Nevertheless, it would appear that the ante-bellum colleges, with their clear-cut Christian convictions, had a more certain grasp of the moral advantage to be looked for and of the doctrines that would bring that reward.

Last among the restrictions on speculation under which ante-bellum science worked were the substantive limitations of natural theology. After 1820, once materialism and Deism had declined, science and theology entered an intellectual *détente,* using as their formula of peace the Paleyan doctrine of "design." This doctrine was able to satisfy both scientific and clerical interests: the former, by sanctioning the empirical study of natural phenomena; the latter, by assigning to natural events a providential, supernatural cause. In the rhetoric of amity that developed, the word "harmony" was constantly used, though not in the same sense as before. Among the philosophers of the Enlightenment, "harmony" had usually

[36] George P. Fisher, *Life of Benjamin Silliman* (2 vols.; New York, 1866), I, 101.
[37] Thomas J. Wertenbaker, *Princeton, 1746–1896* (Princeton, N.J., 1946), p. 233.

signified the uniformity and regularity of nature, the universality of reason, the moral and intellectual likeness of all the members of the human race. To the Deists, representing one element of the thought of the Enlightenment, it also denoted opposition to the special creeds that were dividing the major religions.[38] "Harmony," in the language of ante-bellum science, had different denotations. It meant that Christian revelation agreed with all the conceptions of reason, that the ethical principles of Sinai were borne out in natural law, that the words in the Book of Genesis agreed, when correctly interpreted, with the evidence in the strata of rocks. Nature not only revealed a wondrous plan from which God's intelligence and benevolence could be inferred—this the Enlightenment had not denied; but now Nature was also considered to give evidence of the miracles on which the Christian eschatology was built.

One result of the prevalence of this commodious doctrine of design was that sacerdotal and scientific lines could be easily crossed: ministers could take up science, in the time-honored Mather tradition;[39] scientists could deliver religious sermons based on natural texts.[40] From the point of view of the present, this halcyon accommodation of naturalism to supernaturalism appears as the calm before the storm—or, perhaps, to the positivistic mind, the dark night before the dawn.[41] Darwinism was to loose all the latent antagonisms in the doctrine of design, cleaving it into a

[38] Arthur O. Lovejoy, "The Parallel of Deism and Classicism," in *Essays in the History of Ideas* (Baltimore, 1948), pp. 78–98.

[39] Some of the leading professional clergymen who were also teachers of science in this period were Edward Hitchcock, president of Amherst (1845–54), Congregationalist, geologist and paleontologist; Chester Dewey, professor of mathematics and natural philosophy at Williams College (1810–27), Congregationalist, also professor of chemistry and natural sciences at the University of Rochester (1850–61); Benjamin Hale, professor of chemistry at Dartmouth (1827–35), president of Geneva (Hobart) College (1836–58), Episcopalian, also a geologist and mineralogist; Charles Cogswell Upham, professor of mental and moral philosophy at Bowdoin (1824–67), Congregationalist, psychologist. There is unfortunately no career-line study of clerical personnel in science to answer some of the fundamental questions that this crossing of interests raises—for example, the reason for the large number of Congregationalists, the social and personal motivations that led them to their interest in natural science, the influence of their biases on the teleological flavor of American science.

[40] This was a common practice of scientists in England and America. See the lives of Faraday, Sir David Brewster, William Whewell, Sir Charles Bell, James D. Dana, William Maclure, Louis Agassiz, Benjamin Silliman, Asa Gray.

[41] In his survey of the first century of American education in 1876, Daniel C. Gilman found that "hostility toward scientific pursuits or toward scientific instruction has never in this country been manifested to any noteworthy extent by the religious part of the community or by theological teachers." "Education in America, 1776–1876," *North American Review*, CXXII (January, 1876), 224.

dogma of supernatural election and an hypothesis of natural selection, into a theory of providential intervention and a theory of divine concurrence. But God the Designer and God the Governor become sharply differentiated only when science and theology are at odds. In this period, science worshiped both the active and the passive God.

The accommodation to theology did not, to be sure, work consistently to the disadvantage of scientific thought. For example, the Christian version of design gave the science of geology a sanctuary from attack and a mantle of respectability. By dwelling on the "harmony of [God's] word with the visible creation," Silliman was able to answer the fundamentalist objections of Moses Stuart of Andover Theological Seminary.[42] By insisting that each harvest of fact gleaned from nature corroborated the working of Providence, James Dwight Dana effectively combatted the prejudices against science felt by obscurantist theologians like Tayler Lewis.[43] Had they not quieted qualms and disarmed opposition, it is doubtful that American scientists in the ante-bellum period could have pushed geology as far as they did. Methodologically, geology differed from the older sciences in that it sought the laws of natural development. It raised the question of how things came to be, and not the question, much safer for religion, of how things function as they are. Substantively, geology dealt with events definitively described in Scripture: it was the first science organized to deal not only with the work but with the word of God. With such a jurisdiction and such a basic point of view, geology was a potential threat to theology, natural and revealed. The fact that this threat called up in the scientists new talents for rationalization and compromise does not cancel the significant advances made. Always desiring to answer the interpretative problems of geology in a way least offensive to the Mosaic cosmogony, Silliman nevertheless had the integrity to turn to the anti-Biblical Vulcanist theory of earth-formation when the factual basis of the Neptunist theory of the diluvian crisis seemed to have been destroyed.[44] Eager to keep the peace between

[42] See Moses Stuart, "Remarks on a 'Critical Examination of Some Passages in Genesis 1,'" *American Journal of Science,* XXX (1836), 114–30; Fisher, *Life of Benjamin Silliman,* II, 132–60.

[43] Tayler Lewis, *The Six Days of Creation, or the Scriptural Cosmology* (Schenectady, 1855); James D. Dana, "A Review of Six Days of Creation," *Bibliotheca Sacra,* XIII (January, 1856), 80–129, and XIV (July, 1857), 461–524. See also Agassiz' approval of Dana's rebuttal in Daniel C. Gilman, *The Life of James Dwight Dana* (New York and London, 1899), p. 324.

[44] Dirk J. Struik, *Yankee Science in the Making* (Boston, 1948), pp. 300–301. For comparable developments in England, see Charles Coulston Gillispie's instructive book, *Genesis and Geology* (Cambridge, 1951), *passim.*

science and religion, Edward Hitchcock had the courage to abandon the literal interpretation of the Bible. "The facts of science, rightly understood," he wrote in 1851, "should not contradict the statements of revelation, correctly interpreted." [45] Thus, when "rightly understood," geology furnished irrefutable proof of the late appearance of man, the immutability of species, and the special providences of God, and so backed up both revelation and design at the most significant points. On the other hand, when "correctly interpreted," the Pentateuch was a figurative version of geological truth, and science should construe its metaphors. Thus, the six demiurgic days should be considered spans of geological time, and the ecumenical flood, disputed by science, should be reinterpreted as a local deluge. [46] Even Lyell, whose uniformitarian theory ruled out miraculous intervention in the whole domain of inorganic development, received a hearing in America, [47] though the most popular theories, down to the Darwinian era, were those of Cuvier, whose catastrophist hypothesis of the earth's formation squared more completely with the Biblical account. [48]

But the advance of geological science was the heaviest strain that the theological compromise would endure. As far as biology was concerned, scientists were timid in their generalizations, not out of positivistic caution, but out of concern for moral consequence and because of their theological preconceptions. As Arthur O. Lovejoy persuasively argues, the main proofs of organic evolution, except for the explanatory key of natural selection, were accessible in the writings of Lamarck, St. Hilaire, and, particularly, Robert Chambers. [49] Fifteen years before Darwin, Chambers had marshaled the evidence in favor of the theory of evolution: the general harmony between the theory of evolution and the rest of scientific thought, particularly uniformitarian geology; the presence in animals of rudimentary organs; the paleontological evidence of increasingly complex organisms appearing in succeeding epochs. Yet the scientific fraternity mercilessly attacked his theory when it appeared in 1844. To concede that everything was adapted for use and nothing for beauty and perfection, to

[45] Edward Hitchcock, *The Religion of Geology* (Boston, 1851), p. 4.

[46] *Ibid., passim.*

[47] Struik, *Yankee Science*, pp. 302–3; W. N. Rice, "The Contributions of America to Geology," *Science*, XXV (1907), 161–75.

[48] C. Wright, "The Religion of Geology," *New England Quarterly*, XLI (1941), 335–38.

[49] Arthur O. Lovejoy, "The Argument for Organic Evolution before 'The Origin of Species,'" *Popular Science Monthly*, LXXV (November and December, 1909), 499–514, 537–49.

give over the realm of life to blind chance and mechanical law, would have imperiled the Paleyans' conceptions. To relinquish the anthropomorphic God would have jeopardized the structure of faith on which morality presumably rested.[50] The recoil of scientific thought from such hazards threw it back upon the less plausible theory of repeated acts of "special creation," upon a series of miracles separated by long intervals of time. Here providentialism and moral purpose maimed academic science at a critical juncture of thought.

From the foregoing we conclude that academic freedom in investigation was diminished not by the action of forces alien and antipathetic to science, but by the inhibitions present within science itself. Rationalistic historians like Draper and White, who later presented the relation of science and religion or science and theology as one of inherent and recurring antagonism, missed or misread the ante-bellum record.[51] When Benjamin Silliman, Sr., the arch-exponent of the theological compromise, appended to a geology textbook an orthodox account of Creation,[52] when Professor John McVickar, in a perfect illustration of one tenet of doctrinal moralism, declared that "what religion reproves as wrong, Political Economy rejects as inexpedient," [53] when Louis Agassiz failed to draw what now seems the obvious evolutionary implication from his biogenetic law,[54] they were not making gestures to conformity, with *eppur si muove* spoken under the breath. The weapons which a frightened theol-

[50] There were, to be sure, non-theological reasons for rejecting Chambers—his mysticism, occasional inaccuracies, and other lapses from scientific propriety. But, as Lovejoy demonstrates, many of the weaknesses in the logic and evidence of Chambers' book that called forth biting attack from the scientists were also present in Darwin's work. At least the hypothesis, if not the particular rendering of it, should have been accepted, but scientists damned the author and his idea. Lovejoy, "The Argument for Organic Evolution," pp. 502, and *passim*.

[51] John William Draper, *History of the Conflict between Religion and Science* (New York, 1874); Andrew Dickson White, *A History of the Warfare of Science with Theology* (2 vols.; New York, 1896).

[52] Cf. Silliman's supplement to *An Introduction to Geology* by Robert Bakewell, first American ed. (New Haven, 1829), pp. 3–126. In the second edition Silliman went further, entitling his supplement "Consistency of the Discoveries of Modern Geology with the Sacred History of the Creation and the Deluge" (1833). Thomas Cooper attacked this attempt at conciliation as ruinous to science; see *On the Connection between Geology and the Pentateuch* (Boston, 1833).

[53] Gladys Bryson, "The Emergence of the Social Sciences from Moral Philosophy," *International Journal of Ethics*, XLII (April, 1932), 311.

[54] In his "Essay on Classification" in the first volume of the *Contributions to the Natural History of the United States* (Boston, 1852), Agassiz adumbrated a theory that later became known as the biogenetic law. "The changes which animals undergo during their embryonic growth coincide with the order of succession of

ogy employs to defend its static ideas—such weapons as censorship, heresy trials, economic sanctions, excommunication—were not used against ante-bellum scientists. The absence of open conflict was not owing simply to the unprovocative character of scientific thought. It testified also to the acceptance by the religious of scientific inquiry as an essential social good, to the growing deference to the authoritative pronouncements of science, and to the general confidence that the court of nature would always sustain the vital pronouncements of religion. It was not until Darwin forced science to accept the transmutation theory that the necessary limits of scientific inquiry, the proper sources of authority, and the tribunal role of nature became matters of basic controversy.

PIETY WITHOUT PARTISANSHIP?

To what degree was the demand for academic freedom—both in instruction and in investigation—affected by the proselytizing purpose of the ante-bellum colleges? To what extent was religious orthodoxy also sectarian in character? In their official pronouncements the Protestant colleges invariably claimed to be religious but not sectarian. Credibility was lent to this claim by the all but total absence of religious tests for students,[55] the occasional charter proscriptions against religious tests for faculties,[56] and the frequent absence of formal ecclesiastical control.[57] But the test

---

the fossils of the same type in past geological ages." The astounding thing is that Agassiz could enunciate such a principle and yet oppose Darwinism so vehemently.

[55] Of the 19 state and 32 private institutions studied by Elliott and Chambers, 10 state and 16 private colleges were in existence during the middle period. A perusal of these twenty-six charters reveals not a single reference to the right or intention to disqualify students on religious grounds. Edward C. Elliott and M. M. Chambers, *Charters and Basic Laws of Selected American Universities and Colleges* (New York, 1934), *passim*. On the other hand, 4 private institutions (Columbia, Princeton, Brown, Knox) and all public institutions covered by Elliott and Chambers provide in their charters that *no* such test shall be imposed. There is good reason to believe that this is a representative sample of the charter provisions on student entry at this time.

[56] Elliott and Chambers (*ibid.*) show that 4 state and 6 private institutions of the 26 ante-bellum colleges they covered had charter prohibitions against the imposition of religious tests for faculties. In their list, Yale alone provided for the administration of a religious oath to the faculty in its charter of incorporation.

[57] The Congregationalists relied mainly on sympathetic association with their colleges rather than formal control. The Congregational Society for the Promotion of Collegiate and Theological Education at the West favored the autonomy of individual colleges, preferring to promote Congregational ideals through financial aid.

is not so much the selection of students—where the chronic debt and desire for fees were mitigating factors [58]—as the selection of teachers; not so much the promises and ideals of the charters—which were political documents designed to allay the suspicions of hostile denominations [59] —as the motive for college establishment, the style of the college's religious ritual, the flavor of the college's instruction. Judged on these latter points, and excluding the special cases of Harvard, Pennsylvania, Union, and certain state universities in the early part of this period, the ante-bellum colleges substantiate the aphorism that piety without partisanship is easier to praise than practice.

The enormous expansion of denominational colleges in the first half of the century was impelled by a variety of motives. The founders were animated by the desire to bring the word of God and the chance of salvation to the heathen frontier, to counteract the infidelities and heresies spawned by the Revolution and the Enlightenment, to educate citizens for the duties imposed by the broadening franchise, to open professional careers to youths in the isolated hinterland, to extend the benefits of a liberal education. But certainly one of the most powerful and sustained of their motives was the aggrandizement of sect. The separation of church and state after the Revolution did not bring about the separation of church and college. On the contrary, disestablishment, by ending the monopolistic position of favored religions, opened the educational field to fiercer sec-

---

The Presbyterians also maintained very lax control through their Board of Education until 1883, when the constitution of the central Board of Aid provided that every college receiving aid be organically connected with the church, or else provide by charter that two-thirds of its board of control should be members of the church. On the other hand, the polity of the Lutherans, Baptists, and Methodists favored ecclesiastical control over the institutions receiving aid from the church. See Paul M. Limbert, *Denominational Policies in the Support and Supervision of Higher Education* (New York, 1929).

[58] See Chap. V.

[59] Despite the large number of colleges founded in this period, hardly a single college charter was passed by a state legislature without popular or sectarian opposition. As a result, a good deal of political maneuvering and verbal camouflaging went on. The Georgia Baptists, for example, with unusual candor, wanted to call their college "The Baptist College of Georgia." They found it more politic to settle for a less provocative name, Mercer University. Albea Godbold, *The Church College of the Old South* (Durham, N.C., 1944). Seldom in the charters were the sectarian attachments of the original self-perpetuating board pointed out. For example, Princeton's charter designated twelve Presbyterian ministers and eleven laymen, of whom only two were Quakers and one was an Episcopalian, without explicitly consigning that institution to Presbyterian control. See Willard W. Smith, "The Relation of College and State in Colonial America," unpublished Ph.D. dissertation (Columbia University, 1949).

tarian competition. In the East, where in colonial times the colleges of the established churches had reigned supreme—in Virginia, Massachusetts, Connecticut, New Hampshire, and New York—statehood and disestablishment allowed the pent-up demand for rival colleges to find unrestrained expression.[60] In the West, particularly when the evangelistic sects saw the need for a trained as well as consecrated ministry, the churches fell to the task of college-building with a militant missionary zeal. As imperialistic as the nations in the field of politics were the churches in the field of education. There was the same promoting of wares and searching for markets, the same carving of spheres in semicivilized domains, the same multiplying of jurisdictions. Except for the Congregationalists and Presbyterians, who collaborated (with mounting tension) in the establishment of ten colleges in a Plan of Union that lasted from 1801 to 1852, each denomination worked separately, adding to its own dominion, serving the one God and the particular creed.[61]

The proselytizing of colleges for their sects was rarely admitted or openly condoned. In a typical utterance, the board of trustees of Congregationalist Marietta College declared that "the essential doctrines and duties of the Christian religion will be assiduously inculcated, but no sectarian peculiarities of belief will be taught." [62] But the scope of the verb "to teach" and the definition of the adjective "sectarian" were very ambiguous. Like all the new denominational colleges of the period, Marietta, emulating the early colonial colleges, was founded "mainly to meet the demands for competent teachers and ministers of the Gospel." [63] The number of college graduates going into the ministry between 1816 and 1840 was greater than the number going into any other profession. By one estimate, one third of the graduates entered upon clerical careers in the peak period, 1836 to 1840; [64] the ratio of ministerial to other

[60] See G. Bush, *History of Education in Massachusetts* (Washington, D.C., 1891), pp. 225–79; G. Bush, *History of Education in New Hampshire* (Washington, D.C., 1898); Thomas Le Duc, *Piety and Intellect at Amherst, 1865–1912* (New York, 1946), pp. 1–5.

[61] See Chap. V for a fuller treatment of the post-Revolutionary expansion of the denominational college system.

[62] Charles F. Thwing, *A History of Higher Education in America* (New York, 1906), p. 231.

[63] *Seventh Report* of the Society for the Promotion of Collegiate and Theological Education at the West (1850), p. 61; quoted in Donald G. Tewksbury, *The Founding of American Colleges and Universities before the Civil War* (New York, 1932), p. 83.

[64] According to Burritt's combined statistics for the professional distribution of college graduates in thirty-seven representative colleges and universities, the per-

professional careers was estimated in 1857 as one in four for the Congregational colleges.[65] In addition, indigent preministerial students were heavily subsidized by church organizations. Although in time these new denominational colleges differentiated their theological courses from the rest of the curriculum, not until the end of the period, when the development of separate theological schools was well under way [66] and the proportion of ministerial candidates in the general student body had dropped to as low as one in five,[67] did these colleges lose their seminarial look. Nor was indoctrination confined to the classroom. Use was made of symbol and association: the halls and streets bore the names of the prophets and martyrs of the church.[68] Use was made of ritual and ceremonial: Sunday service and morning devotions were cast in the style of the sponsoring sect.[69] Sometimes two creeds were recognized in worship and ritual, as when the Princeton board in 1802 voted to print "copies of the Westminster Shorter Catechism and that of the Episcopal

---

centage of graduates going into the ministry did not dip below 50 until 1720, except for the 1661–1695 period. From 1721–1745 it held to around 40 percent and dropped until it reached the low point of 20.8 percent in 1791–1795, when it was overtopped by the law. A gradual rise thereafter brought it up to 32.8 percent in the 1836–1840 period. Bailey B. Burritt, "Professional Distribution of College and University Graduates," *Bulletin of United States Bureau of Education*, XIX (Washington, D.C., 1912), 74–83, 142–44.

[65] C. Van Rensselaer, "Commencement Address at Carroll College" (1857), in *Pamphlets on College Education* (Columbia University Library), Vol. VII, No. 9, p. 387.

[66] The establishment of professional schools of theology which were independent of colleges began in the second half of the eighteenth century. In the early nineteenth century, Andover Theological Seminary and Princeton Theological Seminary attained positions of real importance. At Harvard, divinity studies were separated from the college and organized into a distinct school in 1819. The Yale Divinity School was organized in 1822. By 1876, there were 113 seminaries. Still, until the middle of the nineteenth century, many schools preferred to retain the close relation between theological training and the liberal arts. Robert Kelly, *Theological Education in America* (New York, 1924).

[67] Burritt, "Professional Distribution of College and University Graduates," p. 75.

[68] Viz., Emory College, named for a bishop of the Methodist Church, its streets commemorating the names of Wesley, Asbury, and Coke. Godbold, *Church College of the Old South*, pp. 62–63.

[69] Yale was strict. Under Dwight, it denied students the right to attend Episcopalian services, though this permission had been granted under President Clap forty years before. Harvard allowed students to worship at the nearby churches, Brown made provision for Jews to consecrate their Sabbath. But in effect the freedom to worship elsewhere was limited. Traveling off the campus was not encouraged by college authorities; for convenience, if not because of other pressures, students generally accepted the devotional forms of the college. See Samuel Eliot Morison, *Three Centuries of Harvard*, p. 88; Walter C. Bronson, *History of Brown University, 1764–1914* (Providence, R.I., 1914), pp. 98–99.

Church." [70] Furthermore, though religious revivals were encouraged on behalf of an undifferentiated Christian piety, the lists of conversions suggest that the Spirit was likely to visit in the sectarian garb of the college.[71] At all events, parents who sought to keep their sons in the family faith had no difficulty in determining on which side the colleges were "neutral." Cheyney notes that in the first decades of the century, Philadelphia Presbyterians showed a marked preference for Dickinson and Princeton, Philadelphia Lutherans for Franklin, Philadelphia Anglicans for Columbia and William and Mary; the local and more convenient, but truly nonsectarian, University of Pennsylvania was by-passed.[72]

One manifestation of the sectarian spirit was seen in the employment of the faculty. Nine times out of ten, the college president was a minister,[73] and ministers in academic posts were usually ordained in the sponsoring church. Schmidt tells us that "there was no religion of the college president as such; he rather reflected the theological views of the denomination in which he held membership and whose interest he served." [74] On the affiliations of professors, the statistics are less conclusive because they are less complete and accessible. Our survey of the faculty rosters of Harvard, William and Mary, Miami, Oberlin, Lafayette, Princeton, and Middlebury for the period 1800 to 1860 indicates that about 35 per cent of the total were clergymen, which again strongly suggests sectarian choice.[75] The variations among these institutions suggest further that sects with a congregational structure were less able to impose this criterion

[70] This was the way the board interpreted a faculty resolution to allow students "to make choice of the Catechism of that denomination to which he belongs." John Maclean, *History of the College of New Jersey* (Philadelphia, 1877), II, 50–51.

[71] Thus the religious revival that hit Princeton in 1848 brought 25 conversions, of which 18 were to the Presbyterian Church (the sponsors), 6 to the Episcopalian (at Princeton, the minority church, recognized as such), and only 1 to the Methodist. Maclean, *History of the College of New Jersey*, II, 20.

[72] Edward P. Cheyney, *History of the University of Pennsylvania* (Philadelphia, 1940), pp. 176–77.

[73] Schmidt, *The Old Time College President*, pp. 184–86.

[74] *Ibid.*, pp. 187–88.

[75] This percentage was compiled from S. J. Coffin, *The Men of Lafayette, 1826–1893* (Easton, Pa., 1891), pp. 23–33, 113–20, 125–29; *Catalogue of Miami University, 1809–1892* (Oxford, Ohio, 1892), pp. xiii–xxii; *Third and Fourth Triennial Catalogues for Miami, 1840* and *1843; Annual Circulars for Miami, 1847*, pp. 55, 58, 59; Edgar J. Wiley, *Catalogue of the Officers and Students of Middlebury College . . . 1800–1915* (Middlebury, Vt., 1917), pp. ii–xix, xxvii–xxix, xxx–xxxv; Maclean, *History of the College of New Jersey*, II; *The History of the College of William and Mary from Its Foundation, 1660–1874* (Richmond, 1874), pp. 80–81.

than those with a synodal structure.[76] We also conclude that sectarian affiliation was a qualification for professors when subject-competence was not, and that subject-competence was not of prime importance when professors had to "double on the brass" in tiny tutorial orchestras. Thus Unitarian and cosmopolitan Harvard boasted in 1831 a heterogeneous interdenominational faculty—six Unitarians, three Roman Catholics, one Lutheran, one Episcopalian, one Quaker, and one Sandemanian; of them all, only the professor of divinity was required to pass a creedal test.[77] Baptist Brown also prided itself on its broad-minded choice of faculty.[78] At the other extreme, however, Presbyterian Miami in 1831 had three professors, all of them Presbyterian divines.[79] Presbyterian Pittsburgh College, closer to the mean in size if somewhat advanced in urbanity, in 1831 had four ordained Presbyterian ministers and one Catholic priest out of a faculty of five.[80]

The politics of sect intruded even upon the nominally neutral ground of the state universities. Twenty-one state universities struggled to survive in the ante-bellum period.[81] To the more militant sects these universities seemed designed to seduce young minds for either Satan's or Caesar's purposes. Treating them either as prizes to be fought for and won, or as enemies to be countered and destroyed, the churches placed their agents on state boards of trustees or else built competing colleges. The aggressiveness of the sects stymied the growth of the state universities throughout the period.[82] For varying periods of time North Carolina,

[76] See Chap. V, "Presbyterians and Partisans."

[77] Morison, *Three Centuries of Harvard*, p. 242.

[78] Bronson, *History of Brown University*, pp. 100–1.

[79] W. L. Tobey and W. O. Thompson, *Diamond University Volume: Miami University* (Oxford, Ohio, 1899), pp. 192–98.

[80] Agnes Lynch Starrett, *Through One Hundred and Fifty Years* (Pittsburgh, 1937).

[81] These, with their dates of founding, were Georgia (1785), North Carolina (1789), Vermont (1791), Tennessee (1794), Ohio (1802), South Carolina (1805), Miami (1809), Maryland (1812), Virginia (1816), Alabama (1821), Indiana (1828), Delaware (1833), Kentucky (1837), Michigan (1837), Missouri (1839), Mississippi (1844), Iowa (1847), Wisconsin (1848), Minnesota (1851), Louisiana State (1853), California (1855). The names are those in use today; the dates of founding are approximate. See Tewksbury, *Founding of American Colleges and Universities*, pp. 133–207. Several of these universities began as church institutions and lost their sectarian connections.

[82] Control of the board of trustees by certain denominations was easier to acquire and hold when these boards were self-perpetuating than when they were under state control. When originally founded, North Carolina, Delaware, Vermont, Transylvania, Tennessee (Cumberland and East Tennessee Colleges), Miami, Indiana (Vincennes), Mississippi, and California (College of California) had private

Tennessee, Vermont, Kentucky, Transylvania, Miami, Indiana, and Alabama universities fell under the direct influence and control of particular sects.[83] The universities of Missouri, Mississippi, and Michigan bowed to the pressure of several competing denominations.[84] The universities of Georgia, Ohio, Missouri, and Iowa, among others, were stunted by the competition of rival denominational colleges.[85] In the northeastern states and in six of the southern and western states, ecclesiastical opposition prevented the birth of state universities until after the Civil War.[86]

The state universities were not indifferent to religion. From their beginnings, they adopted the practices of religion in education—Bible classes, daily prayers, compulsory chapel, revivalism.[87] That they did not neglect the spiritual welfare of students may be deduced from the backgrounds of their presidents and professors who, in the ratio of one in three, were also recruited from the ministry.[88] Even Jefferson's plan for the University of Virginia, which went further along the road to secularism than

boards of trustees, which encouraged one sect, usually the Presbyterians, to take hold from the start. After the Dartmouth College case, however, the state usually inserted in the charter its right of revision. After prolonged battles, control ultimately came to rest in the hands of the state.

[83] See D. H. Gilpatrick, *Jeffersonian Democracy in North Carolina, 1789–1816* (New York, 1931), p. 129; L. S. Meriam, *Higher Education in Tennessee* (Washington, D.C., 1893), pp. 20–61, 63–105; G. Bush, *History of Education in Vermont* (Washington, D.C., 1900); Niels H. Sonne, *Liberal Kentucky, 1780–1828* (New York, 1939), pp. 160–261; G. W. Knight and J. R. Commons, *The History of Higher Education in Ohio* (Washington, D.C., 1891), p. 34; David D. Banta, "History of Indiana University," in *Indiana University, 1820–1920: Centennial Memorial Volume* (1921), pp. 103–7.

[84] E. Mayes, *History of Education in Mississippi* (Washington, D.C., 1899), pp. 25–117; Wilfred Shaw, *The University of Michigan* (New York, 1920), p. 40; Jonas Viles, *University of Missouri* (Columbia, Mo., 1939), p. 23.

[85] E. M. Coulter, *College Life in the Old South* (Athens, Ga., 1928), Chap. VIII; Knight and Commons, *Higher Education in Ohio*, p. 23, 55–58; Viles, *University of Missouri*, Chap. III; L. F. Parker, *Higher Education in Iowa* (Washington, D.C., 1893), Chap. IX.

[86] Tewksbury, *Founding of American Colleges and Universities*, pp. 169–74.

[87] Earle D. Ross, "Religious Influences in the Development of State Colleges and Universities," *Indiana Magazine of History*, XLVI (December, 1950), 343–62.

[88] Ross, "Religious Influences," p. 349; Curti and Carstensen, *The University of Wisconsin* (Madison, Wis., 1948), pp. 17–19; Coulter, *College Life in the Old South*, p. 19. Between 1804 and 1860, for example, four out of eight presidents of South Carolina College were ministers; ten out of thirty-eight professors were ministers. M. LaBorde, *History of the South Carolina College* (Charleston, S.C., 1874), pp. 527–28 and *passim;* Edwin L. Green, *A History of the University of South Carolina* (Columbia, S.C., 1916), p. 210 and *passim*. Between 1800 and 1860, two out of North Carolina's three presidents and nine out of its twenty-nine professors were ministers. Battle, *History of the University of North Carolina*, I, 51–54, 67–72, 79–80.

any other, permitted a definite amount of "released time" so that students might worship with their own pastors, offered the university's facilities for the use of outside divinity schools, and instructed the professor of ethics to emphasize religious values. Only because he feared sectarian controversy did Jefferson forbid formal instruction in theology, the appointment of clerical professors, and any form of sectarian control. Yet this measured secularism earned for Virginia the sobriquet of "godless" and the immoderate hatred of the militant sects throughout the antebellum era.[89] It was not the irreligion of the universities but their *politique* attitude toward sect that aroused the wrath of the churches.

In this connection too the churches disavowed any narrow sectarian purposes. Indeed, they often claimed that they were acting in behalf of a true nonsectarian policy. Again, it was a question of definition, not one of conscious deception. In the semantics of the religious, it was not sectarian to teach the immortality of the soul, the infallibility of the Bible, or even the existence of the Trinity, provided no pronouncements were made on such truly divisive points as the sanction for voluntary baptism. Conversely, however, it was sectarian—in a "Socinian," Unitarian, or Deistic way—to consider any of these basic Christian postulates open to serious question. Arguing, therefore, that an open mind was a sectarian position, the churches turned the tables on their enemies. The Horace Holley case, referred to above,[90] is an interesting case in point. The Presbyterian Church in Lexington, Kentucky, forced the dismissal of Transylvania's president because he had proved himself to be "violently sectarian." He had indoctrinated students, wrote the editor of the *Western Luminary,* a Presbyterian organ in Kentucky, in a religion "whose confession of faith is to have no confession, and whose sectarianism is to despise all sects." [91] Nor did sectarianism masquerade as its opposite only through a play on words. It was persuasively argued that the only way to stop the abuse of religious favoritism was to distribute faculty chairs in the state universities among the denominations in proportion to their

[89] Philip Alexander Bruce, *History of the University of Virginia* (5 vols.; New York, 1920–22), III, 133–47. Professor D. H. Hill, in his inaugural address as Professor of Mathematics of Davidson College, called the University of Virginia while under Jeffersonian principles "a terror to the land, a curse to the cause of education, in fact a nursery of crime and vice." Godbold, *Church College of the Old South,* p. 15.

[90] See Chap. V.

[91] Robert Peter and Johanna Peter, *Transylvania University, Its Origin, Rise, Decline, and Fall* (Louisville, Ky., 1896), p. 141.

respective strength in the community. This reversal of the Reformation rule, *cuius regio eius religio,* would, it was maintained, be in line with American democratic practice. A state with a large Baptist population should no more be required to have only Congregationalist teachers than a state with a predominance of Democrats should be forced to have only Whig representatives. Responding to this argument, the University of Virginia, having hired with Jeffersonian indifference a Catholic and a Jew, was compelled to right the balance by adding a militant Presbyterian clergyman.[92] Where no sect had clear domination, the nonsectarian course was presumed to lie in an equal division of the spoils. Accepting the premise that sectarianism disappears when a variety of sectarians are brought together, the University of Michigan for years pursued a policy of even-handed injustice, and named a minister of a different sect to each of its professorships.[93]

State constitutions gave little protection to the universities where sectarianism was at high tide. The constitutional provision against *any* religious test for professors could be interpreted in practice to sanction a *different* religious test for each academic office.[94] The "wall between church and state"—a barbed fence when the state tried to nullify a private church-college charter [95]—was a trampled hedge when the churches undertook to dominate the state universities.

For all this, the oppression of sect was not complete nor did it go unchallenged. The anguish and glory of Protestant separatism is that it covets intellectual solidarity but creates intellectual diversity. For one thing, the interchurch rivalry that built the colleges was often continued in the form of intramural conflict for the control of the colleges. Of the forty-nine colleges controlled by the Presbyterians in the ante-bellum period, three fell into the hands of the Methodists; three became state universities; seven fell to the Congregationalists; one began as Anglican, tarried briefly with the Presbyterians, and finally turned independent; one began as a semi-state institution, was associated with the Presbyterians, and was taken over by the Baptists; eight by slow degrees moved into virtual independence; and one (Transylvania) endured the vertiginous experience of passing from the control of the Baptists to the Episcopalians to the

92 Bruce, *History of the University of Virginia,* III, 133–35.
93 Shaw, *University of Michigan,* p. 40.
94 Banta, "History of Indiana University," pp. 72–73.
95 See *Trustees of Dartmouth College* vs. *Woodward* ("The Dartmouth College Case"), *4 Wheaton 514, 712* (1819).

Presbyterians to the Methodists to the Disciples of Christ.[96] Moreover, the schismatic conflict between the Old and the New Light Presbyterians, and the fission of the church into northern and southern branches, brought further intramural conflict to the twenty-six schools that remained in the Presbyterian fold.[97] Designed as shrines to particular truths, the denominational colleges were often embarrassed by a succession of creeds.

These conflicts for control, so threatening to the life and educational continuity of the colleges, set off flashes of rebellion against the denominational system as a whole. The close association of Miami University with the Presbyterians involved it in the fratricidal strife that split this church in the decade of the 1830s. Recognizing that theological controversy was harmful to church and college alike, President Robert Hamilton Bishop fought for unity in the church and for a liberal spirit in the college.[98] At Illinois College, J. M. Sturtevant, a sincere religionist and one of the original Illinois Yale Band, was so incensed by the inquisitions of the Presbyterian Synod into the teaching at his college that he became a vocal opponent of "the passion, the prejudice, the bigotry" of denominationalism in education.[99] In one article, he wrote:

We do not affirm that ecclesiastical governments so conditioned are bad; we do not affirm that they may not accomplish useful and important ends. But we do affirm that they cannot be stable. They must be constantly liable to the rise of minorities, whose views and feelings are in irreconcilable conflict with those of the ruling majority; and whenever this does happen, convulsion and disruption must and do ensue. . . . The tendency of sect [is] . . . to reduce all our Colleges to feebleness and starvation, by multiplying them beyond the demands and necessities of the community . . . [This spirit of sect] elevates minor denominational peculiarities into tests of fitness for the highest and most dignified stations; it tends to fill our most important chairs of instruction with men of inferior talents and attainments, because they are supposed to be right in the matter of denomination, and thereby to impair the efficiency of the Institution in the discharge of its appropriate function.[100]

Decades before Charles W. Eliot proclaimed that "a university cannot be built upon a sect" and made this the guiding principle of the post-

[96] Tewksbury, *Founding of American Colleges and Universities*, pp. 91–102.

[97] R. E. Thompson, *History of the Presbyterian Church in the United States* (American Church History Series, Vol. VI [New York, 1895]).

[98] James H. Rodabaugh, "Miami University," pp. 66–73.

[99] Charles Henry Rammelkamp, *Illinois College, A Centennial History: 1829–1929* (New Haven, 1928), pp. 119–26; J. M. Sturtevant, *An Autobiography* (New York, 1896), pp. 188, 198–99, 245–49.

[100] "Denominational Colleges," *The New Englander*, XVIII (February, 1860), 82.

Civil War era, opposition to sectarianism gathered head within the denominational colleges themselves.

DISORDER AND DEFICIT

We have seen that the educational ideals of the old regime—its traditionalism, authoritarianism, paternalism, doctrinal moralism, and sectarianism—depressed the demand for freedom in two areas of academic expression, instruction and inquiry. The word "depressed" (rather than "suppressed") is chosen in this context advisedly. Freedom thrives on desire and desire on opportunity; and these ideals were an effective prophylactic against the passion and incitement to be free. But educational ideals are not the whole of academic existence, nor are they the only institutional factors relevant to our theme. The college is not only a place where formal teaching and learning go on; it is also a unit of government, an economic entity, a congeries of social relationships. How it functions in these roles influences those opportunities for intellectual conflict, those expectations of indulgence, those inclinations to self-assertion, that kindle the demand for freedom. Seen in the light of these diverse functions, the ante-bellum college was not characterized only by indoctrination and compliance. Throughout the period there was student agitation against the rules, discontent in the faculty with its status and role, and—pushing the colleges toward reform—a hovering, nagging poverty. In sum, two forces were dialectically opposed in the ante-bellum colleges. The first was a conception of education that tended to make the college a monolithic institution. The second—of increasing power as time went on—was an intramural spirit of revolt and reform which, in challenging authority in a system fundamentally authoritarian, acted as one of the agents which eventually destroyed that system.

There is a strong impression among academic men today that fewer and weaker powers are being delegated to them by trustees now than formerly, and that there has been a regression from a Golden Age of faculty self-government to a present state of subservience. We were once "cleric, now we are clerical," says Professor Jacques Barzun, in a witty but mistaken epigram. Actually, in their conventional relations with trustees, faculties were in an inferior position and at a disadvantage all through the seventeenth and eighteenth centuries; in the early nineteenth century a nadir seems to have been reached. In the latter period the system of control by a nonresident board, carried over from the colonial colleges, evolved into an instrument of academic government that was officious, meddlesome, and often tyrannical. One finds the trustees of colleges prescribing the work of the classroom, writing the laws of student government, shaping the curriculum, subjecting the private lives of teachers to scrutiny and espionage. Take the obsessional interest in minutiae exhibited by the board of trustees at Princeton in the early nineteenth century. "When a committee of the board came to examine the faculty's 'minutes'," writes one historian of early Princeton,

it sternly reported that the pages of the minute book were not numbered, that in one place a date was wanting, that there were instances of grammatical construction which it thought incorrect. . . . Worse than all this, however, it was learned that one tutor had been away on a trip, that another had entertained friends in his room . . . all of which showed a great want of proper discipline.[101]

It is doubtful that the most intrusive board of trustees today would ever display toward its faculty so marked an attitude of contempt. Nor was this a unique example: Pennsylvania's board rivaled Princeton's in its concern for petty details,[102] and the trustees of Hamilton and Lafayette were not far behind in their disregard for faculty judgment.[103]

In accounting for this state of affairs it is not enough to conclude that this is how a theocracy always functions, that the ministerial mind turned the colleges into pastorates and made close surveillance a duty. As a matter of fact, clergymen rarely predominated on the early nineteenth-century boards of control,[104] and officiousness was a habit of

---

[101] Varnum Lansing Collins, *Princeton* (New York, 1914), pp. 116–17.

[102] Cheyney, *University of Pennsylvania*, p. 178.

[103] Joseph D. Ibbotson and S. N. D. North, eds., *Documentary History of Hamilton College* (Clinton, N.Y., 1922), pp. 181, 185, 193, 195–226; David Bishop Skillman, *The Biography of a College* (2 vols.; Easton, Pa., 1932), I, 172–78.

[104] Beard claims in *Rise of American Civilization* that clergymen dominated these boards (New York, 1942), II, 470. Schmidt controverts this with his random figures. "Up to 1861, the records list thirty-three clergymen and forty-three laymen [at Williams]. . . . The totals for Union college in 1861 were nineteen clerical and forty-eight lay representatives. . . . The corresponding figures for Amherst in the same year were twenty-four and thirty-eight." Schmidt, *The Old Time College President*, p. 51. Further figures support our contention that laymen usually predominated. The thirty-six charter trustees of Lafayette College were all nonclergymen; between 1830 and 1860, thirty-three were clergymen and forty-six were nonclergymen (Coffin, *Men of Lafayette*). At Middlebury there were seventeen clergymen and fifteen laymen between 1801–1829, twenty-five clergymen and twenty-three laymen between 1830 and 1860 (Wiley, *Catalogue of the Officers and Students of Middlebury College*). At Miami, between 1824 and 1829, ten were clergymen, fourteen were

boards that were almost or entirely nonclerical.[105] Greater emphasis, it would appear, should be given to the status relationships then existing in the colleges. In dealing with the men of large affairs who sat on the governing boards, the president, the professors, and the tutors were often hopelessly outclassed. As in colonial times, the tutor was a functionary to whom deference was never generously paid, and it was only gradually that he was to make his exodus from the nineteenth-century college scene.[106] The professor was not held in much higher regard; dependent on student fees and yet the inquisitor of student morals, he took on the uncertain authority and something of the status of the nursemaid. Most damaging to faculty prestige was the decline in the caliber of the president who, as an ex-officio member of the board of trustees, as the guardian of campus religiosity, and as the head of the college faculty, held a strategically powerful position. While the screen of orthodoxy was tightly woven, it served to keep from the presidency the celebrated, the independent, the truly top-notch man.[107] Powerful personalities like Josiah

---

not; between 1830 and 1836, sixteen were clergymen and seventy were not (*Catalogue of Miami University, 1809–1892*). Finally, McGrath, studying thirteen private institutions—Williams, Wabash, Knox, Yale, Pennsylvania, Princeton, Dartmouth, Lafayette, Amherst, Wesleyan, Hamilton, Lawrence, and Beloit—concludes with the statement that 39.1 percent of the trustees in the year 1860 were clergymen. Earl J. McGrath, "The Control of Higher Education in America," *Educational Record*, XVII (April, 1936), 259–72. Of course, all this does not mean that clergymen were not an enormously important element.

[105] One example is provided by the Board of Trustees at the University of Virginia, which despite Jefferson's democratic leanings kept very close control on faculty doings. "The professors were under as close supervision in the work of the classroom as the students themselves. The chairman of the Faculty was expected to report: (1) how often each instructor had failed to lecture as required; (2) how frequently he had neglected to question the members of his class; (3) how much time was consumed by him in delivering lectures and making his examinations; and (4) how often he had omitted sending in his class report to show the number of his pupils' absences, and the degree of their attention and progress." There were no clergymen on this board. Bruce, *History of the University of Virginia*, II, 132.

[106] In the eastern colleges there was a gradually diminishing proportion of tutors to total faculty between 1820 and 1850. At Harvard, Yale, Columbia, Williams, Union, Hamilton and Amherst, tutors were 30 percent of the whole in 1820, 27 percent in 1830, 25 percent in 1840, 23 percent in 1850. The gradual decline is significant, and represents an important though gradual shift in status relationships and potentialities. The western colleges had fewer tutors than the eastern, and the tradition of the celibate young tutor did not take strong hold there. For figures, see those prepared especially by the New York Public Library for Clarence F. Birdseye, *Individual Training in Our Colleges* (New York, 1907), p. 135.

[107] There were a few notable exceptions: Dwight of Yale (1795–1817), Jeremiah Chaplin of Colby (1820–1833), John Kirkland of Harvard (1810–1829), Joseph Caldwell of North Carolina (1804–1812, 1817–1835), Eliphalet Nott of Union (1804–1866).

Meigs of Georgia and Horace Holley of Transylvania were compelled to resign; giants like John Witherspoon of Princeton and William Smith of Pennsylvania were succeeded by less able and more tractable men; the first two decades of the century found Amherst, Bowdoin, Columbia, Dartmouth, Vermont, and Williams in an interregnum between important presidents. In the dialogues of power that always go on between laymen and professionals, the president's voice can be decisive. When it is loud and clear, it can "cleave the general ear"; too often, alas, it is whispery; in this period, it was, with very few significant exceptions,[108] almost inaudible.

Gradually, by a step forward here and a short gain there, in the course of the next decades the college teacher was elevated from the position of a powerless subaltern to the status of an executive officer in the realm of discipline and instruction. What improved the situation was not any widespread adherence to some overarching principle of professorial autonomy. Rather, the factor that seems to have been crucial in furthering reform was the prosaic and commonplace, but disquieting and relentless, problem of the lack of student discipline. Never have the colleges had so many rules for students and so much student unruliness as in the ante-bellum period. Coulter, in his *College Life in the Old South,* presents some of the laws of the University of Georgia that frustrated student joy:

If any scholar shall be guilty of profaneness—of fighting or quarreling—if he shall break open the door of a fellow-student—if he shall go more than two miles from Athens without leave from the President, a Professor or a Tutor,— if he shall disturb others by noisiness, loud talking or singing during the time of study,—if he shall ring the Bell without order or permission—if he shall play at billiards, cards or any unlawful game—if he shall associate with vile, idle or dissolute persons, or shall admit them into his chamber,—if he shall instigate or advise any student to a refractory stubborn behavior—he shall for either of those offenses, be punished by fine, admonition, or rustication, as the nature and the circumstances of the case may require.

Then, there were laws against more serious offenses, which were gravely enumerated: keeping dogs, robbery, fornication, forgery, striking an instructor, fiddling on Sunday, and defacing the walls with indecent figures. Finally, "Whereas the laws of the College are few and general" [sic],

---

[108] See Franklin B. Dexter, "An Historical Study of the Powers and Duties of the Presidency of Yale College," *Proceedings of the American Antiquarian Society,* New Series, Vol. XII (1897), pp. 27–42.

in cases not covered, the faculty might proceed at their discretion! [109] Unfortunately, for every law to break, there was a febrile adolescent lawbreaker. A semester unmarred by expulsions was memorable in college annals; a chapel that escaped vandalism enjoyed a most unnatural quiet. The chief instrument of student aggression—the firecracker—was part of standard student equipment; the ivied halls would shake to the reverberations of explosions. Needless to say, the safety-valve of college sports had not yet been invented; the effective cajoleries of the kindly dean had not yet appeared; to maintain a system of too much government in an undergoverned society was the task the college set for itself, and the task was truly insuperable.

To be sure, adult authority would always reassert itself against prank and rebellion. An institution so dedicated to discipline engendered dedicated disciplinarians. The offenders would be rounded up; the president would be solemn and severe; the faculty would constitute itself the high court and mete out appropriate punishment. But peace was easier to restore than the faculty's equanimity. These multitudinous acts of student exuberance or irritation—always defined as acts of irreverence or defiance—struck like so many arrows at professorial complacency. Not only did student dismissals damage the reputation of the college and threaten it with financial ruin; not only was the professor's image of himself as remote and benevolent impaired by sorties against students in the night; but these outbreaks invariably brought down on the teachers' heads a plague of trustees, who disrupted the normal course of pacification. Should the trustees, like those at Hamilton College, recognize student petitions of grievance, then students could play the distant authority against the local tyrants with a skill that made discipline impossible.[110] Or should the trustees, like those at Transylvania and Brown, be divided on sectarian lines, then student insubordination might actually be encouraged by one faction of the trustees in order to discredit the other.[111] More common, if hardly less disserviceable, were the trustees who assiduously offered advice though they were out of touch with the situation. Thus the trustees of Princeton, descending into its riotous at-

[109] Coulter, *College Life in the Old South*, pp. 60–62. For other listings of student laws, see Bronson, *History of Brown University*, pp. 153 ff.; Wertenbaker, *Princeton*, pp. 132–214.

[110] Henry David, *A Narrative of the Embarrassments and Decline of Hamilton College* (1832).

[111] Sonne, *Liberal Kentucky*, pp. 88–89; Bronson, *History of Brown University*, pp. 188–89.

mosphere in 1817, counseled the use of civil force against the students to maintain order, a course that outraged the parents, violated academic traditions, and damaged Princeton's reputation for decades.[112]

This dual hazard of student disobedience and trustee interference led to demands by the faculties for greater self-government.[113] The demand was for partial autonomy, not for total independence. Though the plans for reform differed in detail from college to college, they were consistent in this one vital point. No European gild of scholars, autonomous in all its concerns, was envisioned by these reformers of the early and middle nineteenth century. No serious attempt was made to alter the charter so as to shift legal control to professors. The management of funds, the selection and appointment of the chief executive, the preparation and approval of budgets—which all lay within the province of English and Scottish professors—were powers neither sought by American faculties nor tendered by American trustees.[114] Even at Harvard, where a final and unsuccessful move to seat the faculty on the Corporation was made in 1825, the presence of the Board of Overseers was always protection against complete faculty self-rule.[115] The main effort was directed toward convincing the trustees to delegate to the faculty power over education and discipline; toward developing, as it were, a limited faculty *imperium* within a trustee *imperio*.

On this theme each ante-bellum college, tied to its own traditions and past mistakes, worked its own variation. Great powers were yielded to the faculty at Yale, where a line of strong presidents since Thomas Clap had never been interrupted, and where the Corporation had learned from the senior Dwight to respect the authority of the president.[116] In the regime of Dwight's successor, the less majestic and more democratic Jeremiah Day, the president undertook to share his powers with leading

[112] Collins, *Princeton*, pp. 131–32; Maclean, *History of the College of New Jersey*, II, 168–70; Wertenbaker, *Princeton*, p. 109.

[113] This is an unwritten chapter in the various histories of American higher education, partly because of the pre-eminent interest in curricular change and little else. Charles F. Thwing, who is concerned with the wider institutional aspects (he actually devotes a chapter in his history to the financing of the denominational college) almost ignores the informal power relationships in the college. See *A History of Higher Education in America* (New York, 1906). The several doctoral dissertations on this subject tend to slight the denominational era.

[114] For example, the charters of Yale and Knox colleges were issued almost a century apart, yet the changes in the powers of their respective boards were insignificant. Elliott and Chambers, *Charters and Basic Laws*, pp. 283–86, 588–93.

[115] Morison, *Three Centuries of Harvard*, pp. 224–38.

[116] Yale University, *Sketches of Yale College* (New York, 1843), p. 56.

members of the faculty. Not only initiative in making curricular changes and undivided power over disciplinary cases, but the right to approve all new appointments, was conceded to the faculty. So firmly was this tradition planted that in 1871 a Yale president could claim that "with scarcely an exception, no law has been passed, no officer appointed, unless after full consultation and exchange of views between the boards of control and of instruction.[117] Princeton's trustees, unable to cope with financial failure and student unruliness, turned for guidance to Professor John Maclean, whose plan for higher salaries, an expanded curriculum, and alumni contributions they passively adopted. The success of this plan set a precedent for their dependence on faculty initiative, and thereafter the power to establish as well as to execute policy flowed to the side of the faculty.[118] Elsewhere, down through the years, the trustees relinquished numerous powers: the power to revise, unaided, the course of study;[119] to control student admissions;[120] to undertake systematic classroom visitations;[121] to conduct the final oral examination—their last affectation of scholarship. This functional separation of power ranks with the establishment of lay control and the bureaucratization of personnel practices as one of three important milestones in the development of American academic government.

Still the problem of student discipline remained—the rock which even the sanguine Jefferson dreaded as he charted the course for his university.[122] That the faculty was allowed to use its discretion did not mean that it would use its discretion wisely. Doubtless most teachers in the

[117] Pierson, *Yale College,* p. 134.   [118] Collins, *Princeton,* pp. 140 ff.

[119] The revision of the statutes of the University of Mississippi was designed to give the faculty control over educational policy (1856). Prior to that time, they had been framed so as to put the most minute affairs under the discretion of the trustees, "including even such matters as the ringing of the college bell and the arrangement of the hours of recitation." President Barnard argued: "You have appointed us because we are professional teachers and you believe we understand our business; you have prescribed the broad outlines of our work, and we have undertaken to do the work on those lines. Now, if you are to direct the details of the work at every step, you will succeed no better than you would succeed if you were to direct the engineers of the Mississippi Central in the same way. Our professional knowledge and experience will be set aside and rendered useless, and our whole work will probably be badly botched." John Fulton, *Memoirs of Frederick A. P. Barnard* (New York, 1896), pp. 204–5.

[120] Fletcher, *History of Oberlin,* I, 178.

[121] See W. H. Cowley, "The Government and Administration of Higher Education: Whence and Whither?" *Journal of the American Association of Collegiate Registrars,* XXII (July, 1947), 477–91.

[122] Letter to Ticknor (1820), Thomas Jefferson, *Writings* (Washington, 1890), XV, 455.

ante-bellum period remained convinced that the traditional approach to student discipline was best, and regarded the disciplinary problem as the problem of how to make discipline more rigid. Some sought more ascetic laws or a tighter system of espionage, or else worked laboriously at marking up merits and demerits of conduct, as though the whole issue could be resolved into a simple and inexorable arithmetic.[123] Others settled on one cause of disobedience—infidelity—and sought one primary remedy—to extricate fallen students with the hoists of evangelical religion.[124] But there was also a growing minority that attacked the faulty methods of teaching and the uninspiring content of instruction. A small contingent of Americans who had studied at German universities came home to insist that power was better exercised over subjects than over subject schoolboys, that a contribution to philology was far more significant than a contribution to student manners, that the whole emphasis of the college should be shifted from discipline to scholarship.[125] Those who read the works of Fellenberg, Pestalozzi, and that new and exciting theorist, Herbert Spencer, were turning to the view that dull recital did not sublimate the aggressions, that gerund-grinding did not occupy the attention, that prescribed courses did not satisfy the interests of the average boy at college—and that there was the heart of the problem.[126] And, as the period drew to a close, such reformers as Francis Wayland spoke in a native idiom of how the conventional curriculum no longer answered the problems of real life, and of how only a more vocation-centered offering could meet the needs of undergraduates.[127]

Thus the problem of student discipline stirred up doubts on some

[123] See Francis H. Smith, *College Reform* (Philadelphia, 1851). Smith worked out a disciplinary system that defined every duty and punished its negligence with demerit marks. Henry James in his biography of Eliot called this kind of discipline a system wherein "a docile but stupid lamb might outrank a superior scholar who was caught in a good many pranks." *Charles William Eliot* (Boston and New York, 1930), I, 38.

[124] One means was the promotion of revivals in the sectarian colleges of the South. Though they upset college routine, sometimes for a week or more, they were encouraged by college officials. Godbold, *Church College of the Old South*, p. 70.

[125] See Chap. VIII for an analysis of the German contribution to American higher education.

[126] See Chap. VII for an analysis of Spencer's theory of education and its influence on American educational reform.

[127] See Wayland's *Thoughts on the Present Collegiate System in the United States* (Boston, 1842); *Report of the Corporation of Brown University* (1850).

of the most fundamental issues. Was it irreligion or faulty instruction that made students ill-tempered and disobedient? To what extent was doctrine the source and touchstone of morality? If few, perhaps, contended that religion was irrelevant to good morals, some were coming to see that religion was insufficient for good morals. After all, if the University of Virginia had disciplinary problems while under Jefferson's "godless" tutelage, so had those near-by citadels of the faith, Randolph-Macon and Washington colleges.[128] Observing the spectacle of cows in the chapel of the highly Presbyterian LaGrange College, F. A. P. Barnard, president of the state University of Mississippi, concluded that if his institution was less "godly," it was nevertheless better disciplined.[129] The carousing and dissipation that Andrew Dickson White encountered while a student at Geneva College, an institution under "direct Christian influence," must have suggested to him that free thinking and free drinking were not necessarily connected.[130]

As pressing as the problem of disorder, and perhaps even more far-reaching in its effects, was the problem of financial distress. The eastern colleges in the first three decades of the nineteenth century, and the western colleges throughout the period, were poor—but this word does not fully convey their plight. Material undernourishment is an endemic ailment of all academic bodies. Even the richly provided universities of the golden nineties complained of this condition. But whereas theirs was the emaciation of bodies in too-rapid growth, the ante-bellum colleges were atrophied organisms, living at a low ebb. So small was their scale of operations that the slightest shift of fortune was enough to determine life or death. In 1827, Princeton's treasury showed a deficit of $753, not an heroic debt in modern terms, but one that made her reduce the salaries of two professors to what must have been below subsistence level.[131] Twice Rutgers lapsed into the status of an academy for want of funds;[132] once Amherst's income was so low that her professors worked without salaries in order to keep her alive.[133] The western colleges fared worse

[128] Richard Irby, *History of Randolph-Macon College* (Richmond, Va., 1898), pp. 112–13.

[129] Fulton, *Memoirs of Frederick A. P. Barnard*, pp. 203–4.

[130] Andrew D. White, *Autobiography* (New York, 1922), I, 18–19.

[131] Wertenbaker, *Princeton*, p. 170.

[132] William H. S. Demarest, *A History of Rutgers College, 1766–1924* (New Brunswick, N.J., 1924), pp. 184–271.

[133] George Whicher, ed., William Gardner Hammond's *Remembrance of Amherst: An Undergraduate's Diary, 1846–1848* (New York, 1946), p. 10.

and for a longer time.[134] Their high mortality rate is eloquent of their protracted, inescapable poverty.[135] Undoubtedly the hostility to change that was part of the character of the ante-bellum colleges can be attributed to inadequate means. Change meant expansion, expansion meant expense, and theirs was a destitute economy. A scholastic and tradition-bound curriculum was, aside from its other supposed virtues, decidedly cheap.

Put in commercial terms, low sales, inadequate capital, and high operating costs tell the story of these financial failures. In relation to the growth in population, the percentage of college enrollments declined all through the period. In New England in 1826 the proportion of students in college to the population was one in 1,513; in 1855, one in 1,689; in 1869, one in 1,927.[136] At the same time, endowment did not keep pace with the rising cost of education. For the eastern colleges the starvation time in endowments was the period from 1800 to 1830. The loss of carefully nurtured nest eggs in the inflation of the American Revolution,[137] the drying up of English sources of philanthropy after independence,[138] the parsimony of the state legislatures,[139] all worked

[134] In 1871 eight eastern colleges—Amherst, Bowdoin, Dartmouth, Harvard, Middlebury, Vermont, Williams, and Yale—had four times the endowment of eighteen western colleges—Beloit, Berea, College of California, Carleton, Heidelberg, Illinois, Iowa, Knox, Marietta, Oberlin, Olivet, Pacific Union, Ripon, Wabash, Western Reserve, Wilberforce, and Wittenberg. See George F. Magoun, "Relative Claims of Our Western Colleges," *Congregational Quarterly*, XV (January, 1873), 49–75.

[135] Tewksbury, *Founding of American Colleges and Universities*, p. 28.

[136] Taking his figures from President Barnard's reports, Charles Kendall Adams concluded that "the sad fact stares us in the face that the training which has long been considered essential to finished scholarship has been losing ground from year to year in the favor of the people." "The Relation of Higher Education to National Prosperity," Phi Beta Kappa address, 1876, in Northrup, Lane, and Schwab, eds., *Representative Phi Beta Kappa Orations* (Boston and New York, 1915), pp. 160–61.

[137] Colleges such as Harvard, which had Federalist sentiments and had been fortunate enough to have speculated in state and federal paper, recouped their losses in the Hamiltonian windfall, but Princeton invested every penny in United States loan certificates on which the government defaulted in 1782. Morison, *Three Centuries of Harvard*, pp. 157–58; Wertenbaker, *Princeton*, pp. 66–67.

[138] Jesse B. Sears, *Philanthropy in the History of American Higher Education* (Washington, D.C., 1922), p. 22.

[139] The years in which the eastern colleges received their last cash endowments or subsidies from the state were Harvard, 1824; Yale, 1831; Dartmouth, 1809; Columbia, 1819; Hamilton, 1846; Union, 1804; Geneva, 1846; Pennsylvania, 1844. Princeton, Rutgers, and Brown never received grants or appropriations. Vermont received no grants or appropriations but was allowed the remission of a small debt in 1852. Frank W. Blackmar, *The History of Federal and State Aid to*

to reduce the colleges' productive assets to pitiable figures. After a century of existence Columbia's income from all sources was less than two thousand dollars a year.[140] In 1817, Princeton's yield from income-bearing assets was a mere $1,500.[141] As late as 1831, after 130 years of private and public beneficence, Yale's receipts from all sources, including tuition, were slightly less than twenty thousand dollars.[142] The western colleges were even less solvent. The poverty of their frontier communities, the competition of the state universities, which had first claim on the public purse, the fluctuations in the values of land on which their endowments were based, the strain on denominational resources caused by their proliferation, gave them a tenuous hold on life. For the first quarter-century of its life, Illinois College (founded 1835) subsisted more on fervor than funds. Its initial capital was some fourteen thousand dollars and several hundred acres of land, taxable but for a long period unsalable. A subscription of $100,000, the result of its president's fund-raising mission in the east, was repudiated in the crash of 1837. The faculty, sent east to ask alms, returned empty-handed. By 1843, the pay of its professors was in arrears, its debt had mounted to $25,000, and its property was heavily mortgaged. Only the aid of the Society for the Promotion of Theological and Collegiate Education kept Illinois College alive until the late fifties, when secular philanthropy and gifts from alumni pushed it over to the side of solvency. Nor was it able in its time of troubles to seek a more auspicious re-establishment elsewhere. Saddled with debts and chattels, this mendicant college, unlike the poor medieval university, was immobilized by its poverty.[143]

Here again, the remedy prescribed for the problem shook authority out of its settled grooves. One main resource was available and it was used—the sympathy and largesse of the alumni. As individuals, college graduates had always been interested in the welfare of their alma maters. Attachment to class and college had been fostered by the small numbers of students, the close living, and the class unity that characterized the old-time colleges; time and the worse restraints of adult life dimmed

Higher Education in the United States (Washington, D.C., 1890). However, other sources of income were made available to the colleges by the states; for example, exemption from taxation, land endowments, and the right to hold lotteries. See Thwing, *History of Higher Education in America*, pp. 328–30.

[140] Thwing, *History of Higher Education in America*, p. 326.

[141] Wertenbaker, *Princeton*, p. 120.

[142] Sears, *Philanthropy in Higher Education*, p. 37.

[143] Rammelkamp, *Illinois College*, pp. 82–244.

the memory of sophomoric repression. But it was not until the nineteenth century [144] that this sentimental concern was organized, capitalized, and set to earning dividends. Between 1827 and 1853, Princeton, Williams, Rutgers, Pennsylvania, Harvard, Amherst, and Brown, which together had half the total number of all alumni alive in 1829,[145] organized alumni associations.[146] The idea spread to the newer colleges of the Middle West, where organization of alumni associations followed close upon the establishment of colleges.[147] Similarly, the midwestern state universities endeavored to organize their graduating classes and to keep alive their sense of sodality.[148] Results were observable from the start, particularly in the Atlantic Seaboard colleges, whose alumni were relatively numerous and wealthy. Yale's and Princeton's sons tendered large sums in subscription drives.[149] Harvard received spectacular bequests from Christopher Gore and Abbott Lawrence, as well as aid from its organized alumni.[150] These transfusions revivified these colleges, and they quickly forged ahead of all competitors. Columbia, on the other hand, not having founded her alumni organizations until 1854, remained in the doldrums of deficit until almost the end of the period.[151]

Originally, the purposes of alumni organizations were convivial and philanthropic—to renew the friendships of youth and to provide a viable endowment. For a time, the college authorities successfully resisted sporadic attempts by the alumni to secure an official place in college councils. Not until 1865, after a long struggle, did the Harvard alumni obtain the right to elect the members of the Board of Overseers; [152] not until 1872 did the Yale alumni supersede the six state senators on the Corporation and challenge clerical control; [153] not until 1900 did Princeton's alumni secure seats on the board of trustees.[154] But long before they secured formal recognition as a law-giving as well as a fund-raising group, the alumni influenced the course of educational policy.

[144] Except at Yale, where the records of class organization date back to 1792. Wilfred B. Shaw, "The Alumni," in Raymond A. Kent, ed., *Higher Education in America* (New York, 1930), p. 657.

[145] *American Quarterly Review*, I (April, 1829), 224–55.

[146] Shaw, "The Alumni," pp. 658–59.

[147] *Ibid.*, p. 658.   [148] *Ibid.*, p. 659.

[149] Thwing, *History of Higher Education in America*, p. 325.

[150] *Ibid.*   [151] *Ibid.*

[152] John Hays Gardiner, *Harvard* (New York, 1914), pp. 296–98, 301.

[153] Bernard C. Steiner, *History of Education in Connecticut* (Washington, D.C., 1893), pp. 178–79.

[154] Collins, *Princeton*, p. 249.

Status-wise, the alumni were at least on a par with the trustees. Social deference did not have to be paid to any group by an alumni association like Harvard's, whose first officers were John Quincy Adams; Joseph Story, justice of the Supreme Court; Edward Everett, governor of Massachusetts; John Pickering, president of the American Academy; Horace Binney, member of Congress; Lemuel Shaw, chief justice of the Massachusetts Supreme Court; Leverett Saltonstall, member of Congress; Nathaniel L. Frothingham, overseer and fellow of the American Academy; Peleg Sprague, judge of the United States District Court and United States Senator; Benjamin R. Curtis, afterward judge of the Supreme Court.[155] The very presence of so distinguished a group made the faculty feel accountable to another will than that of the trustees. In some cases the alumni and the faculty made common cause against the conservative book-balancers on the board of trustees.[156] At Princeton, the result of faculty-alumni collaboration in the 1830s and 1840s was the transfiguration of Old Nassau, founded to raise up men for the gospel ministry, into a school that excelled in science and modern languages, that hired scholars rather than mere pious pedagogues, that already glimpsed its future as a university.[157] Its thought became secularized, slowly, almost imperceptibly. In 1812 the Princeton trustees, choosing a teacher, had recommended him as "pious, prudent and highly respectable," and then had mentioned his attainments in mathematics and natural philosophy. Twenty years later, scholarship was the major requirement, and Joseph Henry could write to Maclean that his prime goal in accepting an appointment at Princeton was to win "the reputation of a man of science." [158] With the help of the alumni, the needs of the nation started to replace the needs of the church.

The organization of the alumni produced effects that often were not premeditated. Graduate loyalty was often attached, then as well as now, to infantile or regressive projects. No doubt the main objective of the alumni was to preserve the old college they had known, not to submerge

[155] Gardiner, *Harvard*, pp. 304–5.
[156] This, of course, depended on a spirit of reform existing within the faculty. In certain cases the faculty resisted the lay interests of the alumni which threatened their vested interests in the classical subjects. In 1872, the Dartmouth faculty joined with the president and the trustees to beat down a request of the alumni that they be seated on the board of control to hasten educational reform. See Richard T. Ely, *Ground Under Our Feet* (New York, 1938), pp. 29–30.
[157] Wertenbaker, *Princeton*, pp. 215–55.
[158] *Ibid.*, pp. 153, 220.

her identity in a large university. No doubt they were, on the whole, more inclined to build a new chapel than to build a new scientific school. But their very presence was an incentive to experimentation. Knowing that the generosity of the alumni would catch up with him, Silliman the younger organized a school of science at Yale before he had acquired an endowment for it. In time, the alumni responded handsomely. When they did, the exclusiveness of the college that had been their pride, the homogeneity of the college that had won their praise, were in part destroyed. The Silliman school, which was differentiated from the college proper, required no compulsory prayers, no compulsory chapel, no compulsory hours of study. Its students, more mature than the average undergraduate, worked on their own in the laboratories, and its professors were guides, not goads, to learning. Soon there were Yale men who knew chemical laws but did not know Latin hexameters, and it was not less upsetting to staid tradition that these students did not receive the same liberal-arts degree awarded other Yale graduates.[159]

The breeding ground of institutional change is the sense of institutional failure. Student disorder and chronic poverty created grave inner doubts about the value of the education offered and led men to question the proposition that sound doctrine breeds sound morals. The organization of the alumni and the growth of faculty autonomy opened certain of these "strongholds of ancient prescription" to lay interests and liberal ideas. These changes in the roles of alumni and faculty were, to be sure, undirected movements; the old system was still substantially intact. The purposeful construction of a new system awaited the social and intellectual changes of the postwar period. It should not, however, be forgotten that the great builders of that period—Gilman, White, Eliot, Barnard—were schooled in the ante-bellum college. Not only did they acquire a sharp distaste for the old rigidities; they were inspired by its stirrings toward reform. And it should not be forgotten that it was, after all, Ticknor, not Eliot, who first suggested the elective system at Harvard; Silliman, not Hadley, who first breached the intrenched positions of Greek and Latin at Yale; Wayland, not White, who offered the first large-scale plan for a vocationalized higher education.

By 1860 the signs were pointing to a drastic revision of the goals of the college system. The growing emphasis on scholarship, the questioning of old pedagogical assumptions, the enlarging scale of philanthropy,

[159] Chittenden, *History of the Sheffield Scientific School,* I, 49–50.

were converting the larger colleges into institutions geared for research. At the same time, as the result of deeper social forces at work, the "conserving" function of the college no longer loomed so large. The unhinging of moral certainties by urban living, the fading out of the evangelical impulse, the depersonalization of human relations in the process of industrial expansion, were destroying that integral vision, that firm and assertive credulity, required of institutions devoted to conservation. Two other forces were to consummate this shift from "conserving" to "searching" in the universities of postwar America. The first was to be the powerful impact of Darwinism, which would unlock the creative potential of American academic science. The second was to be the influence of the German university, whose scholarly lore and academic traditions Americans admired and adapted. By 1860, the American colleges stood at the verge of a new outlook; two or three decades later, they would possess it fully.

The shift from conserving to searching portended great changes in the conception of academic freedom. As long as conserving was the foremost ideal, academic freedom was a freedom *for,* not *in,* the colleges. The conserver, taken as an ideal-type within the ranks of the men of knowledge, regards the knowledge inherited from the past as the seasoned wisdom of the race or the afflatus of God. As priest, he celebrates it; as scholastic, he systematizes it; as fundamentalist, he applies it, reverencing *ipsissima verba.* The pre-Civil War academic, by filling all three roles, maintained a certain intellectual autonomy—a freedom and isolation as a member of the community of the educated. In a New World, peopled by the uprooted, he kept alive a respect for traditions. In a democratic society, tending to be plebiscitarian in taste as well as in politics, he resisted the attempts of public whim and vulgarity to depreciate the college education. A good part of his opposition to a more secular university and a more vocationalized curriculum stemmed from his desire to protect very fragile values from the crush of a rough society. He sought the freedom not to acquiesce in the philistinism of his age.

This was the contribution of our academic conservers. But it is also in the character of the conserver to submit to the ideas he protects, and this is his major defect. The pre-Civil War college teacher considered the fundamental questions settled, the great truths possessed and funded and waiting only to be drawn upon. Alas, his fundamental questions, answered too didactically, were often empty of educational significance. Subjected to the parochialism of the denominational college, his great truths were transformed into dogmas. Screened for piety and correct belief, he was more alarmed by the attacks of outside parties than by the smothering influence of his own. His demand for freedom in instruction and investigation was, as a consequence, unemphatic and occasional: in a prisonhouse of one's own making, there are few incentives to escape.

The advent of the searcher into academic life reversed the relationship and relative importance of outer and inner freedoms. Characteristically, the searcher regards accumulated knowledge as no more than lore and hypothesis, as fallible as the men who made it. He may be the religious reformer, who strips the veil of mystery from arcane symbols; the artist, who rebels against the academy's official vision; the philosopher, who seeks a new starting point for thought. In the new university that was about to be born, the searcher was most often to wear the vestments of the scholar, seeking facts upon which to base new interpretations of the past; the social scientist, distinguishing what is myth and what reality; the physical and natural scientist, applying a disciplined test to current theories. The cultural autonomy of the college would matter less to the college teacher in these roles. Imbued with German ideals of scholarship, he would hope to contribute to progress by knowing more and knowing it more exactly, not by holding fast to values and a sense of the totality of things. Believing that progress was a social law, he would not only assume that tradition was mere opinion and experience, but that opinion improves as society ages and that experience grows stale with senescence. Without truths to speak for or purposes to defend, the new university would incline toward utility, and jeopardize its initiative and independence in order to answer client needs.

But these weaknesses were to be paid for by new strengths. The academic searcher was to develop arguments for freedom *within* the university that had not been strong before. Armed with the assumption that truth was something progressively to be discovered and provisionally held, he was to attack the presence of sectarianism in American higher education. By appealing to scientific methods of verification, he was to shift the emphasis from results to procedures in the warranting of belief. By introducing German methods of teaching and the German ideal of academic freedom, he was to attack those parental controls that curbed teacher and student alike. Finally, his prolonged apprenticeship, his specialized training, and his close ties with workers in his field, were to enable him to develop a professional *esprit* that would shield him against coercive administrators.

II: DARWINISM AND THE
NEW REGIME

Political revolutions, we are told, have certain traits in common. They are engendered by a series of events that inflame a segment of the population and reveal the injustice of the rulers. They are inspired by an ideology of resentment against those in positions of authority. They invoke the name (even as they transform the sense) of vital, though often dormant, human freedoms. The American academic revolution, foreshadowed in the ante-bellum period and fomented in the era of Darwin, reveals roughly analogous traits. The dismissals and harassments of teachers of evolution were the inflammatory events. The attack upon religious authority in science and education was the ideology of resentment. Freedom for academic inquiry, for which a new rationale was developed, was the freedom that was invoked. Under headings provided by this analogy, we shall analyze the decisive influence of Darwinism on academic thought and institutions.

INFLAMMATORY EVENTS

By any reckoning, the acceptance of Darwinism by American scientists was remarkably rapid. Darwin had surmised, with characteristic shrewdness, that the "young and rising naturalist" would be more receptive to his views than the men of the older generation who had staked their reputations on the special-creations theory.[1] And this was true. No sooner did the *Origin of Species* appear in 1859 than the younger scientists fell to work to test its hypotheses, fill in its gaps, and prove its prophecies.[2] But the great biologist had underestimated, with a

[1] Charles Darwin, *On the Origin of Species by Means of Natural Selection* (London, 1859), p. 417.
[2] Particularly Charles C. Abbott, William A. Hyatt, E. D. Cope, George B. Goode, William K. Brooks, Burt G. Wilder, O. C. Marsh, David S. Jordan, A. E. Verrill, A. S. Packard. The detailed work done in zoology to prove evolution is

humility that was also characteristic, his ability to convince older scientists, once their preconceptions had been challenged. To be sure, Louis Agassiz never did come around to accepting the mutability of the species, although he retreated from his first contention that Darwinism was "a scientific mistake, untrue in its facts, unscientific in its method, and mischievous in its tendency" to the view that Darwin had used "scientific methods" but had claimed more than was warranted by the facts.[3] Nevertheless, awesome as was Agassiz' authority, and important as it was in delaying the complete acceptance of evolution by American scientists,[4] it did not deter his colleague Asa Gray from at once championing Darwin's ideas—and this was the Gray who once had written that the fixity of species "has been settled by human observation." [5] Much against Darwin's expectations, James Dwight Dana, the inheritor of Benjamin Silliman's professorial chair and theological convictions, slowly gave his assent.[6] More quickly, Jeffries Wyman, in the twilight of his career, and Joseph Leidy, at the height of his fame,

summarized in Edward S. Morse, "Address," *Proceedings of the American Association for the Advancement of Science,* XXV (1877), 137–76.

[3] "Professor Agassiz on the Origin of Species," *American Journal of Science and Arts,* XXX, Second Series (July, 1860), 142–55; Louis Agassiz, "Evolution and the Permanence of Type," *Atlantic Monthly,* XXXIII (January, 1874), 94.

[4] See Bert J. Loewenberg, "The Reaction of American Scientists to Darwinism," *American Historical Review,* XXXVIII (July, 1933), 687–93.

[5] Asa Gray, "Explanation of the Vestiges," *North American Review,* LXII (April, 1846), 471. The first review by Gray of Darwin's book was cautiously favorable. "The Origin of Species by Means of Natural Selection," *American Journal of Science and Arts,* XXIX (March, 1860), 153–84. "Under the circumstances," he wrote to Darwin, "I suppose I do your theory more good here, by bespeaking for it a fair and favourable consideration, and by standing non-committed as to its full conclusions, than I should if I announced myself a convert; nor could I say the latter, with truth." Letter of Gray to Darwin, January 23, 1860. Francis Darwin, ed., *The Life and Letters of Charles Darwin* (New York, 1898), II, 66. Subsequent articles in the *Atlantic Monthly* (July, August, October, 1861) revealed that Gray had become a complete convert, though one more interested in squaring evolution with natural theology than in merely proving the empirical adequacy of the hypothesis.

[6] Darwin did not expect his friend Dana to be convinced. In a letter to the Yale scientist in 1863, Darwin wrote that he did not suppose that "with your strong and slowly acquired convictions and immense knowledge, you could have been converted. The utmost that I could have hoped would have been that you might possibly have been here or there staggered." Daniel C. Gilman, *Life of James Dwight Dana* (New York, 1899), 315. The 1870 edition of Dana's *Manual of Geology* considered the attempt to prove evolution as "vain"; the 1874 edition considered evolution a conclusion "most likely to be sustained by further research" though man was exempted from its laws; the final edition of the *Manual* (1895) put man in the evolutionary process. Loewenberg, "The Reaction of American Scientists to Darwinism," pp. 700–701.

cast in their lot with Darwinism.[7] The response of American scientists was more affirmative than that of the French (Darwin's candidacy for membership in the French Academy was at first rejected), more immediate than that of the English (not until twenty years after the appearance of the *Origin of Species* did Cambridge, Darwin's university, award him an honorary degree).[8] By contrast, the American Philosophical Society awarded Darwin honorary membership as early as 1869, and the gesture was soon repeated by other American societies.[9] By 1873, the year of Agassiz' death, the theory of evolution was no longer a disputed hypothesis within the American scientific community, though some scientists entertained strong doubts as to whether natural selection was the major evolutionary agent,[10] and a few were reluctant to place man in the evolutionary process.[11] When one considers the prolonged enthronement of the miracle-working God in organic science, the enormous pre-Darwinian resistance to the theory of transmutation, the entrenchment of the Aristotelian-Christian doctrine of fixed forms and final causes, fifteen years of scientific inquest were a very brief period of doubt.

But it happened that, as scientific doubts subsided, religious opposition rose. At first, the spokesmen of orthodox religion were mostly content to attack the new theory as grossly hypothetical or untrue. Remembering the fate of Lamarck and St. Hilaire, they were confident that science would refute what appeared to be a new perpetration of old errors.[12] When, however, it became increasingly clear that science

[7] Burt G. Wilder, "Jeffries Wyman, Anatomist: 1814–1874," in David Starr Jordan, ed., *Leading American Men of Science* (New York, 1910), pp. 193–94. "The Joseph Leidy Centenary," *Scientific Monthly*, XVIII (June, 1924), pp. 422–36.

[8] *Popular Science Monthly*, II (March, 1873), 601. *Atlantic Monthly*, XXX (October, 1872), 507–8.

[9] Thomas Huxley, "On the Reception of the 'Origin of Species,'" in Francis Darwin, ed., *Life and Letters of Darwin*, II, pp. 538–41.

[10] Under Edward Drinker Cope there arose a neo-Lamarckian school—misnamed because the school stressed the direct action of the environment on organic structure (which had been denied by Lamarck) as well as the effects of use and disuse. See Cope, *The Origin of the Fittest* (New York, 1887). A neo-Darwinian school, consisting of the American followers of August Weismann, emphasized natural selection exclusively, which had never been Darwin's position. See George Gaylord Simpson, *The Meaning of Evolution* (New Haven, 1949).

[11] A respectable though not authoritative view, propounded by St. George Mivart and Alfred Russel Wallace, alleged the discontinuity between sentient and rational forms of life. St. George Mivart, *On the Genesis of Species* (New York, 1871); Alfred Russel Wallace, *Criticism of the Descent of Man* (New York, 1871).

[12] Cf. Heman Lincoln, "Development vs. Creation," *Baptist Quarterly*, II (July, 1868), 270; W. C. Wilson, "Darwin on the Origin of Species," *Methodist Quarterly Review*, XLIII (October, 1861), 605–25.

would return a favorable verdict, and when, furthermore, Darwin bluntly declared that his theory included man, the pitch of opposition rose and was sustained for several decades.[13] In this chapter we shall enlarge upon the character of the religious opposition to Darwin. Suffice it for the moment to say that it too diminished in time. In the 1880s, certain religious leaders came to see that science would not be swerved from its course by clamor and vituperation, and that the rigid opposition of the churches would serve to isolate them, insulate them, and destroy their ancient power.[14] The fading appeal of the Protestant churches for the working masses in the cities underscored the need for change, for some concession to the times.[15] Hence, one group of theologians, taking their cue from the compromises effected during the controversy over geology, endeavored to prove that the Biblical text supported the evolution of animals, and that the whole process of evolution was another indication of design.[16] A second group went further and undertook a thorough revision of theology in the light of evolutionary science. Applying Darwin's laws and Spencer's optimism to a wide range of Christian dogma, they maintained that sin was not a falling from grace but the heritage from man's brutal ancestry, that revelation was not a visitation from above but the product of developing reason, that God's will does not work from outside nature, but works through nature immanently.[17] In the eighties such doctrines were still regarded by the orthodox as abominable theological heresies. By the last decade of the nineteenth century, however, many religious spokesmen, especially in the Northeast, had crossed over to evolution on just such causeways of rationalization.[18] Talk of conflict between

[13] An analysis of the trends in religious opposition to Darwinism can be found in Windsor Hall Roberts, "The Reaction of American Protestant Churches to the Darwinian Philosophy," unpublished Ph.D. dissertation (University of Chicago, 1936).

[14] There had, of course, been moderates in the religious camp from the beginning. See S. R. Calthrop, "Religion and Evolution," *Religious Magazine and Monthly Review*, L (September, 1873), 193–213.

[15] Arthur M. Schlesinger, Sr., "A Critical Period in American Religion," *Proceedings, Massachusetts Historical Society*, LXIV (June, 1932), 423–47.

[16] See James McCosh, *The Development Hypothesis: Is it Sufficient?* (New York, 1876); Arnold Guyot, *Creation or The Biblical Cosmogony in the Light of Modern Science* (New York, 1884).

[17] See Henry Ward Beecher, "The Sinfulness of Man," in *Evolution and Religion* (New York, 1885), p. 81; Lyman Abbott, *The Evolution of Christianity* (New York, 1893), pp. 112 ff.

[18] The turn of opinion in the Northeast is neatly exemplified by the articles that appeared in a popular journal, the *North American Review*. In 1860, the magazine published Francis Bowen's violently antagonistic review of Darwin's book ("Dar-

science and religion was then discounted in the very journals that had cried it up a decade or two before.[19] By the end of the century, antievolutionism had lost its place in serious theology,[20] though it remained astonishingly strong as part of a folkish fundamentalism.[21]

How may we account for the hostility of the religious community to this new development in biology? The modern ear, jarred by fundamentalist idioms, may hear only the accent of unreason. That some of Darwin's critics were shallow and ignorant is certainly true. On one obtuse level of criticism, for example, some of Darwin's opponents foreshortened the steps in the process of evolution and described it as "the tendency of favourable varieties of turnips to become men," or as the theory that "man, having first been a tadpole, became a monkey, and then wore off his tail by sedentary habits." [22] Others, exhibiting a kind of phylogenetic snobbery, seemed to think that Darwin had libeled the race by discovering simian rather than seraphic ancestors.[23] Still others, not grasping the distinction between probable and demonstrative reasoning, thought the absence of fossil remains linking man with the other primates completely disproved evolution.[24] But ignorance

---

win on the Origin of Species," XC [April, 1860], 474–506). In 1868, Francis E. Abbot, reviewing Spencer's *Principles of Biology,* attacked the special-creation hypothesis (CVII [October, 1868], 378). In 1870, C. L. Brace, in an article entitled "Darwinism in Germany," lauded Darwin's "incomparable carefulness and diligence" (CX [April, 1870], 284–99). Finally, Chauncey Wright's three articles appeared in defense of Darwin, Darwinism, and the Darwinian method of inquiry, "Review of Wallace's Contributions to the Theory of Natural Selection," CXI (October, 1870), 282; "Review of Darwin's Descent of Man," CXIII (July, 1871), 63–103; "Evolution by Natural Selection," CXV (July, 1872), 1–30.

[19] William North Rice, a geologist and an eminent Methodist layman, had castigated the clergy in the 1870s for their unmovable opposition to Darwinism. In 1891, Rice reported that "now and then . . . some theological Rip Van Winckle attempts the old Sinaitic thunders in denunciation of the essential atheism of evolution; but his utterances are regarded by his brethren in the church not with sympathy, but with amusement or mortification." "Twenty-five Years of Scientific Progress," *Bibliotheca Sacra,* L (January, 1893), 27–28.

[20] Frank H. Foster, *The Modern Movement in American Theology* (New York, 1939), p. 160.

[21] Stewart G. Cole, *The History of Fundamentalism* (New York, 1931), *passim.*

[22] Cited in *The Index,* Vol. III, Supplement (April 13, 1872), p. 3; see, also, Sidney Ratner, "Evolution and the Rise of the Scientific Spirit in America," *Philosophy of Science,* III (January, 1936), 108–9.

[23] "Modern Atheism," *The Southern Review,* X (January, 1872), 121–58.

[24] Frederick Gardiner, "Darwinism," *Bibliotheca Sacra,* XXIX (April, 1872), 240–89; "Darwinianism," *American Quarterly Church Review,* XXI (January, 1870), 524–36.

alone would not have attached so much passion to these objections. At the core of the religious resistance, making it hard and bitter and giving it desperate strength, was not so much ignorance as fear. "Nothing is more evident," wrote the Andover theologian, William J. Tucker, "than that a certain sense of fear . . . has begun to seize the heart of our generation. We are literally afraid of the world in which we live." [25] The fact was that while Darwin had labored to make the natural world intelligible and pellucid, to many of the men of his generation he had rendered that world cold and repellent, and they fought to keep it safe from his negations.

Generally speaking, two eventualities were feared: the annihilation of spirit and the destruction of moral sanctions. Darwin's extension of natural law to organic life, following upon its extension to the heavens and to the history of the earth, seemed to exclude divine and ideal ends from the whole theater of existence. Until vitalism and finalism were reconstructed in evolutionary terms, it did not seem that any of the old truces between spirit and matter, purpose and law, could survive under Darwin's influence. The idea of the evolution of the species cut straight under the belief that all living things attain a preordained form; the idea of the evolution of the species through chance variations refuted the belief in divine contrivance; the idea of the evolution of man through chance variations destroyed all hope of spiritual favor. By thus denying spirit, Darwin was thought to doom the whole moral economy based on salvation and retribution. For, in a world where man was mere matter, a being perhaps ultimate but not unique, the ideas of immortality and redemption were errors based on delusions. In a world directed by impersonal force, insensible to the suffering through which it achieved blind goals, prayer and propitiation were wasted on a void. In a world that was lawful through and through, and not susceptible to miracles, the mission and the message of Christ could not have been supernaturally decreed. If in such a world values were to have any meaning or pertinence at all, this could only be achieved by seizing on brute existence and calling it ideal—a course that the popular Herbert Spencer was taking, to the destruction of transcendental ethics and all absolute good. As though this were not enough, Biblical scholarship had come on the scene to complete the unholy work.

[25] Quoted in Daniel Day Williams, *The Andover Liberals: A Study in American Theology* (New York, 1941), p. 46.

Just as the evolutionists linked man with lesser organisms, so the anthropologists linked Scripture with heathen fable. Where Darwin put God beyond the frontiers of nature, the critics of the Bible put His word in the limbo of myth. Who, then, could look on theories that turned Christianity into a mere quotation, theology into an erroneous physics, the universe into something soulless and friendless, and not call these doctrines false, their perpetrators anathema?

This was the psychological background for the attack upon evolution in the colleges. Inevitably, as science was converted to evolution and the curriculum was converted to science, the heresies broached by Darwin bid for academic acceptance. This was inevitable and not at first far-reaching, but in the catastrophic vision of the faithful, where small things loomed as great and innocuous acts as enormities, the attempt to teach evolution seemed part of a devilish plot. Determined efforts were made in the sixties, seventies, and early eighties to hold the line of education by the tactic of exclusion where possible, by threats and tirades where necessary. Synods gave warnings to trustees and trustees instructed presidents to reject the applications of Darwinians. Attacks in the local pulpits, alarms in the religious press, were employed to make colleges toe the mark and professors mend their ways. Once again, a battle of ideas became a battle for the schools.

Because the religious reaction was intense, the colleges experienced difficulties; because the religious reaction was also variable, the colleges experienced rebellion. Had a policy of excluding the proponents of evolution been uniformly applied, it is very possible that deviants would never have appeared to disturb the peace of the academy. If professors could always have known the penalties, they might never have been willing to run risks. But the fact was that academic policy was not consistent and the wages of heresy were not always known. Whether evolutionists would be hired or not depended on a number of factors: the strength of the college's tie to a church or sectarian sponsor; the rigidity of the religious creed binding trustees and staff; the importance of science and scientists in the college's scheme of education; the ambition of college leaders to defend their institution's reputation. In general, the theological seminaries practiced exclusion more rigidly than the state universities, the colleges under close church governance more consistently than those whose church connections were looser. But even in a theological seminary, a Woodrow or Smyth could gain admittance, and even in a church-dominated college, a Winchell could be engaged. Moreover, the religious forces did not agree on the kind of teaching they should proscribe. Lacking ecclesiastical unity, Protestants could not be consistent in their policies, positions, and plans. Some thought it dangerous mischief to teach evolution even as an hypothesis; others were roused to action only when it was taught as the truth. In certain places, any sort of evolutionary exegesis would incur the wrath of the religious; in others, a barrier would be erected solely around the field of philosophy. Furthermore, there was a division in religious councils as to the possibilities of reconciliation: in certain places the old faith was to be kept pure, free from any foreign admixture; in other places it might be combined with some of the findings of science. In fostering academic friction, uncertainty is as important as repression. In a situation where the margin of safe divergence is obscure, the pale of orthodoxy undiscernible, the penalties of heresy unpredictable, the cautious man will blunder and the man of moderation will be martyred. One of the consistent and significant features of these academic-freedom cases was that the participants were temperate evolutionists who, in the course of events, were trapped into conflict with authority and were surprised into suffering for the cause.

The clearest illustrations of this can be found in the cases that arose in the theological seminaries.[26] In these institutions a large proportion of the faculty was cut to the denominational pattern; the purposes of instruction were creedal, the interest in science undeveloped. This was particularly true in the southern theological seminaries. John M. Mecklin, who knew the southern seminaries in this period at first hand, described them as living in "peaceful monastic seclusion" untroubled by the new discoveries of science. Their mental outlook, he wrote, was "not essentially different from that of Bernard and the monks of Clairvaux. It was naively assumed that this orthodox point of view coincided

[26] Valuable secondary works on these and all the academic-freedom cases involving Darwinism are few. The chief source of information is Andrew Dickson White's *A History of the Warfare of Science with Theology* (New York, 1896), and every subsequent treatment of these cases has followed at least the valuable leads of these volumes, if not their biases. This work's compilation of cases and use of not readily available newspaper materials are invaluable, but its simple Manichean interpretation, suggested by the militant title, leaves much to be desired. Supplementary to this work are Bert J. Loewenberg, "The Impact of the Doctrine of Evolution on American Thought," unpublished Ph.D. dissertation (Harvard University, 1933), and Howard K. Beale, *A History of Freedom of Teaching in American Schools* (New York, 1941), pp. 202–7.

with the truth." [27] Yet even these schools for ministers, in their conservative southern setting, were not consistent enough in their demands to eliminate all uncertainty.

In 1857 the Presbyterian Theological Seminary in Columbia, South Carolina, established "The Perkins Professorship of Natural Science in Connexion with Revelation, the design of which shall be to evince the harmony of science with the records of our faith, and to refute the objections of infidel naturalists." [28] The controlling synods chose for this task a Presbyterian minister who had studied science under Agassiz and had received a Ph.D. from Heidelberg. For twenty-five years James Woodrow labored to fit the odd-shaped pegs of science into the existing holes of theology, and his long tenure may be taken as evidence that he was thought to have succeeded.[29] Meanwhile, however, Darwin had appeared on the scene to complicate the problem of apology. The suspicion arose that the professor had accepted evolution, and that, in holding to this theory as his standard, he had reversed the fitting process and was now attempting to adapt theology to his scientific beliefs. Requested by the seminary's board in 1884 to expound his views on evolution, Woodrow replied that he accepted the "divine inspiration of every expression which [the Bible] contains"; that he thought, however, that the Bible had nothing to say on the mode of man's creation; that where it did speak in contrary terms, as in the story of the origins of Eve, he was willing to reject evolution.[30] As Woodrow expected, the Board of Directors was appeased by an approach to evolution that let the Bible decide its applications. But the governing Synod declared Woodrow out of bounds by that small but all-important fraction of belief which sets sectarians apart. The issue, resolved one group in the South Carolina Synod, did not hinge on whether "the said views of Dr. Woodrow contradicted the Bible in its highest and absolute sense, but upon the question whether they contradict the interpretation of the Bible by the Presbyterian Church in the United States." [31] The

---

[27] John M. Mecklin, *My Quest for Freedom* (New York, 1945), pp. 60, 61.

[28] Marion W. Woodrow, ed., *Dr. James Woodrow as Seen by His Friends* (Columbia, S.C., 1909), p. 13.

[29] Woodrow's conflict with the obscurantists in his church preceded this crisis. See Thomas Cary Johnson, *The Life and Letters of Robert Lewis Dabney* (Richmond, Va., 1903), pp. 339–49.

[30] James Woodrow, "Address on Evolution," delivered May 7, 1884, to the Alumni Association of the Columbia Theological Seminary. In Marion Woodrow, *Dr. James Woodrow*, pp. 617–45.

[31] White, *History of the Warfare . . .* , I, 317.

Board of Directors yielded to pressure, and Woodrow was dismissed for fostering the kind of compromise it was the duty of his office to promote.[32]

The southern seminary was not the only place where trials and ordeals for vague infidelities were endured. In 1886, the Board of Visitors of the Andover Theological Academy (Congregational), which by charter was charged with the task of admonishing or removing professors for heterodoxy,[33] tried five members of the faculty for defection from the Andover Creed. As a result, one of the accused, Professor Egbert C. Smyth, Brown Professor of Ecclesiastical History and President of the Faculty, was dismissed. The defendants had not been entirely unaware that they had been earning the displeasure of the Visitors. For some years their teachings had been subjected to mounting criticism in the church. According to the most orthodox theologians, Calvinism was based on the absolute trustworthiness of Scripture, the inherent sinfulness of man, the certainty of future punishment. The Andover professors, using the *Andover Review* as their organ, had accepted the higher criticism of the Bible, the doctrine of natural evolution, and the dogma of probation after death for those who had never known Christ.[34] But these did not seem to them gross enough divergences to warrant indictment and trial. After all, their heresies, in any large view, were marginal, and their tenure of office had been long. In no vital respect did they disavow the fundamental dogmas of Calvin. Certainly they had always opposed the aberrant views of the Unitarians and the agnosticism of such evolutionists as Spencer. *Progressive Orthodoxy,* the title of one of their books, was the proper name for their position. Moreover, when appointed to their positions, they had reserved the right to interpret the Andover Creed in accordance with their consciences, and had not been disturbed for doing so—Smyth for as long as twenty-five years. The fact that the trustees sided with

[32] A similar case occurred at the Southern Baptist Seminary at Louisville, Kentucky, where in 1879 Professor Crawford H. Toy was expelled for expounding advanced Biblical criticism. This came after a ten-year incumbency. Charles C. Torrey, "Crawford H. Toy," *Dictionary of American Biography*, XVIII, 621–22; *National Cyclopedia of American Biography*, VI, 94.

[33] William J. Tucker, *My Generation* (Boston and New York, 1919), p. 186. Tucker, one of the defendants in the trial, gives the clearest picture of the Andover controversy. See also Henry K. Rose, *History of Andover Theological Seminary* (Boston, 1933), pp. 168–79.

[34] Daniel Day Williams, *The Andover Liberals,* gives an excellent presentation of the New Theology as promulgated at Andover; pp. 64–83, and *passim*.

the accused at the trial,[35] and the fact that the Visitors dismissed only Egbert Smyth, though his colleagues shared his opinions, reveal the divided and unpredictable character of the orthodox attack. As it happened, the case had a happy outcome. The Visitors' decision was appealed and set aside in the Supreme Court of Massachusetts and Smyth was restored to his position.[36]

The Winchell affair at Vanderbilt presents another variation on the same theme. A large gift from Commodore Vanderbilt in 1873 converted Central University in Nashville, Tennessee, from a school for the training of ministers to a large, multipurpose university. Under the terms of the gift the institution retained an ecclesiastical system of control: the bishops of the Methodist church comprised the Board of Supervisors, and Bishop Holland N. McTyeire was named permanent president of the trustees.[37] The addition of wealth to evangelical zeal had the effect of broadening perspectives. Desiring to make this university supreme among the institutions of the region, and possessing a money endowment unmatched in the impoverished South, McTyeire engaged eminent men for his faculty, among them the able Alexander Winchell, an avowed, though conservative, evolutionist. It was logical to assume that once ambition had opened the gates to an evolutionist, ambition would thereafter protect him. No doubt this was Winchell's assumption when in 1878 he wrote a tract on the pre-Adamite origin of man.[38] The argument, based on the assumption that Negroes were racially too inferior to have stemmed from the Biblical Adam, had appeared in southern race mythology before.[39] The book was liberally sprinkled with reverent allusions to the scientific truth of Scripture. Winchell, moreover, was not yet ready to concede that the law of evolution included man, and he always believed that the law of evolution but administered the will of the Maker.[40] Yet even these conciliatory

[35] The arguments of the complainants and the defendants can be found in *Arguments on Behalf of the Complainants in the Matter of the Complaint against Egbert C. Smyth* (Boston, 1887); *The Question at Issue in the Andover Case* (Boston, 1893); *The Andover Heresy: Professor Smyth's Argument, Together with the Statements of Professors Tucker, Harris, Hincks and Churchill* (Boston, 1887).

[36] *Egbert C. Smyth vs. Visitors of the Theological Institution in Phillips Academy in Andover,* 154 Massachusetts Reports, 551–69 (1892).

[37] Edwin Mims, *History of Vanderbilt University* (Nashville, Tenn., 1946), pp. 32–33.

[38] Alexander Winchell, *Adamites and Preadamites* (Syracuse, 1878).

[39] For a systematic discussion of this point see William Sumner Jenkins, *Pro-Slavery Thought in the Old South* (Chapel Hill, N.C., 1935), pp. 254–75.

[40] Alexander Winchell, *The Doctrine of Evolution: Its Data, Its Principles and*

ideas proved offensive to the faithful. Religious journals, one of them under the editorial direction of the dean of Vanderbilt's Biblical Department, accused Winchell of attempting to destroy the truths that were given in the Gospel.[41] In the face of this criticism, the President's ambition quickly surrendered to caution. Winchell was dismissed, under circumstances that again reveal the incalculable consequences of nonconformity. We quote Winchell's published account in full:

Forty-five minutes before the hour appointed for my late lecture at the University on "Man in the Light of Geology," I met Bishop McTyeire casually, and he embraced the opportunity to introduce a business which caused me extraordinary surprise. He said, in effect:

"We are having considerable annoyance from the criticisms which are passed by our people on some of your positions in matters of opinion, and it is likely to increase."

"What positions?" I asked.

"The positions taken in your pamphlet on Adamites and Pre-Adamites. Our people do not believe those things; they object to evolution."

"But," said I, "evolution is not professed in that pamphlet; there is not a single position in it which is not generally accepted, save the opinion that perhaps the black races are older than the white and brown."

"Well, our people are of the opinion that such views are contrary to the 'plan of redemption.'"

"The redemption of man," I replied, "could as well operate retroactively from Christ to races older than Adam, as from Christ to Abraham or Adam."

"I am not offering any objections myself," replied the Bishop, "but our people are complaining and the University will suffer, and I thought, perhaps, you might relieve us of our embarrassments. The Board," he continued, "will be in session in a few minutes, and they will meet again, after your lecture."

"I am unable to understand you. I think you exaggerate the complaints. Besides, the complaints are groundless."

"Well," said the Bishop, "the St. Louis *Advocate* has been hostiling the subject, and you know what the attitude of our *Advocate* has been."

The latter mention aroused equal surprise and indignation; for only a few days previously the Bishop, in a lengthy and confidential interview, which of course I am not at liberty to report, had made statements—revelations—to me, such that I did not expect to see Dr. Summers' perversions and insinuations turned to my disadvantage at the hand of a high official occupying an inside position. I reminded the Bishop of what he had said in the conversation with a view to inducing me to remain till commencement and deliver a

Its Theistic Bearings (New York, 1874), lectures delivered at Drew Theological Seminary, December, 1873; *Reconciliation of Science and Religion* (New York, 1877), p. 144; "Grounds and Consequences of Evolution," *Sparks from a Geologist's Hammer* (Chicago, 1881), p. 332.

41 Mims, *History of Vanderbilt University*, p. 100.

lecture. "And you, yourself," I added, "proposed that I should lecture on Evolution."

"That is true," he replied, "for I wanted you to have an opportunity to put yourself right."

He did not explain whether he wished me to recant, or assemble [sic] or avow and defend my belief.

Referring again to the two discontented newspapers, he said, "These are feathers—straws."

"A great University ought to know how to withstand feathers and straws," said I.

"But they are likely to become stones," added the Bishop.

"These complaints are puerile," I continued. "They are themselves misconceptions of the facts, and they are prompted by bigotry. There has been no attempt to disprove the positions of my pamphlet. Besides that, I have not been heard; I have had no opportunity to explain or defend."

On repeating his request that I would relieve the Board of an embarrassment, I declared that I did not understand his meaning, and he then explained that he thought I might considerately "decline a reappointment."

"Are professors subject to annual appointment?" I asked.

"Well, yes; special professors are," he replied.

"No," said I, with indignation and scorn, "I will not, on such grounds, decline a reappointment. If the Board have the manliness to dismiss for cause, and declare the cause, I prefer they should do it. No power on earth could persuade me to decline. But the action which you foreshadow will be unjust and oppressive, as well as discrediting to the University. It will recoil upon its authors."

"We do not propose to treat you as the Inquisition treated Galileo," said the Bishop.

"But what you propose is the same thing," I rejoined. "It is ecclesiastical proscription for an opinion which *must be settled by scientific evidence.*" [42]

In the older eastern colleges, the cases arising over evolution formed a somewhat different pattern. Here religion and science had lived together in better accord. Steeped in irenic traditions, these colleges proved to be far more receptive to evolutionary ideas. Gradually, without fanfare, Darwinists were appointed to their expanding departments of science. In 1880, the roster at Yale included such evolutionists as O. C. Marsh in paleontology,[43] Addison Emery Verrill in zoology,[44]

[42] Letter of Alexander Winchell to the Nashville *Daily American,* June 16, 1878. The italics are in the text. The Library of Congress newspaper collection.

[43] Marsh was a distinguished advocate of the evolution of all life from simple forms, and his thoroughgoing evolutionism admitted no exceptions. "To doubt evolution to-day is to doubt science and science is only another name for truth." *Proceedings of the American Association for the Advancement of Science,* XXVI (1877), 212. "One of the main characteristics of this epoch is the belief that *all*

Sidney Irving Smith in zoology and comparative anatomy,[45] and James Dwight Dana in geology;[46] at Brown there was Alpheus Spring Packard, a neo-Lamarckian entomologist;[47] at Princeton, though Cope's application was refused,[48] Arnold Guyot in geography,[49] Charles A. Young in astronomy, and Cyrus Brackett in physics[50] were evolutionists to some degree. At Harvard, the oldest college, which was becoming under Eliot also the greatest, every naturalist on the staff—Gray, Hagen, Goodale, Whitney, Shaler, James, Farlow, Faxon, and the younger Agassiz—accepted the theory of mutability.[51] To be sure, the pace of acceptance was not everywhere rapid: in 1880, the Reverend Mr.

---

life, living and extinct has been evolved from simple forms. Another prominent feature is the accepted fact of the *great antiquity of the human race.*" Presidential Address, *Proceedings of the American Association for the Advancement of Science,* XXVIII (1879), 33. Winchell had been dismissed only a year before for saying what Marsh could say with complete impunity. Indeed, even at Nashville, Marsh was bold enough to say in 1877 that "every sensible man is an evolutionist." Mims, *History of Vanderbilt University,* p. 60. In paleontology, Marsh's reconstruction of the development of the horse through geologic ages was acclaimed by Darwin as the best support of his theory that had appeared since the *Origin of Species.* Charles Schuchert and Clara Mae Le Vene, *O. C. Marsh, Pioneer in Paleontology* (New Haven, 1940), p. 247.

[44] See Wesley R. Coe, "Addison Emery Verrill," National Academy of Sciences, *Biographical Memoirs,* XIV (1929), 39; Wesley R. Coe, "A Century of Zoology in America," *A Century of Science in America* (New Haven, 1948), pp. 410–12.

[45] "An eager disciple of the then controversial Darwinian theory of Evolution, he sought for verification of this hypothesis in all he saw around him." Wesley R. Coe, "Sidney Irving Smith" in National Academy of Sciences, *Biographical Memoirs,* XIV (1929), 8.

[46] See p. 321n.

[47] With Cope and Hyatt, Packard founded the Neo-Lamarckian school of evolutionary thought. *Popular Science Monthly,* LXVII (May, 1905), 126–27. Packard's textbooks for high school and college students declared for evolution. See *First Lessons in Geology* (Providence, R.I., 1882), and *Zoology for High Schools and Colleges* (New York, 1880).

[48] In 1873, Cope failed to receive consideration for a newly created chair in natural science. His impression was that this was because of his pronounced views on evolution, but there is no factual proof that this was so. Benjamin Marcus, "Edward Drinker Cope," in Jordan, ed., *Leading American Men of Science,* p. 335.

[49] "While adopting the law of development and applying it to all history, still [he] believed that true species came into existence only by divine act. In his later years, as his work on 'Creation' shows, he was led to accept, though with some reservation, the doctrine of evolution through natural causes. He excepted man, and also the first of animal life." James Dwight Dana, "Arnold Guyot," National Academy of Sciences, *Biographical Memoirs,* II (1886), 334.

[50] There is nothing in their textbooks that would reveal acceptance of evolution, but it was claimed in the *Popular Science Monthly* that they were evolutionists "without reserve." "Scientific Teaching in the Colleges," *Popular Science Monthly,* XVI (February, 1880), 558.

[51] *The Index,* XI (March 4, 1880), 112–13.

Chadbourne, President of Williams, held forth against evolution in the college's only course in biology;[52] Amherst did not offer a course on evolution until 1897.[53] Taken as a group, however, these colleges were not proscriptive in the area of science: their scientists could find facts in Darwin's favor and not be denounced as unclean. Yet even here there was an area where ideas collided. This was the vague and indeterminate zone where science impinged on philosophy. It fell to the clerical presidents to try to police that zone, and friction arose when they laid down the rule: "Evolution so far but no further."

We are able to describe the attitudes of these pivotal figures, the eastern college presidents, on the basis of a questionnaire addressed to nine of them in the year 1880.[54] The question they were asked was whether they allowed it to be taught that "man, at least so far as his physical structure is concerned," was evolved from irrational animals. The answer they gave was "No!" and the reasons they gave are instructive. Several referred to the lack of evidence for such a sweeping hypothesis. The Reverend Julius H. Seelye, President of Amherst, wrote:

So long as the notion that man is evolved from the monkey has not a single fact to rest upon, and is in flat contradiction to all the facts of history, I think we may leave it with the sciolists. . . . This college does not yet teach groundless guesses for ascertained truths of science.[55]

[52] Cf. Paul Ansel Chadbourne, *Lectures on Natural Theology* (New York, 1867), and *Instinct, Its Office in the Animal Kingdom and Its Relation to the Higher Powers in Man* (New York, 1872).

[53] The catalogue of 1884–85 said: "While one special aim of the department is to furnish the student of medicine with a broad foundation for his future studies, its general aim is to lead every student to a careful examination of the laws which govern the structure, actions and occurrence of all living forms" (p. 32). The catalogue of 1897–98 went further: "The evolution of the Animal Kingdom. In this course the student traces, *as far as possible* [our italics], the line of evolution leading from the protozoon to man" (p. 52). The catalogue of 1900–1901 completely accepted evolution: "Zoology 2a. The evolution of lower invertebrates. 2b. The evolution of higher invertebrates and of vertebrates. 2c. The evolution of man" (p. 62).

[54] The presidents polled were Noah Porter of Yale, Martin Brewer Anderson of Rochester, James McCosh of Princeton, William Cassaday Cattell of Lafayette, Julius H. Seelye of Amherst, Eliphalet Nott Potter of Union, Paul Ansel Chadbourne of Williams, Samuel Gilman Brown of Hamilton, Ezekiel Gilman Robinson of Brown. Taken by the orthodox and vigilant *New York Observer*, the poll was designed to disprove the assertion that the evolution of man was taught in the colleges. The presidents of Harvard, Pennsylvania, and Johns Hopkins were not polled, for the probable reason that these presidents would not have given the desired answers. For commentary on the liberal side, see *The Index*, IX (March 4, 1880), 112–13.

[55] *Ibid.*, p. 112.

On the same tack, President Samuel Gilman Brown of Hamilton declared that

the doctrine of the "evolution of man from irrational animals" has never to my knowledge, been taught at Hamilton College. I trust it never will be till it has been proved true, as in my judgment it has not been, and I do not think it ever will be.[56]

The modern commentator cannot help observing that while these presidents paid their respects to the data, they ignored the verdict of science; that whereas they wished to put alien doctrines to test, they artfully or credulously supposed that their own assumptions were true. Others relied on the arguments of doctrinal moralism. The Reverend William Cassaday Cattell of Lafayette declared:

I have never known of any of my colleagues expressing either in private or in the classroom, the opinion referred to. . . . We are keenly alive to the danger from what is manifestly the infidel *trend* of the views generally held by evolutionists. It is a great relief to me to know that there is such a cordial acceptance of the old faith, which it has been the tendency or avowed aim of these materialistic teachers to destroy." [57]

And the Reverend James McCosh of Princeton replied:

I teach that man's soul was made in the image of God, and his body out of the dust of the ground. I do not oppose development, but an atheistic development.[58]

This was a half-way covenant that Francis Abbot called an "oil-and-water mixture of miracle and law." The two conventional arguments of the religious opposition were the pseudoscientific "not proven" and the theological "infidel trend."

Neither argument would pacify or convince the evolutionists on the faculties of institutions governed by antirevolutionists. Both arguments invited contradiction: the first through different readings of the record, the second through denials of the charge. The Porter-Sumner case at Yale in the late 1870s illustrates the point that once evolution had been accepted in the commerce of academic ideas, no selective blockade or embargo could thereafter easily be enforced. Hostilities began at Yale in 1879 when President Noah Porter demanded that Sumner abandon the use of Spencer's *Study of Sociology* as a textbook. Yale's venerable president had no objection to the teaching of evolution in the field of

[56] *Ibid.*   [57] *Ibid.* (Italics in the text.)   [58] *Ibid.*

natural science; [59] but he saw a great difference between Darwin's scientific synthesis of variation, adaptation, and selection and Spencer's philosophical trinity of matter, environment, and force. The difference, as he saw it, lay primarily in the implications of each for theistic religion. Porter wrote to Sumner:

The freedom and unfairness with which it [Spencer's book] attacks every Theistic Philosophy of society and of history and the cool and yet sarcastic effrontery with which he assumes that material elements and laws are the only forces and laws which any scientific man can recognize, seem to me to condemn the book as a textbook for a miscellaneous class in an undergraduate course.[60]

This pronouncement took Sumner by surprise. Porter had appointed Sumner to his post in 1872 over considerable religious opposition.[61] Spencer's works had been used in Porter's classes, and though there they became foils for Christian doctrine,[62] their use in other classes had not been proscribed. It would seem, wrote Sumner in reply, that "the use of Spencer's books is a privilege of the President and his use of them does not . . . constitute a precedent for anybody else; but I confess that this view of the matter never suggested itself to me." [63] Here again the unpredictable character of the religious riposte made prudence all but impossible. On the other hand, it is doubtful that the arrogant and opinionated Sumner would have taken the prudent course even if he had known it. To him, Porter was identified with a group that was opposing everything modern in education, from the elective system to alumni representation.[64] As a minister of the Episcopal church, Sumner had fought to liberalize theology and to correct the follies of sectarianism.[65] In Spencer, Sumner found scientific support for his rigid ethic of self-reliance and his strenuous belief in *laissez faire*.[66] A

[59] Schuchert and Le Vene, *O. C. Marsh*, pp. 238–39. Porter was no obscurantist in religion. He was opposed to fanaticism and pietistic fervor, and to sectarian bickering in missionary work. See Walter James, "Noah Porter," unpublished Ph.D. dissertation (Columbia University, 1951).

[60] Harris E. Starr, *William Graham Sumner* (New York, 1925), pp. 346–47. Starr's account of this controversy is indispensable.

[61] Cornelius Howard Patton and Walter Taylor Field, *Eight O'Clock Chapel, A Study of New England College Life in the Eighties* (Boston and New York, 1927), p. 102.

[62] Henry Holt, *Garrulities of an Octogenarian Editor* (Boston and New York, 1923), pp. 306–7.

[63] Starr, *William Graham Sumner,* p. 361.

[64] *Ibid.,* p. 75.   [65] *Ibid.,* p. 114.

[66] See William Graham Sumner, *What Social Classes Owe to Each Other* (New York, 1883).

powerful controversialist, a strong personality, a man who became a tradition at Yale while he lived and the idol of a cult after his death, Sumner was a formidable adversary for even a president of Yale.[67]

Sumner's defense was contained in a letter which he circulated to the faculty and the members of the Yale Corporation. He did not undertake to defend the merits of Spencer's book in any serious way— "what could be gained by an argument about that question? Where should it be carried on? Who wants to hear it?" The essential issue, as he saw it, was whether a professor who was competent enough to be allowed to teach should teach without restraint from religious taboos. In pitching his answer on this level Sumner wrote neither an *apologia pro vita sua* nor a brief for evolutionary philosophy, but an important document of academic freedom.

Sumner's arguments were directly opposed to those offered by the nine clerical college presidents. First of all, he rejected the *ad hominem* test so dear to the doctrinal moralists:

Mr. Spencer's religious opinions seem to me of very little importance in this connection, and, when I was looking for a book on sociology, the question whether it was a good or available book in a scientific point of view occupied my attention exclusively. Neither did I take into account the horror of Spencer's name, which, as I have since learned, is entertained by some people. If I had known of it, however, I should not have thought that it was a proper consideration to weigh much in the question which presented itself to me.[68]

Nor, said Sumner, was the argument that sociology was undeveloped as a science in any sense sufficient or compelling:

Pres. Porter affirms that sociology is inchoate and tentative. So is psychology; so are many new developments of physics, biology and other sciences. To object to what is inchoate and tentative is to set up a closed canon of human learning.[69]

Above all, he would not concede that any part of science should be quarantined:

His [Porter's] position was that the students might better get no sociology than run the risk of getting agnosticism in getting sociology, and he even seems to maintain that they might better get no sociology than get it from a book by Spencer. I resisted this and maintained that they should have sociology anyhow, from the best means available, and I would not submit to a restraint the

---

[67] Biographical material on Sumner may be found in Sumner's autobiographical sketch in *A History of the Class of 1863 of Yale College* (New Haven, 1905).
[68] Starr, *William Graham Sumner*, pp. 358–59.   [69] *Ibid.*, p. 360.

motive of which was consideration for metaphysical and theological interests.[70]

The immediate outcome was a draw. The Corporation, aware of Sumner's powerful support in the faculty and in a segment of the public press, refused to accept his resignation. On the other hand, Sumner did withdraw the text, claiming that its usefulness had been impaired by the publicity the contest had received. But one may agree with Harris E. Starr that, in the long run, the laurels rested with Sumner. Sumner "made his fight, and thereafter every professor at Yale who was devoted to truth rather than tied to dogma had greater confidence and courage." [71]

Except for Harvard,[72] the older eastern colleges in the early eighties

[70] *Ibid.*   [71] *Ibid.,* p. 369.

[72] Harvard was the first college to provide a lectureship for the exposition of evolutionary thought, this being John Fiske's course on "The Positive Philosophy" delivered during the academic year 1869–70 and again in 1870–71. It was a measure of the change brought about by the election of Charles W. Eliot to the presidency in 1869, for eight years before, as an undergraduate, Fiske had been threatened with expulsion from Harvard for lecturing to his schoolmates on Comtism. See John Spencer Clarke, *The Life and Letters of John Fiske* (Boston and New York, 1917), I, 231–35. Spencer wrote to Fiske: "That eight years should have wrought such a change as to place the persecuted undergraduate in the chair of lecturer is something to wonder at, and may fill us with hope, as it must fill many with consternation." Clarke, p. 356. A good deal of doubt, however, appears as to why Fiske, who had received a temporary appointment as instructor in history and then as assistant librarian, failed to receive a permanent professorship at Harvard. Clarke writes that the publication of Fiske's lectures in the New York *World* immediately produced a "wave of bitter objurgation and denunciation" in the "religious and a portion of the secular press" in protest against "Harvard's Raid on Religion." Many writers have subsequently followed Clarke in assuming that there was a great religious outcry over Fiske's lectures. Our own investigation of contemporary newspapers does not support that assumption. There is no defense of Fiske or mention of the attack in the New York *World* in the year those lectures were given, which surely would have been the case had that paper's favorite author been attacked. There is no mention of it in the New York *Tribune* (Nov. 13 to April 1, 1869–70) or the New York *Times* (Nov. 13 to Feb. 1, 1869–70). No reference to the Fiske lectures appears in the New York *Evangelist,* a Presbyterian weekly (Nov., 1869 to Feb. 10, 1870), or in the orthodox New York *Observer* (Nov., 1869 to March, 1870). The Boston newspapers are equally negative.

It is true that the Harvard University Board of Overseers had religious objections to Fiske. According to Clarke, when Fiske was nominated to his instructorship in history, "the orthodox element in the Board of Overseers, chafing under the steady progress of President Eliot's liberalizing policy, was roused to opposition, and vigorous protest to Fiske's confirmation was promptly made. It was openly charged that Fiske was a pronounced atheist, and the more dangerous because of his learning and ability. It was alleged that the Board had gone to the extreme limit of toleration in confirming him as Lecturer on Philosophy; to go further and sanction his occupancy of the chair of History, even temporarily, would be an insult to all the traditions of the college" (p. 374). But there are cryptic aspects in the Board's

were still provincial and religious in tone. They had not yet entered on their careers as universities. Although they swallowed, even stomached, evolution, it was not truly to their taste. By contrast, two secular private universities established after the Civil War—Cornell and Johns Hopkins—were broad and free in design. By their charters' terms and their founders' wishes they were nonsectarian institutions.[73] To their presidents and faculties evolution was not gall and wormwood, but everyday nourishing fare.[74] Cornell's students learned about evolution from President Andrew Dickson White in history, from Burt G. Wilder in biology, and, somewhat later, from Edward Titchener in psychology.[75] President Daniel C. Gilman of Johns Hopkins appointed Newell Martin, a disciple of Huxley, as professor of biology, and invited Huxley himself to speak at the university's opening ceremonies.[76] But there were limits to tolerance here too. Generally, evolution could thrive in the open, and doctrinaire Darwinists were safe, but scholarly critics of religion, or materialists in philosophy, were not. The weakness and strength of these universities lay in their newness and secular approach. More worldly than the New England colleges, they were less sure of themselves in the world; more openly committed to tolerance, they lacked a tradition of dissent; more secular in outlook and spirit,

---

attitude too. Clarke states that "broad-minded clergymen" like James Freeman Clarke supported Fiske, yet a letter by J. F. Clarke on file in President Eliot's correspondence, dated February 5, 1870, objects to Fiske on the grounds that his espousal of the positive philosophy of Auguste Comte disqualified him for instructional duties at Harvard. (Letter of David W. Bailey, secretary of the Harvard Corporation, to the author, January 28, 1953.) Furthermore, the Board at this time carried Fiske's nomination through despite the opposition, which would suggest that Fiske's subsequent failure to obtain a permanent position did not stem exclusively from religious considerations.

[73] Cornell's charter provided that "persons of every religious sect or of no religious denomination, shall be equally eligible to all offices and appointments." Carl L. Becker, *Cornell University: Founders and the Founding* (Ithaca, N.Y., 1943), p. 93. For Johns Hopkins' antisectarianism, see Fabian Franklin, *The Life of Daniel Coit Gilman* (New York, 1910), pp. 184, 186, 219–22.

[74] See Walter P. Rogers, *Andrew D. White and the Modern University* (Ithaca, N.Y., 1942), p. 79; Daniel Coit Gilman, "The Sheffield Scientific School," in *University Problems* (New York, 1896), pp. 113–14.

[75] For a discussion of Burt G. Wilder's contribution to evolution, see J. H. Comstock, "Burt Green Wilder," *Science*, LXI (May 22, 1925), 531–33. For Andrew Dickson White's, see C. K. Adams, "Recent Historical Work in the Colleges and Universities of Europe and America," *Papers, American Historical Association*, IV (January, 1890), 39–65; for Edward Titchener's work, see Edwin G. Boring, *The History of Experimental Psychology* (New York, 1929), pp. 402–13.

[76] Daniel Coit Gilman, *The Launching of a University* (New York, 1906), p. 20; Franklin, *Life of Gilman*, pp. 220–21.

they were not chafed by the Puritan conscience that would brook no outer restraint.

Thus, in the early eighties, the trustees of Johns Hopkins turned down a liberal English minister, James Ward, presumably because he was not orthodox enough for their chair in philosophy.[77] In 1877, Cornell refused to reappoint the philosopher Felix Adler, whom President White had secured to lecture on Hebrew and Oriental literature. Returning from graduate studies abroad, Adler had given lectures that, in the words of an editorial in the Cornell *Review,* were "calculated to develop in young minds, at least, strongly rationalistic views." [78] When he went so far as to suggest to a public audience that some of the central doctrines of Christianity were discoverable in other religions as well, he was roundly attacked in the local religious press. The university authorities warned him to desist, and at the end of his three-year appointment did not again offer him a place.[79] Since Adler's lectureship had been supported by the funds of an outside philanthropist, Vice-President Russel tried to make it appear that the trustees had not objected to Adler but to the donor's control over nominations.[80] White gave a different account, implying that Adler voluntarily withdrew.[81] But a letter from Russel to Adler, written toward the end of the latter's term, shows that the actual reason was the administration's faintness of heart:

You are surprised at my silence about your chances of returning here. One who walks a very narrow path over which he can safely guide his charge ought not to be very talkative. My charge is this university. Besides my children I have no other interest. Truth and Liberty will take care of themselves, their triumph is secure, but an institution may be injured irreparably, and no such great injury can befall it as a collision with either Truth or Liberty. Should one who guides it expose it to such a chance? . . . True wisdom, it seems to me, forbids my bringing on a contest where victory would not be of greatest importance, but where defeat would be lasting injury. This is the reason why I said nothing to you about returning on a new engagement. Had I the power I would make such an engagement, for I believe that your lectures here did nothing but good.[82]

[77] J. Mark Baldwin, *Between Two Wars: 1861–1921* (Boston, 1926), I, 118.

[78] Article in the New York *Times,* May 21, 1933.

[79] Rogers, *Andrew D. White,* p. 77.

[80] Letter of William C. Russel to Joseph Seligman, May 5, 1877. Furnished by Professor Horace L. Friess of Columbia University.

[81] Andrew Dickson White, "An Open Letter," April 5, 1877. Reproduced in *The Index,* VIII (June 21, 1877), 292–93.

[82] Letter of William C. Russel to Felix Adler, March 12, 1877. Furnished by Horace L. Friess of Columbia University.

Ironically, Russel was dismissed by the trustees four years later, for reasons that are still obscure, but which may have had to do with his own (as Lyman Abbott charged) "pronounced nonreligious convictions." [83]

All together, these incidents had a shattering effect on the colleges' inner harmony and poise. Formerly, the presidents had played the rebel, and their ethos of resignation had usually shortened the part. Now the role was taken by professors who, though reluctantly, played it lustily and at length. Winchell told his story to the papers; Smyth and friends fought their case in court; Sumner wrote a letter to his colleagues that was by former standards insubordinate. Disaffection, in becoming a movement, shunned the usual disguise.

Behind this break in the convention of acquiescence one perceives a shift in the faculties' groups of reference—that is, the groups toward whose judgment they were oriented, by whose values and demands they were controlled. Customarily, professors had deferred to their trustees. To be sure, long before the fight for evolution, the wisdom of the trustees had been challenged in the sphere of classroom teaching and control. Trustees had ceased to be the source of expert judgment on problems relating to technique. But they had not lost their moral authority over the wider sphere of deportment. As elders of the church and shepherds of the fold, they had the minister's and the prelate's prestige. As they were in close contact with the college community, their influence was personal and direct. Generally, in the ante-bellum era, the trustees ruled *de jure* as in fact. But their blunders in the conflict over Darwinism squandered this inheritance of respect. Their policy of repression, since it wavered, was seen by professors as caprice, and no rule can keep its moral nimbus when it seems to be a fickle changing thing. Again, the waverings of their policy of repression gave professors the courage to dissent, since there was always another college to go to should home grounds prove at any time unsafe. In addition there now appeared a new group of reference which rivaled and replaced the trustees. One result of the Darwinian crisis was that it brought together like-minded teachers—scientists, scholars, and philosophers—who believed in evolution and who developed new standards of conduct from their interaction and mutual support. To dissent, in their frame of reference, was not to be disloyal or obstructive, but to light a

[83] Rogers, *Andrew D. White*, p. 157.

beacon of reason in a fog of orthodox fears. Professors on trial for their opinions thus spoke to a larger jury than the one which adjudged their tenure. In fighting for scientific freedom, Winchell addressed not only his employers, but also his cohorts outside; he failed before the Methodist board, but he reached his allies and friends, and there was the greater reward. Nor did this shift in the axis of allegiance bring only intangible satisfactions. The evolutionists, scattered throughout the profession, were in a position to give concrete help, so that the victims of religious repression often improved their statuses and careers. Winchell received an appointment to a chair at the University of Michigan; Woodrow was eventually appointed to the presidency of the University of South Carolina; Crawford Toy was the recipient of a first-class position at Harvard. The other aspect of alienation from the trustees was a broader academic connection that encouraged and rewarded dissent.

The significance of the academic-freedom cases lies not only in the professorial attitudes they illustrated but in the public reaction they caused. These trials over matters of belief, with their openly inquisitorial spirit, their solemn invasions of privacy, their blatant idealizations of sect, were notoriously inept. The spectacle of a trial at Andover to decide whether the "Universal Atonement" claimed by the Andover professors agreed with the "General Atonement" in the Creed—agreement, not truth, being the issue—was a revival of a kind of heresy-hunt the age was confident it had outgrown.[84] To a people in search of solidarity after years of fratricidal war, a Presbyterian standard for Gospel, exclusively and coercively applied, seemed almost as perverse and as factious as a Methodist brand of mathematics or a Baptist rendition of Greek.[85] Attempts to put a good face on these actions (at which sophisticated secularists would have been successful) were defeated by the artless exultation of sectarians whenever they tasted success. Thus,

[84] "Heresy" trials occurred in the churches as well as in the colleges. In 1883, W. Heber Newton, a prominent Episcopalian clergyman, was indicted but not prosecuted. *The Nation*, XXXVIII (February 28, 1884), 179. Another Episcopalian minister, Howard MacQueary, was condemned by an Episcopalian council in 1891 for his *Evolution of Man and Christianity*. See "Intellectual Liberty," *Popular Science Monthly*, XXXVIII (April, 1891), 844. In 1898, however, when Arthur Cushman McGiffert, a Presbyterian minister, wrote a book that advanced opinions contrary to the Westminster Confession, the Assembly of the Presbyterian Church merely made it a question of honor as to whether he should withdraw from the church. It was a tacit admission that the heresy trial had become inappropriate. Loewenberg, "The Impact of the Doctrine of Evolution," p. 268.

[85] See the compilation of northern and southern newspaper opinion in Marion Woodrow, *Dr. James Woodrow*, pp. 646–720.

when the president of Vanderbilt tried to justify his ousting of Winchell by citing the need to retrench,[86] his more ingenuous coreligionists gave the underlying reason away. "The university has afforded us intense gratification by its recent action," declared the Tennessee Conference after Winchell's dismissal.

This is the age in which scientific atheism, having divested itself of the habiliments that must adorn and dignify humanity, walks abroad in shameless denudation. . . . But our university alone has had the courage to lay its young but vigorous hand upon the man of untamed speculation and say: "We will have no more of this. . . ."[87]

To call the religious and conciliatory Winchell a "man of untamed speculation" was to add the mistake of hyperbole to the sin of naiveté of mind. Liberal opinion took this as the cue for its counterattack. Vanderbilt University, wrote the editor of the *Popular Science Monthly,* "follows the exploded precedents of past centuries, and puts forth its power to muzzle, repress, silence and discredit the independent teachers of scientific truth."[88] Winchell was compared with Galileo. Something musty and medieval seemed to emanate from the scene of these purgations, something altogether out of keeping with the forward movement of the age.[89] In this new age of enlightenment, intellectual coercion meant regression; in this age of automatic progress, regression was a cardinal sin. The chief benefit and utility of these cases, therefore, was that they stuck in the craw of the public. Even before the phrases of academic freedom had become common American catchwords, these infringements on academic freedom came to be regarded as anachronisms.

Finally, the evolutionary cases spurred a fresh assault on sectarianism in the colleges. Heretofore, sectarian control had been attacked on financial grounds as inadequate, or on administrative grounds as unstable. Now it lay open to attack as the foe of scientific advance.[90] By reveal-

---

[86] See Hunter Dickinson Farish, *The Circuit Rider Dismounts: A Social History of Southern Methodism, 1865–1900* (Richmond, 1938), pp. 295–98.

[87] As reported in an editorial, "Vanderbilt University Again," *Popular Science Monthly,* XIV (December, 1878), 237.

[88] "Religion and Science at Vanderbilt University," *Popular Science Monthly,* XIII (August, 1878), 493.

[89] *The Index,* IX (July 11, 1878), 325.

[90] Thus Andrew Dickson White linked denominationalism to ancient oppressions of thought: "Here we have survivals of that same oppression of thought by theology which has cost the modern world so dear; the system which forced great numbers of professors, under penalty of deprivation, to teach that the sun and planets revolve

ing the intolerance of sectarian minds, the incompetence of clerical trustees, the excesses of religious authority, these widely noticed cases hastened secular reform. They did so, however, only because the intellectual ground was being prepared. An ideology of resentment against religious authority, emerging from the crucible of the Darwinian debate, was effectively undermining the philosophical supports of sectarianism. We turn now to explore the main ideas in that ideology.

THE ATTACK UPON RELIGIOUS AUTHORITY

The attack of the evolutionists upon religious authority was not a "war between science and religion." However certain it appeared to their opponents that atheism was their goal and the anti-Christ their collaborator, the evolutionists' mood was conciliatory. To be sure, most of the evolutionary scientists thought Darwin had delivered the *coup de grâce* to the main tenets of natural theology. No longer did they accept literally the Adamite version of creation. No longer did they resort to Paley's arguments. To maintain that the usefulness of natural organs proved God's existence, prevision, and moral aim seemed an anthropomorphic mistake fit for a cruder day. But it was still very much a matter of argument among them as to whether science, having overthrown certain tenets of natural theology, had also liquidated its concerns and biases. There were evolutionary positivists, like Chauncey Wright, who staunchly maintained that science should no longer be concerned with matters beyond factual description.[91] They believed that science should answer *hypotheses non fingo* to every question of spiritual meaning, cosmic purpose, and final ends. Their unwillingness to combine science with natural theology was shared by Darwin himself. As presented in the *Origin of Species,* the metaphor of natural selection was a principle for ordering facts, not an ethical or ontological law.[92] But other evolutionists still were eager to salvage the

---

about the earth; that comets are fire-balls flung by an angry God at a wicked world; that insanity is a diabolic possession; that anatomical investigation of the human frame is sin against the Holy Ghost; that chemistry leads to sorcery; that taking interest for money is forbidden by Scripture; that geology must conform to ancient Hebrew poetry." White, *History of the Warfare* . . . , I, 318–19.

[91] Gail Kennedy, "The Pragmatic Naturalism of Chauncey Wright," *Studies in the History of Ideas* (New York, 1935), pp. 484 ff.; Philip P. Wiener, "Chauncey Wright's Defense of Darwin and the Neutrality of Science," *Journal of the History of Ideas,* VI (January, 1945), 19–45.

[92] See Francis Darwin, ed., *Life and Letters of Charles Darwin,* pp. 274–86.

intellectual estate of natural theology. Spencerians like John Fiske believed that science could disclose the plan and purpose of the universe, provided that in adhering to law it disclosed a master plan, an immanent purpose.[93] Still others, like William James, holding scientific laws merely probable, thought that the "will to believe" could resuscitate faith and religion.[94] There were, in addition, conservative theists like Asa Gray who still saw the hand of Providence working in mysterious ways, and more pantheistic scientists like Joseph Le Conte who ascribed the unpredictable products of evolution to a spiritual force in nature.[95] Truly, evolution proved compatible with a wide diversity of religious beliefs.[96]

Similarly, the evolutionists' attack upon religious authority over education was not an attack upon religion *per se*. The evolutionists who became university presidents—Charles W. Eliot, Andrew Dickson White, Daniel C. Gilman, and David Starr Jordan—could be considered irreligious only by narrow orthodox standards. To be sure, they were hostile to the religious bias that prevented acceptance of Darwin, and they opposed sectarian control of colleges. But each was loyal to what he considered the core-beliefs of religion, though that core might be practically devoid of dogma. Eliot's evolutionism led him to a conception of God as a glorious "Transcendent Intelligence," [97] and the quality of his piety was not strained. "He who studies Nature," he wrote in justifying his early choice of a scientific career, "studies the thoughts and works of God. God is revealed in His works as well as in His word, and he who reverently contemplates the works, worships

[93] John Fiske, *The Idea of God as Affected by Modern Knowledge* (Boston, 1886), pp. 95–96, and *passim*.

[94] William James, *The Will to Believe* (New York, 1903). See, also, Ralph Barton Perry, *The Thought and Character of William James* (2 vols.; Boston, 1935), II, 207–44.

[95] Asa Gray, *Natural Science and Religion* (New York, 1880); Joseph Le Conte, *Evolution: Its Evidence and Its Relation to Religious Thought* (New York, 1894).

[96] We still await a full-scale treatment of the conciliations of science and religion undertaken by the evolutionary scientists. Valuable articles have appeared, notably Sidney Ratner, "Evolution and the Rise of the Scientific Spirit in America," *Philosophy of Science*, III (January, 1936), 104–22; Bert J. Loewenberg, "The Controversy over Evolution in New England," *New England Quarterly*, VIII (June, 1935), 232–57; Loewenberg, "Darwinism Comes to America, 1859–1900," *Mississippi Valley Historical Review*, XXVIII (December, 1941), 339–68; Herbert W. Schneider, "The Influence of Darwin and Spencer on American Philosophical Theology," *Journal of the History of Ideas*, VI (January, 1945), 3–18. See also Edward A. White, *Science and Religion in American Thought: The Impact of Naturalism* (Stanford, 1952).

[97] Henry James, *Eliot*, I, 318.

as truly as he who reads the word." [98] For all his reputation for rationalism, Andrew Dickson White firmly believed in the Scriptural plan of salvation.[99] David Starr Jordan scorned the atheist, and though his God was more like Spencer's Great Unknowable than the Christian personal God, he used consecrated phrases to describe Him—the "power that made for righteousness," that which "transcends humanity." [100] Perhaps there was something genteel and colorless about the religion of these educators, perhaps something underdeveloped and oversimple; but they were not, as their religious enemies made them out to be, godless, faithless, unmindful of the need of worship.

But this is not to say that all the ideological conflicts were apparent, and that none of them was real. For the great Darwinian debate was richer in significant issues than any in the American annals of disputation. It went far beyond the substantive problem of whether evolution was true, and far beyond the psychological problem of how to hold to acquired science while retaining birth-right beliefs. Touching on the nature and sanctions of authority, the methods and problems of verification, the standards of scientific debate, the Darwinian controversy eventually implicated all that was problematic in the area of human judgment. The philosophy of science, the psychology of learning, the metes of intellectual freedom, all entered the purview of this controversy. In consequence there was not *a* war, but many particular wars: a war between two kinds of men of knowledge—the clerical and the scientific; between two sorts of educational control—the sectarian and the secular; between two fundamental ways of knowing—the authoritarian and the empiricist; between two basic approaches to instruction —the doctrinal and the natural. We can summarize these conflicts by saying that science and education joined forces to attack two major objectives—the authority of the clergy and the principles of doctrinal moralism—and that one of the effects of this coalition was the hastening of academic reform.

ANTI-CLERICALISM IN SCIENCE AND EDUCATION

In Chapter VI we noted that in the days before Darwin, the Protestant pastor and the scientific worker had usually walked in step. One

[98] *Ibid.*, I, 64.   [99] Rogers, *Andrew D. White*, p. 83.
[100] Edward McNall Burns, *David Starr Jordan: Prophet of Freedom* (Stanford, 1952), p. 189.

reason for their rapport was the effect of the Protestant spirit and heritage upon the office of the minister. Opposed to any priestly exclusiveness, the Protestant minister shared the intellectual interests of his communicants. Because he was outside the infallible Church, he had to buttress religious doctrine with the facts and theories of science. Quite often, as we have seen, he dabbled in science himself. But, paradoxically, once Darwin caused a parting of the ways, these same clerical Protestant attitudes only served to widen the breach. Because he was close to the views of his congregation, the Protestant minister tended to reflect its unenlightened ideas and give voice to its unreasoning fears. In a sense, therefore, clerical anti-Darwinism became the spearhead of popular anti-intellectualism. Worse yet, since he could trade on his scientific reputation, the Protestant minister felt no qualms in challenging expert opinion, in searching the scientific literature for anti-revolutionary testimony, in declaring with pontifical assurance that Darwin was factually wrong. What made clerical anti-Darwinism so imprudent, so powerful, and also so resented was that it carried the fight against evolution into the court of science itself.[101]

The reaction of the evolutionists was to attack the competence of the clergy to judge the issues of science. Huxley's retort to Bishop Wilberforce at the 1860 meeting of the British Association for the Advancement of Science became a favorite anecdote and then a legend of American scientific anticlericalism. "Is it on his grandfather's or his grandmother's side that the ape ancestry comes in?" the fatuous Bishop had inquired. Huxley had been unsparing in his reply: "If there were an ancestor whom I should feel shame in recalling, it would be a man . . . who, not content with success in his own sphere of activity, plunges into scientific questions with which he has no real acquaintance."[102] This moral was soon recited by native Huxleys.[103] The clergy

---

[101] Selectively, the Protestant ministers quoted from the scientist Richard Owen to prove natural selection ineffective; from the scientist Quatrefois to prove the species in nature immutable; from the scientist St. George Mivart to prove Darwin in error at many points. See Loewenberg, "The Impact of the Doctrine of Evolution," p. 268.

[102] Various eyewitnesses to this colloquy have presented different accounts. The version quoted above can be found in Henshaw Ward, *Charles Darwin: The Man and His Warfare* (Indianapolis, 1927), pp. 313–15.

[103] We have relied heavily on the *Popular Science Monthly,* a crusading journal of evolution, and on *The Index,* the organ of the Free Religious Association. While these journals were on the "left" in the evolution controversy, they are of inestimable value for the accounts of a wide range of events and opinions contained in their

are not competent to make scientific judgments, wrote John Trow-bridge in the *Popular Science Monthly.*

Ministers who are only general readers in science can have no conception of the scientific spirit which comes through investigation. There is a cultivated interest which arises only from familiarity with methods, processes, and instruments. A minister lives apart from the seething turmoil and progress of the scientific world; and, if he should attempt to dispute with innovators, he will meet the same fate as any comparative recluse who attempts to dictate to the world from his retirement.[104]

Not only occupational, but mental and temperamental disabilities, were charged against the clergy. The clerical mind, wrote Francis Abbot, editor of *The Index,* can never accept the fact of its own fallibility.[105] The clerical mind, wrote David Starr Jordan, is irrevocably committed to untestable assumptions.[106] The key argument of the disciples of evolution was that science and religion, while not necessarily different as to content, were quite separate as spheres of competence.[107]

Like the doctrine of design in an earlier day, the doctrine of scientific competence was one of the large and influential ideas that have altered the course of intellectual history and the historical relations of intellectuals. It took the form of two theories: a theory of the scientific elite, in which the function of competence was judicial; and a theory of scientific procedure, in which the function of competence was methodological. Both can be found in the writings of Francis E. Abbot, the leader of the Free Religion movement. Opposed both to the transcendentalists, who relied mainly on private illumination, and the Biblical fundamentalists, who sought a fixed and infallible authority, Abbot pro-

pages. *The Index* was published from 1870 to 1886; cf. Stow Persons, *Free Religion* (New York, 1947), pp. 85–90. The *Popular Science Monthly* was launched in 1867 and continues to the present day.

[104] John Trowbridge, "Science from the Pulpit," *Popular Science Monthly,* VI (April, 1875), 734–35.

[105] Francis E. Abbot, "Authority in Science and in Religion," *The Index,* III (Dec. 20, 1871), 412.

[106] David Starr Jordan, "The Church and Modern Thought," *Overland Monthly,* XVIII (1891), 392.

[107] This argument was presented by so conservative a scientist as St. George Mivart, an English Catholic, whose book arguing for psychogenesis in evolution was placed on the Roman Catholic Index, and who, in arguing for the right of science to decide matters within its province, was excommunicated. In an article entitled "Modern Catholics and Scientific Freedom," printed in *Nineteenth Century,* Vol. XVIII (July, 1885), Mivart argued that the past blunders of the Church in scientific matters disqualified it to be the supreme arbiter in scientific affairs and that even loyal Catholics might refuse to submit to its decisions (pp. 35–36).

posed that a "tribunal of science" be created—a court of trial and appeal for the provisional determination of truths. On it, would sit the leading authorities of science; to it, the problems of science would be submitted; from it, a "consensus of the competent" would be derived; by it, the world would be purged of imposture by continuing applications of expertise. The idea of a scientific tribunal was, of course, an old and vulnerable one—a Baconian dream easily rebuffed by realities. But the idea that the competence of scientists was exclusive and that their judgment for the moment was authoritative—this was a formidable conception, and it endured in the ideology of science.[108]

Competence, to Abbot, did not rest merely on acquired skill and knowledge; it also was dependent upon the discipline of the scientific method. "I vindicate," he wrote, "the rights of the human intellect as the sole *discoverer* of truth; I maintain the unique and exclusive claim of the scientific method as the sole *organon* of its discovery." [109] To Abbot there was nothing recondite about the scientific method: it was ordinary thinking corrected and refined by caution. It began, as he understood it, with facts—not with innate ideas or intuitions; it proceeded through hypothesis and deduction—through the pure operations of reason; it ended in verification—in the empirical test of conclusions; it submitted to public inspection—to the verification of others. It differed from other ways of knowing: from the ways of faith, intuition, and authority. It accepted no prerequisite beliefs from faith, no untestable propositions from intuition, no final decrees from authority.

These two conceptions of competence were in some ways closely related. The judicial competence of the scientist depended upon his ability to perform the operations of the scientific method; the methodological competence of the scientist depended upon the use of his acquired knowledge in perceiving and formulating problems. On the other hand, in certain ways, the two conceptions of competence were opposed. In the one—the conception of the "wise men"—competence was depicted as uncommon, antecedent, and adjudicative; in the other—the theory of the "wise means"—competence was depicted as more common, projective, participative. The first conception set the scientist apart

[108] Francis E. Abbot, "A Tribunal of Science," *The Index,* IX (June 6, 1878), 270; "The Individual at the Bar," *ibid.,* X (April 17, 1879), 186–87; *ibid.,* X (Dec. 25, 1879), 613.
[109] Francis E. Abbot, "The Scientific Method in Religion," *The Index,* VIII (March 22, 1877), 136.

from other men: he was an oracle who spoke truthfully and to the profit of those who heard him; he was an esoteric specialist comprehensible only to his kind. The other drew the scientist closer to the run of men: he was the exponent of their artisan interest in facts and causes and effects; he represented their moral interest in detachment and in mental candor. Those who were concerned with the relations of science to the common life would find it difficult to strike a balance between these two notions of competence. But however this may be, both notions upheld the claim that scientists were exemplary men of knowledge, and this is their significance for our theme. Both discounted the qualifications of the priest to control the dominion of knowledge. Both asserted that cultivation rather than consecration, accomplishments rather than observances, skill and method rather than piousness, accredited the man of knowledge. Not before the Darwinian controversy did scientists present so pre-emptive and imperious a claim to gnostic superiority.[110]

These anticlerical, panscientific notions soon found expression within the colleges, where the position of the Protestant minister was undergoing changes. No longer did he address a student body bent on emulating his career. Whereas in 1830 the proportion of ministers among the graduates of Harvard, Yale, and Princeton had been one in three, by 1876 the proportion had dropped to one in thirteen.[111] There had been a time when the only systematic professional training in America had been for the ministry. Lawyers and doctors had learned their trades as apprentices, and scientists had practically trained themselves. By the 1880s the universities were taking over the professional and pre-professional training of doctors and lawyers,[112] and a trend toward

[110] This assertiveness, of course, did not stem only from the discoveries of evolution, but also from the refutation by science of religious conceptions in psychology and anthropology. The development of experimental psychology, by connecting psychic phenomena to the functioning of the nervous system, refuted spiritualistic theories; the development of pathological psychology, by connecting mystic phenomena to the unconscious, took from the former their supernatural character; the development of historical and ethnological studies, connecting religion to the solemn moments in collective life, undermined classic notions of the origin of religion. See Antonio Aliotta, "Science and Religion in the Nineteenth Century," in Joseph Needham, ed., *Science, Religion and Reality* (New York, 1926), pp. 154–55.

[111] Charles W. Eliot, "On the Education of Ministers," *Princeton Review*, LIX (May, 1883), 340–56.

[112] For example, of the 156 medical schools in existence in 1900, 86 were founded between 1876 and 1900. The real boost in medical standards, however, did not take place until after Abraham Flexner published his report on medical education in

specialized training in the sciences was going on apace.[113] Even the classics departments were becoming less congenial haunts for clergymen, as philological and historical scholarship cast a shade over classical discipline. The passage from the pulpit to the classroom, once a natural and unremarkable event in a clergyman's career, now seemed less warranted; with the decline in enrollment of divinity students it was less necessary, and with the development of lay scholarship it was more strange. In this propitious setting, a movement was begun to rid the colleges of the symbols and the presence of clerical power.

In the attack upon clerical control, no argument figured more prominently than the contention that the clergy were incompetent in science. Professor F. W. Clarke of the University of Cincinnati scored the situation that allowed "almost any decayed minister, seeking an asylum" to beat an American Laplace in a race for a professorship.[114] The *Nation* was of the opinion that "clergymen were no longer *par excellence* the learned men of the community" and that "the increased demands of the natural sciences in the universities call for an amount of administrative talent and experience which ministers rarely possess." [115] Charles W. Eliot believed that the clergy, with their fixation on creed and rigidity of belief, had never learned to practice or respect the scientific method. The scientific spirit of inquiry, wrote Eliot,

seeks only the fact, without the slightest regard to consequence. . . . The achievements of scientific inquirers, animated by this spirit of sincerity and truth, have been so extraordinary within the past sixty years . . . that the educated world has accepted it as the only true inspiration of research. . . . No other method of inquiry now commands respect. . . . Protestant theologians and ministers must rise to that standard, if they would continue to command the respect of mankind.[116]

Medical Education in the United States and Canada, Bulletin 4, Carnegie Foundation for the Advancement of Teaching (1910).

[113] By 1880, Johns Hopkins, California, Pennsylvania, and Rutgers boasted six teachers in science apiece, and Harvard had as many as fourteen. Nicholas Murray Butler, ed., *Monographs on Education in the United States,* II (Albany, N.Y., 1900), 3–42.

[114] F. W. Clarke, "American Colleges versus American Science," *Popular Science Monthly,* IX (August, 1876), 472.

[115] Rogers, *Andrew D. White,* p. 80.

[116] Charles W. Eliot, "On the Education of Ministers," pp. 345–46. Eliot did not, as did some of his contemporaries, despair of winning the ministers over to the scientific method; consider his reorganization of the divinity school at Harvard on a nondenominational and, as he saw it, "scientific" basis. See William J. Potter, "Theology at Harvard," *The Index,* X (April 24, 1879), 198–99; Eliot, *Annual Report,* 1878–79.

Educational anticlericalism and scientific anticlericalism, feeding on the same ideas, were part of a single movement.

The outcome—if we can apply such a word to a campaign that knew no instant of victory or article of capitulation—was the disappearance of the clergy as an academic force. Earl McGrath, in a well-known study, gives a statistical picture of the exodus of clerical trustees from the nation's private colleges. In 1860–61, 39.1 percent of the members of the boards of 15 private institutions were clergymen; by 1900–1901 the percentage had dropped to 23 percent, and clergymen were outnumbered for the first time by lawyers and businessmen; by 1930–31, the percentage had dwindled to 7.2 percent.[117] At Harvard, 7 of the 36 governors (Overseers and Fellows) were clergymen in 1874–75; in 1894–95 only one was. Between 1884 and 1926 the number of clergymen on the board of trustees at Amherst was reduced by half, at Princeton by two thirds, and at Yale by 60 percent.[118] The secularizing of the office of the president—a traditional benefice of the clergy—took longer to accomplish. Harvard appointed its first lay president, Eliot, in 1869; Yale did not follow until 1899, with Arthur T. Hadley. Cornell and Johns Hopkins began with lay presidents, but Princeton, Amherst, and Dartmouth did not appoint lay presidents until the twentieth century. Oberlin did not unfrock the presidency until 1927. In certain of the larger institutions the exit of the cleric coincided with the entry of the scientist. President Gilman of Johns Hopkins was a geographer, Eliot of Harvard a chemist, Hall of Clark a psychologist, Jordan of Stanford a biologist, Hadley of Yale an economist, Wilson of Princeton a political scientist. But the apostolic succession of the scientist was far from automatic or assured. More often than not, the seats vacated by the clergy fell to incongruous occupants—politicians, businessmen, lawyers, professional administrators, and, later, generals—whose competence in science or educational administration seemed at times extremely doubtful.

[117] Earl McGrath, "The Control of Higher Education in America," *Educational Record*, XVII (April, 1936), 259–79.

[118] The trustees of these institutions were identified through the *Dictionary of American Biography*, the *National Cyclopedia of American Biography*, *Who Was Who in America, 1897–1947*, and from school catalogues, where the designation of "Rev." or "D.D." was taken as fully descriptive. It could not be determined whether about 10 percent of the members of these boards were clergymen.

The notion of competence was not the only ideological product of the Darwinian debate. Equally important was the rejection in science and in education of the tenets of doctrinal moralism. It will be recalled that, as a standard of reliability, doctrinal moralism was the view that veracity was a function of faith, that only the believer could be believed. As a criterion of verification, it held that the truth of any idea was determined by its envisioned moral consequences. The religious opponents of evolution were unbridled in their use of both tenets. No theist could believe in evolution, wrote Enoch Fitch Burr, lecturer on the scientific evidence of revealed religion at Amherst, because evolution was "founded by atheism, claimed by atheism, supported by atheism." [119] To a Catholic writer, the theory of evolution, since it "opens the gate to the free indulgence of passion . . . cannot be a sound one; for no sound system produces such fruit, and from the fruits one comes to know the tree." [120] Again and again, the orthodox churchmen "refuted" evolution by casting aspersions on its proponents or by predicting its evil effects.

The use of doctrinal moralism as a standard of reliability infuriated the evolutionists. "Charges of 'heresy,' 'infidelity,' or 'atheism' are beside the question," insisted one writer in the *Popular Science Monthly*. "If a theory in astronomy, in geology, in physics, chemistry or biology, is in doubt, let it be judged on its own evidence." [121] A scientific work, the evolutionists held, should not be judged by the character of its author, but should stand clear and dissociated, held to account only for itself. Moreover, the charge of faithlessness was not only irrelevant, but, if recklessly and indiscriminately applied, was also insubstantial. When Andrew Dickson White was vilified as an atheist for keeping the works of Channing, Renan, and Strauss in his library, the inanity of the argument was clear enough; when Louis Agassiz was accused by a clergyman of preaching "atheism and Darwinism," the dangerous inaccuracy of the name-calling device was even more clearly

[119] Enoch Fitch Burr, *Pater Mundi, or the Doctrine of Evolution* (Boston, 1873), II, 14.
[120] F. S. Chatard, "Darwin's Mistakes," *Catholic World*, XXXIX (June, 1884), 292.
[121] *Popular Science Monthly*, IX (July, 1876), 328.

exposed.[122] "Denounce the thought or the word as much as you please," wrote Francis Abbot,

but if you denounce the thinker because of his honest thought, you are a tyrant to the extent of your power—all the worse if you quote morality and religion to justify your tyranny. . . . Show the theory to be false, and you have proved it be injurious; turn aside from the theory to denounce the theorizer, and even if you succeed in overwhelming both with odium, you have won the victory by a cruel, false and wicked trick, which will yet return to plague the inventor.[123]

In scientific criticism, the dissociation of the man from his work became a cardinal principle.

Subtler, more profound, and less consistent objections were raised against the use of doctrinal moralism as a method of verification. One significant rebuttal was offered by the astronomer and mathematician Chauncey Wright.[124] In seeking to clarify scientific debate, Wright opposed both the use of inflammatory words that had entered from the side of theology and the use of metaphysical generalizations that had entered from the side of philosophy. He argued for rules that would "demand of the criticism . . . the same judicial attitude that is demanded of the investigation."[125] This devoted apostle of Darwin and Mill demanded that every subjective element be eliminated from scientific concerns. Knowledge becomes objective and science comes into its own

when it ceases to be associated with our fears, our respects, our aspirations— our emotional nature; when it ceases to prompt questions as to what relates to our personal destiny, our ambitions, our moral worth; when it ceases to have man, his personal and social nature, as its central and controlling objects.[126]

In short, science must seek the "true"—the conformity of ideas to reality—and not the "good"—the conformity of reality to ideals.[127] He drew a distinction between the "scientific mind," which holds rigidly "to the truth of things, whether good or bad, agreeable or disagreeable,

[122] Andrew Dickson White, *Autobiography*, I, 424.

[123] Francis E. Abbot, "Argument and Denunciation," *The Index*, III (April 20, 1872), 125.

[124] See Philip Wiener, *Evolution and the Founders of Pragmatism* (Cambridge, Mass., 1949), pp. 31–69.

[125] "Evolution by Natural Selection," in *Philosophical Discussions* (New York, 1877), p. 170.

[126] "The Philosophy of Herbert Spencer," *loc. cit.*, p. 49.

[127] "Natural Theology as a Positive Science," *loc. cit.*, pp. 40–41.

admirable or despicable," and the " 'philosophical habit of mind,' trained in the school of human life, . . . viewing and interpreting nature according to its own dispositions." [128] Here, then, was one answer to the argument that the ethical consequences of an idea were its primary test of truth. Rather, thought Wright, science and ethics—the "true" and the "good"—belonged in separate and incommensurable categories.

Wright articulated the ideas of the practicing scientist. His precept—objectivity—was the fetish of the laboratory and the field. Refusing to see in the succession of events an ideal or dramatic tendency, he exalted piecemeal research. Assuming the ethical and metaphysical neutrality of science, he supported the scientist's austere craving for "the disenchantment of the world." [129] But few evolutionary philosophers took joy in his icy neutrality, his self-denying ordinances, his divorce of contemplation from desire.[130] A rift, opened by temperamental differences, was expanded by philosophical disagreements. Wright's metaphysical neutrality of science was to James a derogation of metaphysics, to Peirce an emasculation of science.[131] To Dewey, the ethical neutrality of science meant the surrender of the issues of ethics to fixed authority and outmoded sanctions.[132] Though these philosophers shared Wright's disdain for verbal solutions and emotional appeals in debate,[133] they did not be-

[128] "Evolution by Natural Selection," *loc. cit.,* p. 196.

[129] See Max Weber, "Science as a Vocation," in Logan Wilson and William L. Kolb, eds., *Sociological Analysis* (New York, 1949), pp. 5–16.

[130] See Perry, *Thought and Character of William James,* I, 522.

[131] Though James was close to Wright on many philosophical points—both were empiricists and both opposed the gospel of evolutionism as presented by Spencer and Fiske—James would not take Wright's "anti-religious teaching" which he labelled "philosophical nihilism." Perry, *Thought and Character of William James,* Vol. I, Chap. XXXI. See Charles Peirce, "What is Pragmatism?" *Monist,* XV (1905), 161–81; Charles Hartshorne and Paul Weiss, eds., *Collected Papers of Charles Peirce* (6 vols.; Cambridge, Mass., 1935), VI, 33.

[132] A recurrent idea in Dewey's works, which perhaps appears most clearly in a much later work, *The Quest for Certainty: A Study of the Relation of Knowledge to Action* (New York, 1929), pp. 40 ff.

[133] There is no doubt that the standard of empirical adequacy that Wright espoused was also adhered to by his evolutionary opponents. Even in so improbable a place as the writings of John Fiske, we find a vigorous defense of the empirical test in science. Take Fiske's statement that "the truth of any proposition, for scientific purposes, is determined by its agreement with observed phenomena, and not by its congruity with some assumed metaphysical basis" (*Cosmic Philosophy,* I, 272), and his castigation of Agassiz for having intruded his "preferences" into scientific debate. "A scientific inquirer has no business to have 'preferences' . . . . What matters it whether we are pleased with the notion of a monkey ancestry or not? The end of scientific research is the discovery of truth, and not the satisfaction

lieve that the cognitive and moral interests of the scientist could or should be dissociated. Whereas Chauncey Wright, starting from the logic of Mill and the methods of Darwin, emphasized the disciplined, objective, mirroring aspects of knowing, William James, using as a basis the ethics of Mill and the functional psychology of Darwin, emphasized the conative, purposive, active aspects of knowing. From this other corner of the evolutionary camp—one that may loosely be called pragmatist—came another reply to the canons of doctrinal moralism.

On the surface, as principles of verification, pragmatism and doctrinal moralism had much in common. Both assumed that the truth of an idea was disclosed in some way by its consequences. Both denied that cognition existed as an end in itself, or that science should be divorced from human purposes. But here the resemblances ended. For pragmatism took the significant step of divorcing morality from doctrine and rooting it in changing experience. Thus, whereas in doctrinal moralism the "good" was absolute and unconditional, in pragmatism the "good" was plural and contingent. Whereas the former accepted new theory if it agreed with an older stock of beliefs, the latter accepted new theory if it resolved an ongoing human problem. Whereas the former regarded the existing stock of beliefs as inviolable and eternal, the latter regarded accepted beliefs as guides to problem-solving action, always subject to revision, required to work and give satisfaction or else to relinquish their title.

Thus the assault on doctrinal moralism was mounted on two major premises—the ethical neutrality of science and the experimental status of ethics. We need not, for our immediate purpose, dwell on the tensions between practicing science and scientific philosophy that these different premises point to. For the moment, their significance may be said to lie in the preferences and aversions they shared. Differing as to whether truth was something found or made, both asserted that truth was temporary, growing, and contingent, not permanent, static, and absolute. Differing as to whether values were a subject matter for science, both agreed that values were not disclosed by the properties of antecedent reality or by knowledge supernaturally established. Differing as to scope

of our whims or fancies, or even of what we are pleased to call our finer feelings. The proper reason for refusing to accept any doctrine is, that it is inconsistent with observed facts, or with some other doctrine which has been firmly established on a basis of fact." "Agassiz and Darwinism," *Popular Science Monthly,* III (October, 1873), 697. But the difference between Wright and Fiske was that the latter was confident that *his* major preference—cosmic benevolence—had been proved beyond doubt inductively.

of inquiry, both assumed that no belief was so inherently valuable as to be immune to the tests of inquiry. Both, in short, were profoundly hostile to the fundamental axioms of religious authority.

Again we find the evolutionists in education preaching on much the same text. Nowhere had the assumptions of doctrinal moralism been more firmly fixed than in the American college. Yet in the seventies and eighties, as a reflection of the impact of evolution on educational psychology, an attitude hostile toward these assumptions came to prevail even here. Where the philosophers of science sought to clarify terms and to avoid logomachic argument, the philosophers of education sought to prevent the teacher from inculcating verbal abstractions. Where the positivists in science urged the scientist to be ethically neutral, the secularists in education urged the teacher to be doctrinally neutral. Where the pragmatists in science based values on utility and experience, the pragmatists in education did very much the same thing. Here, again, in animus and assumption, education and science were allied.

As a sign of the changing times, England, once the cradle of academic classicism, produced Herbert Spencer, the great philosopher of these new trends in education, and Thomas Huxley, their major publicist. In the United States, Edward L. Youmans and Charles W. Eliot were Huxley's and Spencer's important advocates. Spencer made his mark on the educational world with four essays written between 1854 and 1859 which were compiled in a volume called *Essays on Education*.[134] Huxley put his epigrammatic style into the service of Spencer's ideas in the public forum here and in England.[135] Youmans, the editor of the *Popular Science Monthly*, of more than fifty volumes of the "International Science Series," and of an influential book entitled *The Culture Demanded by Modern Life*, gave Spencer a wide American audience.[136] Eliot served

[134] The book was first published in the United States in 1861. References in the following pages are the Everyman's Library edition published in 1910 in New York. An interesting analysis of Spencer's educational theory is provided by Elsa Peverly Kimball, *Sociology and Education: An Analysis of the Theories of Spencer and Ward* (New York, 1932).

[135] Volume Three of his *Collected Essays* contains some of Huxley's leading addresses (New York and London, 1914).

[136] For Youmans' work in popularizing the ideas of Spencer, see John Fiske, "Edward Livingston Youmans," *A Century of Science and Other Essays* (Boston and New York, 1902), pp. 61–95; H. G. Good, "Edward Livingston Youmans, A National Teacher of Science," *The Scientific Monthly*, XVIII (March, 1924), 306–17. The contributors to *The Culture Demanded by Modern Life* were a galaxy of the scientific stars of that time: John Tyndall, Arthur Henfrey, Thomas Huxley, James Paget, Michael Faraday, W. B. Hodgson, Herbert Spencer, F. A. P. Barnard,

the cause with numerous addresses and articles [137] and used his position at Harvard to put the theory into practice. One need not go beyond the works of this talented quadrumvirate to perceive the main lines of the argument, though an enormous polemical literature reveals the interest the dispute aroused.

The plea of these thinkers for a scientific education was the springboard for their attack on doctrinal moralism. The case for a scientific education was consummately argued by Spencer in his essay "What Knowledge Is of Most Worth?" "Worth," to this worthy successor of Bentham, was equated with usefulness, and his essay was a persuasive disquisition on behalf of practical training. To Spencer, the leading kinds of human activities, in their order of importance, were those that administered to self-preservation, those that secured the necessaries of life, those whose end was the care of offspring, those which were involved in the maintenance of good citizenship, and lastly, those which gratified taste and feeling. These, thought Spencer, were the activities that education should cultivate, the first most, the last least. The current emphasis on the ornamental studies was in inverse relation to need, he thought, and had little articulation with life.[138] But education should prepare for life, the curriculum should be as broad as life—which meant that the subjects that were concerned with life should receive primary consideration. To Spencer, the sciences, natural and social, pre-eminently filled the bill. They enabled man to survive, to manufacture, to guard against disease, to produce fit offspring. They equipped him for the tasks of civic life and even furthered the creative arts. With prophetic insight, Spencer foresaw the day when science would conquer the curriculum.[139]

In his effort to give science the highest credentials, Spencer did not disdain the disciplinary goals and faculty psychology of the classicists. He and his followers were not loath to claim that science sharpened the judgment, inculcated many virtues, flexed the muscles of memory.[140] But this derivative psychology, placed in a new context of evolutionary naturalism, lost all its old authoritarian associations. Since mind was a phe-

---

Justus von Liebig, and Youmans himself. (International Science Library, Akron, 1867).

[137] For some of Eliot's more famous addresses and articles, see *Educational Reform* (New York, 1898).

[138] *Essays on Education*, p. 32.   [139] *Ibid.*, p. 44.

[140] Thomas Huxley, "Scientific Education," *Collected Essays*, pp. 127–28; Youmans, *The Culture Demanded by Modern Life*, p. 6.

nomenon of nature and its growth an evolutionary process, the content and the method of teaching must conform to the laws of the mind's development. Since all evolutionary movement was a progressive integration of matter, the course of effective teaching must go from the simple to the complex. Since instincts, tropisms, and propensities played a vital role in survival, student interest and desire must be consulted and engaged in teaching. Like Rousseau, the evolutionists drew a sharp distinction between a "natural" and an "artificial" education. The natural way in education was to put mind into contact with fact through all of the intaking senses, to let thought be the reflective result of direct and immediate experience. The artificial way was merely to transmit words, to funnel truths into passive receptacles. And the natural way, to these evolutionary naturalists, was doubly blessed: first, because nature was good and guaranteed human perfectibility; second, because control of nature was good, and insured competitive success.

The ultimate goal of these educators was to shift the center of gravity from the teacher to the student. Nowhere was this more apparent than in their approach to moral education, a field that had so long been preempted by parental wish, adult restraint, and the imposing "shalt nots" of the Decalogue. Character development, Spencer and his followers agreed, was the primary objective of every system of education. It was their opinion, however, that this result could not be achieved by a prescribed adherence to creed, but only by adherence to the laws of Nature when those laws were inductively discovered. For Nature was the supreme instructor in the art of moral conduct. Her disbursement of pleasures and pains was in relation to man's obedience to her laws, and obedience to natural laws was the essence of moral action. Her punishments and rewards were just, because they were exactly proportionate to the offense; they were fair, because they were invariant effects of causes; they were instructive, because they followed immediately upon the act. To train the individual to cope with nature and her requirements was the meaning of "education"—the *leading out* of the mind. "Important as may be the mental preparation for dealing with certainties," wrote Youmans, "it is still more important to prepare for uncertainties; to ignore this, arrests education at an inferior stage and but ill prepares for the emergencies of practical life." [141] To eliminate mediate authority was

[141] Youmans, "Mental Discipline in Education," *The Culture Demanded by Modern Life,* p. 36.

to foster individual responsibility and the courageous assumption of risks.

These doctrines were accepted in the colleges, not immediately, not in all areas, and not all at once, but they were accepted conclusively. In helping them take effect—whether in the curriculum, in the classroom, or in the chapel—one institution, Harvard, was always in the vanguard. Under Eliot, the free choice of subjects by students was officially and almost fully allowed. Between 1872 and 1894, subject requirements were abolished for all classes of students except the freshmen, who had to endure the coercion of one required course in English and one in a foreign language.[142] Other colleges followed suit, without, however, going quite so far. Between 1875 and 1886, Amherst more than tripled the number of electives in the junior and senior year; at Yale 50 percent of the courses for juniors and 80 percent of the courses for seniors were made elective; Brown, Dartmouth, and Williams took long strides in the same direction.[143] In 1901, a survey of ninety-seven institutions showed that the elective system had penetrated 70 percent of the program of thirty-four, 50 to 70 percent of twelve, less than 50 percent of fifty-one.[144] In the teaching of the sciences, Eliot was one of the first to champion laboratory methods—i.e., first-hand observation and experiments by students.[145] By 1899, James B. Angell could proclaim that "the method of scientific instruction has been revolutionized. In the last half century no more important step in education has been taken than in the universal introduction of the laboratory methods."[146] In other subjects, the technique of rote recitation was replaced by lecture and discussion—at Harvard by 1880, according to its president's report.[147] The statutes and laws of Harvard College, which had grown harsh and picayune, were pruned to a mere five pages and made considerably more forbearing.[148] At many other institutions the same reforms were accomplished.[149] In

[142] See Samuel Eliot Morison, "College Studies, 1869–1929," in *Development of Harvard University*, pp. xxix–l.

[143] George Herbert Palmer, "Possible Limitations of the Elective System," *Andover Review*, VI (December, 1886), 581.

[144] E. D. Phillips, "The Elective System in American Education," *Pedagogical Seminary*, VIII (June, 1901), 206–30.

[145] Eliot wrote a chemistry textbook with Francis H. Storer that "caused a revolution in the teaching of elementary chemistry by making it a laboratory subject in the United States." James, *Eliot*, I, 164.

[146] James B. Angell, "The Old College and the New University," in *Selected Addresses* (London, 1912), pp. 136–37.

[147] Morison, *Three Centuries of Harvard*, p. 347.

[148] James, *Eliot*, I, 242.

[149] Walter C. Bronson, *The History of Brown University, 1764–1914* (Providence,

the establishment of voluntary worship, Harvard far outdistanced contemporary institutions of her type. In 1886, compulsory chapel—that ancient combination of a ritual observance and a penal system—was abolished at Harvard.[150] In the other private eastern colleges, however, compulsory chapel remained—at Dartmouth until 1925, at Yale until 1926, at Williams until 1927. Princeton commuted the obligation to informal Sunday discussion classes in 1932.[151] Despite the unevenness of change, the authoritarian method everywhere fell on the defensive, and at most important points gave way.

The exodus of clerical trustees, the eclipse of authoritarian norms, the evisceration of the traditional course, doomed the collegiate system that had prevailed in America for centuries. But yet, with that hardihood and unconscious tenacity that age imparts to old forms, church-controlled institutions did not die or disappear from the scene. In 1906, the Carnegie Foundation for the Advancement of Teaching, set up to provide retirement allowances for professors in private, nonsectarian colleges, initially labeled only fifty-one institutions as completely nondenominational.[152] Sectarian control was maintained in a variety of ways. Though all colleges were open to all students without restriction as to creed,[153] 109 were re-

---

R.I., 1914), pp. 404–20; Thomas J. Wertenbaker, *Princeton, 1746–1896* (Princeton, N.J., 1946), pp. 315–19.

[150] Morison, *Development of Harvard University,* pp. li–lviii.

[151] *Ibid.,* p. lviii. The *Dartmouth College Catalogue* for 1895–96 provided that "Prayers are conducted by the President each week-day morning. . . . All undergraduate students are required to be present," or might attend other churches (p. 112). First provision for voluntary attendance is to be found in the *Dartmouth College Catalogue* for 1925–26, p. 14. See also, Leon B. Richardson, *History of Dartmouth College* (2 vols.; Hanover, N.H., 1932), II, 780. The *Yale Catalogue* for 1924–25 provides that "attendance at the daily and Sunday chapel services is required of all freshmen. Exemption from this requirement is granted for the Sunday services. . . ." (p. 105). The next year's catalogue omits all mention of that requirement. The *Princeton Catalogue* for 1893–94 required all undergraduates to attend morning prayers, and gave permission to attend elsewhere "on special occasions" and on "application to the president" (p. 148). By 1907–8 this had become a twice-a-week requirement, with "at least one half of the Sunday Chapel services each quarter" required (p. 321); by 1915–16, the twice-a-week requirement was dropped; finally, by 1932–33, it was announced that "[a] service of worship is held in the chapel each Sunday morning at eleven o'clock. For those who object to required attendance at a religious service, an alternative is offered in the form of an informal discussion class on Sunday evenings" (p. 222).

[152] The Carnegie Foundation for the Advancement of Teaching, *First Annual Report of the President and Treasurer* (1906), p. 28. Hereafter these documents are referred to as *First Annual Report, Second Annual Report,* and so on.

[153] There were still, on the other hand, examples of students required to attend a specified church in the neighborhood: Olivet, Park, and Wake Forest Colleges were cited. *Second Annual Report* (1907), p. 46.

ported as still requiring all or part of the trustees to belong to a specified sect. Formal creedal restrictions on teachers were rare, though there were instances of this as well. The Carnegie Foundation listed 200 institutions that were either owned outright by a church (these were largely the Roman Catholic colleges and universities) or whose boards of trustees were elected by a governing body of the denomination. In certain places, only the right to nominate trustees was vested in an organ of the church; in others, only the right to confirm them. Control was exercised by church assemblies, by high ecclesiastical officers, or by subsidiary or allied corporations.[154] These were only some of the varied designs of the formal machinery of control. The Carnegie Foundation did not enumerate, nor did it exclude, colleges merely in sympathy with a church.[155]

But numbers did not tell, nor the forms of control describe, the decline and attenuation of American academic sectarianism. In many of these institutions, the control of the church was barely nominal, a mechanical adherence to form which convention had managed to preserve and lethargy alone defended.[156] In many places, church control was an incubus which the college was attempting to throw off, or which it endured merely because the charter made remedial action difficult.[157] In few institutions was it reckoned a positive, necessary good. When the Carnegie Foundation inquired as to "whether denominational connection or control ministers to the religious or intellectual life," the respondents in the denominational colleges declared "almost without exception that such connection played little, if any, part in the religious or intellectual life of the student body." To the question whether such a connection improved the organization of the college the answer was "almost universally" couched in the negative.[158] How meaningless was the sectarian form is indicated by the alacrity with which certain colleges proclaimed their independence and revised their charters and by-laws in order to receive the Foundation's benefits. Bowdoin gave up a lucrative sectarian endowment in order to be eligible for membership in the Foundation. Drake University and

---

[154] *Ibid.*, pp. 42–50.

[155] It is difficult to ascertain how many were in sympathetic and traditional association. The College Board of the Presbyterian Church rated 471 colleges and universities denominational in 1911, using this broader standard. The figure may be too high considering the over-generous definition of "college" that denominational rating boards used. W. S. Plumer Bryan, *The Church, Her Colleges and the Carnegie Foundation* (Princeton, N.J., 1911), p. 57n.

[156] *First Annual Report* (1906), p. 49.

[157] *Second Annual Report* (1907), p. 60.　　　　　[158] *Ibid.*, pp. 53–54.

Drury College quickly abolished all tests and conditions. In four years, twenty institutions qualified under the Foundation's rules; after that, in a change of policy, the Foundation required contributions from participants and the process of conversion slowed down.[159] To be sure, several hundred colleges remained sectarian despite these blandishments. But they were marginal institutions, financially, educationally, intellectually. Sectarian colleges are still with us today. But generally they are in the lag, not in the forerank of history, serving as illustrations of the disparities in American education.

A NEW RATIONALE OF ACADEMIC FREEDOM

In interpreting the history of ideas, the belief that nothing under the sun is ever new competes with the Heraclitean doctrine that nothing in the world is abiding. It is with qualifications, therefore, that we conclude that a "new" rationale of academic freedom grew out of the Darwinian debate. For example, we conclude that science invested the theory of academic freedom with a special conception of truth and a formula for tolerating error. But this should not be taken to mean that these ideas came altogether unanticipated upon minds totally unprepared. An academic preference for truth and an academic attitude of tolerance predated the articulation of these ideas and insured their ultimate success. Similarly, we conclude that the concept of scientific competence gave the faculties new leverage against misuses of administrative power. But it would be a mistake to assume that the merits of an argument for competence had never before been grasped by academics: we have seen that the medieval masters used it, as did certain American college presidents, in pre-scientific contexts. Lastly, we conclude that the assimilation of the values of science made academic freedom an ethic, an affirmative moral position, and not merely a negative condition, the absence of overt restraint. Even so, the morality of science did not denote a complete transvaluation of existing values, nor should we count, in the derivation of this ethic, the two thousand years since Socrates as a barren and insignificant age. Without the canons of evolutionary science, we contend, the modern rationale of academic freedom would not exist. But this does not imply that, for science or academic freedom, yesterday was the common date of birth.

With this *caveat* in mind, we shall proceed briefly to explore the three

[159] *Third Annual Report* (1908), pp. 12–29.

contributions of science: the formula for tolerating error; the limitation upon administrative power; the set of positive values.

THE FORMULA FOR TOLERATING ERROR

All justifications for intellectual freedom rest upon a conception of the nature of truth which implies a reason for tolerating error. A concise review of some of the older formulas may help to illuminate the contribution of science. As we have seen,[160] it had been argued in the past that since truth is consistent with itself, the new discoveries of reason will but confirm the dogmas of faith and close the breach against error. Or, that, since only certain beliefs have import for salvation, the rest, however erroneous, carry no penalty of sin. Or, again, that though the truth is already known and needs no further corroboration, the persecution of error is inexpedient since it hardens men in their mistakes. Or, once more, that truth, being invincible and unmistakable, can never be defeated by error, since "who ever knew Truth put to the worse, in a free and open encounter?" The evolutionists devised another formula. To them, all beliefs are tentatively true or tentatively false, and only verifiable through a continuous process of inquiry. Embodying this idea, the modern rationale of academic freedom has become more categorical than any of its predecessors: all seeming errors must be tolerated, for what is truth is never fully known and never finally knowable.

At the same time, the emphasis on disciplined inquiry set important limits to the permissible tolerance of error. The evolutionists' formula did not level every opinion to equal value. It held that every claim to a discovery of truth must submit to open verification; that the process of verification must follow certain rules; that this procedure is best understood by those who qualify as experts. Hence, academic freedom does not theoretically justify all kinds of intellectual nonconformity, but only that kind of nonconformity that proceeds according to rules; not any private belief, but that kind of private belief that allows itself publicly to be tested; not a perfect competition of ideas, but rather an imperfect competition, to which certain opinions come enhanced with a special professional warranty. In this respect, it makes fewer allowances for vagaries of opinion than do, say, the doctrines of Milton and Mill. In the modern theory, though no conclusion is unchallengeable, the method for arriving at conclusions is prescribed.

[160] See above, Chap. I, "The Idea of Toleration"; Chap. IV, "The Secularization of Learning"; Chap. V, "The Idea of Academic Freedom."

LIMITATIONS UPON ADMINISTRATIVE POWER

The prerogative of judging the fitness of professors is lodged by established usage in college boards of trustees; consequently, the institutional aspect of the struggle for academic freedom has turned on whether and to what extent trustees should exercise their prerogative. Since the Darwinian era, the argument for limitation has effectively made use of the notion of scientific competence. When one hears it argued that the professional standing of a professor can only be established by experts, that these experts must be chosen from among his professional peers, that the general consensus of peers is the highest available wisdom in such matters, the argument for judicial competence is called to mind. Sometimes the argument for methodological competence is heard, as, for example, when a professor's dismissal is protested on the ground that the trustees had an inadequate knowledge of the facts, that they admitted prejudiced testimony, or that they were swayed by irrelevant considerations. Again, it would be unwise to exaggerate the novelty of these arguments. They also reflect an affection for "due process"—for basic rules of fair play—that is as old as the common law. Nevertheless, it is also clear that the argument for scientific competence, used in the Darwinian debate as an answer to clerical presumptuousness, has been turned to useful account as a reply to trustee presumption.

These arguments have had a practical effect. They have been implemented by innumerable faculty committees on appointment, tenure, and promotion; by occasional faculty hearings to determine the fitness of a colleague; and by a standing committee of investigation set up by the American Association of University Professors. This investigating committee, composed of professors, investigates complaints over dismissals, seeks out the relevant data, evaluates *ex parte* evidence, and publishes the results of its findings.[161] There is a striking parallel between its operations and assumptions and those upheld by the Darwinian advocates of scientific competence.

THE MORALITY OF SCIENCE

Finally, the rationale of academic freedom has been endowed with certain fundamental values, values not original to science, but implicit in scientific assumptions and inherent in scientific activity. Such values as tolerance and honesty, publicity and testifiability, individuality and co-

161 See Chap. X.

operativeness, have been part of the scientific bequest. Two other values deserve particular emphasis. The scientific criterion of reliability—the dissociation of a scientific work from the beliefs and associations of its author—has bestowed on academic freedom the value of universalism. By universalism is meant the elimination of particularistic criteria— creedal, racial, or national—in judging the merits of a work, and the elimination of unearned advantages—connections, rank, and caste—in considering the merits of a man. The second value is that of neutrality, an interest in disinterestedness that is deeply ingrained in science. By assimilating the value of universalism, academic freedom has come to signify the brotherhood of man in science that is akin in aspiration to the brotherhood of man in God. Attempts to foist upon the academic community an American or a Presbyterian science, or a class or color yardstick in appointments and promotions, are thus infringements of academic freedom. By acquiring the value of neutrality, academic freedom has come to stand for the belief that science must transcend ideology, that professors must renounce all commitments that corrupt the passion for truth. Attempts to suborn professors by pay or other preferences, attempts by professors themselves to hold departments to a particular "line," are thus infringements of academic freedom. As the symbol and the guardian of these two values, academic freedom has come to be equated not only with free intellectual activity, but with an ethic of human relations and an ideal of personal fulfillment.

We should not interpret these changes in the colleges and in the rationale of academic freedom as evidences of a law of progress. Leaving the cocoon of religious authority, the colleges did not emerge at once into sunlit freedom. Taking over the concepts of science, the rationale of academic freedom was not thenceforth complete and unambiguous. In the next chapter, when we examine the last stage in the educational revolution—the building of the graduate school on the model of the German university—we shall see that the new university in some ways compromised the independence of the academic. We shall see—by comparing American academic freedom with German *Lernfreiheit* and *Lehrfreiheit*—that the principles of neutrality and competence were susceptible to restrictive interpretations. The paradox of revolutions—and here our analogy holds too—is that the freedom in the name of which they conquer is often gravely endangered by the new conditions they create.

III: THE GERMAN INFLUENCE

THE FULL STORY of the contacts between the American university and the German university has never been told.[1] Fully treated, it would reveal, first of all, a relationship of one-sided dependence. More than nine thousand Americans studied at German universities in the nineteenth century. Through these students, through the scores of Americans who knew Germany from books and an occasional *Wanderjahr,* through German expatriates teaching in American colleges, the methods and ideals of the German university were transported into this country.[2] The story of this contact would also show the effects of cultural selection. America took from German sources only that which fitted her needs, only that which was in harmony with her history. In a certain sense, the German academic influence, powerful as it was, reinforced rather than initiated native American tendencies toward change. Before 1850, for example, comparatively few American candidates for academic posts followed the trail to Göt-

[1] This is a wide gap in American historiography. There is only one study that attempts directly to relate the German and the American universities: Charles Franklin Thwing, *The American and the German University, One Hundred Years of History* (New York, 1928). While this book has the virtue of regarding the German impact comprehensively, taking into account institutional, personal, and scholarly influences, it is skimpy on details and superficial in analysis. John A. Walz, *German Influence in American Education and Culture* (Philadelphia, 1936), is a little essay too thin to justify its title. B. A. Hinsdale, "Notes on the History of Foreign Influences upon Education in the United States," *Report of the Commissioner of Education,* I (1897–98), 610–13, gives a list of the names of American students at Göttingen, Halle, Berlin, and Leipzig, a valuable but unfortunately incomplete listing. On the over-all impact of German culture on the United States, there are several studies of tangential value. Albert B. Faust, *The German Element in the United States* (New York and Boston, 1909), is a two-volume compendium of bits of information that overstresses the German contribution to American culture. Orie W. Long, *Literary Pioneers* (Cambridge, Mass., 1935) is an excellent study of literary influences, and contains much that is illuminating on the reaction of Everett, Bancroft, Cogswell, Ticknor, Longfellow, and Motley to the German university. Two studies of the American magazines' reaction to German literature contain bibliographical references pertinent to this theme: Scott H. Goodnight, "German Literature in American Magazines Prior to 1846," and Martin H. Haertel, "German Literature in American Magazines, 1846 to 1880," both in *Bulletin of the University of Wisconsin Philology and Literature Series,* IV (1908).

[2] Thwing, *The American and the German University,* p. 41.

tingen blazed by Ticknor and Bancroft.[3] Of those who went, a dispro-portionate number were graduates of atypical Harvard.[4] The denomina-tional college was neither eager for German-trained scholars nor ready for German-trained scholarship. German theology was too skeptical, German philology too specialized, German *Wissenschaftslehre* too strenuous.[5] It was not until a German degree offered advantages to career chances at home—which is to say, it was not until the American college had already grown more secular, specialized, and intellectually ambitious—that the great exodus of American scholars began. It must be assumed, therefore, that the increase in the number of Americans going to Germany in the second half of the nineteenth century—the figures are roughly 200 before 1850 and go up to 2,000 in the peak decade of the 1880s—tells as much about the pace of indigenous change as about the growth of our cultural debt.[6]

Finally, the story would reveal the effects of cultural modification. The Germany seen through American eyes was bound to be, in part, a figment of American preconceptions. Brought into contact with our own ideals

[3] Harold S. Jantz objects to the traditional view that the publication of Mme. de Staël's *De l'Allemagne* in this country in 1814 and the pioneer activities of the Göttingen Four were America's first introduction to German culture and the German university. See "German Thought and Literature in New England, 1620–1820," *Journal of English and Germanic Philology,* IV (1942), 1–45. But his evidence hinges on the interests of a few scholars of particularly broad reading and not on those of the mass of American college graduates, whose interest in English culture was dominant before 1820.

[4] Hinsdale, "Notes on the History of Foreign Influences," pp. 610–13; William Goodwin, "Remarks on the American Colony at Göttingen," *Proceedings of the Massachusetts Historical Society,* XII, Second Series (1897–99), 366–69.

[5] Particularly was there a great reluctance to admit German-trained theological students into the colleges. George Bancroft, though he was provided with a three-year scholarship by the Harvard Corporation to become a philologist and Biblical critic, felt that he had to make his Christian invulnerability to German skepticism quite clear to his Harvard sponsors. Writing to President Kirkland of Harvard in 1819, he assured him that he had nothing to do with German theology except insofar as it was merely critical. "Of their infidel systems I hear not a word: and I trust I have been too long under your eye, and too long a member of the Theological Institution under your inspection to be in danger of being led away from the religion of my Fathers. . . . I say this explicitly, because before I left home I heard frequently expressed fears, lest I join the German school." Long, *Literary Pioneers,* pp. 114–15. A folkish fear of German theology remained long past the midpoint of the century. In 1863, William Graham Sumner, deciding to acquire a German theological training, was thought by his family to do so with considerable risk to his immortal soul. Harris E. Starr, *William Graham Sumner* (New York, 1925), p. 56. Similarly, George Sylvester Morris' family feared for his orthodoxy when he decided to go to Germany in 1866. R. M. Wenley, *The Life and Works of George Sylvester Morris* (New York, 1919), p. 115.

[6] Thwing, *The American and the German University,* p. 42.

and on our own ground, German academic ideals were bound to be greatly altered. The analysis that follows covers briefly only two of many German contributions—the ideal of academic research, and the ideals of *Lernfreiheit* and *Lehrfreiheit*. But even this incomplete account of a complex cultural connection illustrates the three-fold process of dependence, selection, and modification.

ACADEMIC RESEARCH

The conception of a university as a research institution was in large part a German contribution. In this country, the meaning of "university" had been depreciated and obscured by an inflation of institutional claims. Before the mid-century, the word "university" variously denoted: (1) a college with at least one professional school attached to it, such as the University of Pennsylvania or Harvard University; (2) simply a state-controlled institution of higher learning, such as the University of Georgia and the University of North Carolina; (3) a state-controlled institution with one or more professional schools which also offered a wider assortment of elective courses, such as the University of Virginia; (4) any college that aspired to be grand, as did numerous institutions in the South and West.[7] Neither the word nor the thing it referred to encompassed the activity of research. As long as the techniques of research could be self-taught, as long as private libraries could keep pace with the growth of knowledge, there was no cause for a Franklin to seek a professorship, for an Emerson to soliloquize before schoolboys, for a Jefferson, an Irving, or a Motley to try didactically to reproduce his kind. The adoption of research as an academic function awaited changes in the conditions of inquiry—the vast extension of empirical knowledge and the refinement in the techniques of investigation; the overcoming of academic resistance; and, very important, a greater familiarity with the German university which, in the nineteenth century, was a model for reformers and a spur.

[7] Daniel C. Gilman, first president of Johns Hopkins, tells in his memoirs of a dignitary who visited Yale and introduced himself as "chancellor of the University." " 'How large a faculty have you,' asked Dominie Day. 'Not any,' was the answer. 'Have you any library or buildings?' 'Not yet,' replied the visitor. 'Any endowment?' 'None' came the monotonous and saddening negative. 'What have you?' persisted the Yale President. The visitor brightened as he said, 'We have a very good charter.' " *Launching of a University* (New York, 1906), pp. 5–6. For a brief account of the evolution of the word "university" in American academic life, see Carnegie Foundation for the Advancement of Teaching, *Second Annual Report of the President and Treasurer* (1907), pp. 81–85.

The German universities had not always been famed as research in-stitutions. For two centuries following the Reformation they had been little more than agents of the prescribed theology, drowsy centers of scholasticism, branches of the state bureaucracy. Leibnitz' refusal to accept a position at a German university is one indication of their lack of appeal for scholars.[8] That they forged ahead of all others in the nine-teenth century and became the cynosures of richer and older institutions was the result of many factors, among which two—their peculiar struc-tural advantages and the revival of academic philosophy—deserve our special notice.

In organization the German universities in the late eighteenth and early nineteenth centuries were stronger than the clustered colleges of Oxford and Cambridge and the independent technical and professional schools that emerged in France after the Revolution.[9] First of all, the German universities had retained the philosophical faculty in its old medieval conjunction with theology, law, and medicine. Thus they had been, even in their darkest days, something more than theological semi-naries or professional schools. Secondly, the relegation of preparatory courses to lower schools, the abandonment of the communal student life in *Bursen* and colleges, the gradual rise in the age of entering students, liberated the German professor from most parental responsibilities. There was less danger, where the student-teacher relation was an *entente cordiale* and not a forced alliance, that the presence of students would spoil the inspiration of searchers; there was a greater chance, in the freer devotion of mind to mind, for the habit of discipleship to be reborn. Thirdly, the German universities were the possessions and the pride of the several territorial states—which, if not an unmixed blessing, at least allowed them to benefit from the princely penchant for display.[10] Finally, the develop-ment of a civil bureaucracy and the adoption of the Roman law in the

[8] See Paul Farmer's excellent but all too brief essay on this break between academic and intellectual life in Europe, in "Nineteenth Century Ideas of the University: Continental Europe," Margaret Clapp, ed., *The Modern University* (Ithaca, N.Y., 1950), pp. 3–24.

[9] See Stephen d'Irsay, *Histoire dès universités françaises et étrangères des origines à nos jours* (2 vols.; Paris, 1933–35), II, 168–77; John Theodore Merz, *A History of European Thought in the Nineteenth Century* (4 vols.; Edinburgh and London, 1907–14), Chap. I: "The Scientific Spirit in France."

[10] Friedrich Paulsen, *The German Universities: Their Character and Historical Development* (New York, 1895), pp. 57–64; Paulsen, *The German Universities and University Study* (New York, 1906), pp. 44–46, 137–39. The debt of this sec-tion to Paulsen is very large.

German states in the eighteenth century created a need for officials with university training. Even the nobility had to study the new jurisprudence in order to maintain its supremacy in the German bureaucracies—and this did much to enhance the power and the prestige of the German professor and the university.[11]

The flowering of German philosophy came in the eighteenth and early nineteenth centuries. The history of universities provides no example of a philosophical movement so academic in origin (unless it be the development of Scottish common-sense realism at Edinburgh and Glasgow);[12] the history of philosophies hardly recounts a phase so thoroughly academic in flavor. Whereas French Encyclopedism and the English Enlightenment flourished outside the universities, their German counterpart was well ensconced at Göttingen from the year of its founding (1737), at Halle after the reinstatement of Christian Wolff by Frederick the Great in 1740, at Königsberg during the glorious reign of Immanuel Kant (1755–1797).[13] Long before romantic idealism infiltrated the French and English universities, it prospered under Fichte and Schelling at Jena, and under Fichte, Hegel, and Schelling at Berlin. It is worth noting that whereas the great philosophers of England, from Bacon to John Stuart Mill, were men of affairs, the great figures in the heroic age of German philosophy were academic men. From this circumstance may be traced both the glory of English philosophy and the grandeur of the German university.

The philosophical revival revitalized the universities by redefining the idea of searching. Under the long-reigning scholastic system, to philosophize had meant to explain dogma, to deduce its consequences, and to demonstrate its validity: searching, within this confine, was an act of ratiocination. To philosophize, according to the philosophical rationalists, was to submit all belief, even the very conditions of knowledge, to the verification of reason: with them, searching became an act of intellectual criticism.[14] With the rise of German idealism, searching was defined as a positive act of creation: to philosophize, in Fichtean terms, was to find

[11] Paulsen, *German Universities and University Study*, pp. 119–21; W. H. Bruford, *Germany in the Eighteenth Century: The Social Background of the Literary Revival* (Cambridge, 1935), p. 251.

[12] See Gladys Bryson, *Man and Society: The Scottish Inquiry of the Eighteenth Century* (Princeton, N.J., 1945).

[13] Frederick Lilge, *The Abuse of Learning: The Failure of the German University* (New York, 1948), Chaps. I and II. Lilge is a good antidote to the idyllic view of the German university presented by Paulsen.

[14] Immanuel Kant, *Der Streit der Fakultäten* (Königsberg, 1798), Rossmann ed. (Heidelberg, 1947), pp. 21–26.

the content of reality through the very activity of thought.[15] In part, this apotheosis of mind was compensation for the German's failure in action. It helped make amends for defeats on the field of battle to seek spiritual and moral goals in a sphere that was free from contingencies. It was to counteract the materialism of French philosophy that the Idealists sought a suprasensual reality behind the screen of perceived appearances. In addition, deep religious aspirations, evidenced in disguised religious symbols, were met by this abstruse metaphysics. Fichte's selfless scholar may be identified with the celibate priest; the intellect conscious of the Absolute, with the mystic union of man with God; the search for philosophical truth, with the quest for religious certainty.[16] Each of the several schools of idealism was like a militant church whose creed was revealed to its founder. To these academic philosophers, the search for truth was not an occupation, but a calling—a transcendent necessity, a requirement for salvation.

The hegemony of philosophy in the German universities broke down in the 1820s and 1830s with the introduction of the natural and experimental sciences. For decades a war of methods was fought between the scientists, who sought to explain nature through quantitative measurement and careful observation, and the speculative philosophers of Schelling's school, who regarded nature as knowable through *a priori* schemes, more or less intuitively derived. With the success of Johannes Mueller's pioneer work in physiology, the wide acclaim given to Liebig's chemical laboratory, the popularity of Alexander von Humboldt's lectures on natural science, the victory of the methods of science was assured. After 1840, intense specialization, rigid objectivity, the mustering of footnoted evidence, became the hallmarks of German scholarship. But the philosophic spirit was not rooted out of academic thought by these empirical procedures. The idealistic mood lingered over the German universities long after it was severed from the circumstances of its origin. Nineteenth-century German scholarship, even when it exhibited the most painstaking empiricism, was polemical and subjective. "In no other country," Santayana has written, pointing to this characteristic,

has so large, so industrious and (amid its rude polemics) so co-operative a set of professors devoted itself to all sorts of learning. But as the original motive was to save one's soul, an apologetic and scholastic manner has often

[15] J. G. Fichte, "Bestimmung des Gelehrten," *Nachgelassene Werke*, III, 183–93.
[16] See George Santayana's brilliant analysis of this philosophy in *Egotism in German Philosophy* (New York, 1940), Chaps. I and II.

survived: the issue is prejudged and egotism has appeared even in science. . . . If the controlling purpose is not political or religious, it is at least "philosophical," that is to say, arbitrary. . . . Hence a piece of Biblical or Homeric criticism, a history of Rome or of Germany, often becomes a little system of egotistical philosophy, posited and defended with all the parental zeal and all the increasing conviction with which a prophet defends his supernatural inspirations.[17]

The very notion of *Wissenschaft* had overtones of meaning utterly missing in its English counterpart, *science*. The German term signified a dedicated, sanctified pursuit. It signified not merely the goal of rational understanding, but the goal of self-fulfillment; not merely the study of the "exact sciences," but of everything taught by the university; not the study of things for their immediate utilities, but the morally imperative study of things for themselves and for their ultimate meanings.[18]

The German university undertook to train as well as to maintain its scientists and scholars. The lecture, through which the results of new research was transmitted, replaced the old medieval *praelectio,* the exposition of canonical texts.[19] The seminar, which once had been the means for training acolytes in the art of disputation, became, along with the laboratory, a workshop of scientific practice. Working in the vineyard of knowledge side by side with his master, the student learned the methods of his discipline and undertook his own investigations.[20] Gradually, as the faculty of philosophy grew in size and importance, this technique was extended to the other professional faculties. The joining of teaching and research gave the four-part German university a distinctive purpose and character. To a large extent, though not entirely, it arrested the tendency of theology to seek antecedent certainties, of law to become the study of procedures, of medicine to become exclusively clinical.[21] Not pastors

[17] *Ibid.,* pp. 17–18.
[18] See John Theodore Merz's discussion in *A History of European Thought in the Nineteenth Century,* pp. 90, 168–74, 170n, 172n.
[19] Herbert Baxter Adams, "New Methods of Study in History," *Johns Hopkins University Studies in Historical and Political Science* (Baltimore, 1884), II, 64–65.
[20] See Rudolph Virchow, Rectorial Address, "The Founding of the Berlin University and the Transition from the Philosophic to the Scientific Age," in *Annual Report of the Board of Regents of the Smithsonian Institution* (Washington, D.C., 1896), pp. 685 ff.
[21] One exception to this was to be found in theological instruction in the Catholic faculties. Religious compromise had provided for parallel Catholic and Protestant faculties of theology at Bonn, Breslau, Strasbourg, and Tübingen, and Catholic theology faculties at Freiburg, Munich, Münster, and Würzburg. The presence in a university of a faculty over which the Roman Catholic Church exercised a con-

but theologians, not lawyers but jurists, not practitioners but medical scientists, were the desired products. The German university was not a place where anyone could study anything, nor was it a place, despite the practical preparations demanded by state examinations, where the interest in practice was predominant. Technological training in nineteenth-century Germany, by no means neglected, was usually made available in separate schools and institutes; basic courses and tool subjects, by no means disregarded, were offered in the efficient *Gymnasien*. This indifference to vocational ambition, this insistence on disinterested research, created a gulf between the spirit of the university and that of everyday life. Like an independent spiritual order, the German university trained its own personnel, held novitiates to its own standards, and kept the secular world at a certain remove.

To these radiant ideals and great accomplishments, many Americans reacted enviously, and with contempt for their own institutions. "What has heretofore been the idea of an University with us?" wrote the young Henry Wadsworth Longfellow while a student at Göttingen in 1829. "The answer is a simple one:—Two or three large brick buildings,— with a chapel, and a President to pray in it!" How inferior was this to the Göttingen idea "of collecting together professors in whom the spirit moved—who were well enough known to attract students to themselves, and . . . capable of teaching them something they did not know before." [22] As the Gilded Age approached, contrasts of this sort became more and more common. Reform-minded intellectuals, unhappy in the universe of Ulysses Grant, yet sharing its spirit of expansionism, held up the achievements of the German university as indictments of American education. To Benjamin Apthorp Gould, the noted Harvard astronomer, it was intolerable that America, like Rome, should have to send her sons abroad for intellectual nourishment.[23] The reviewer of Noah Porter's book on American education compared the German *Gelehrte* with the

---

trolling influence both in appointments and dogma was a source of friction throughout the nineteenth century. The argument against removal to separate institutions relied on the fear of communal divisionism in Germany and on the hope, not unwarranted, that the scientific method would penetrate Catholic theology too. See Max Müller, *Die Lehr- und Lernfreiheit: Versuch einer systematisch-historischen Darstellung mit besonderer Berücksichtigung der französischen, deutschen und schweizerischen Verhältnisse* (St. Gallen, 1911), pp. 191–200.

[22] Long, *Literary Pioneers*, p. 166.

[23] Benjamin A. Gould, "An American University," *American Journal of Education*, II (September, 1856), 289.

American professor, and found the native product to be "a nondescript, a jack of all trades, equally ready to teach surveying and Latin eloquence, and thankful if his quarter's salary is not docked to whitewash the college fence." [24] Almost all of those destined to become presidents of the great new universities compared the frowsiness of Alma Mater with the charms of the foreign Lorelei. Andrew Dickson White, as a student at the University of Berlin, saw his "ideal of a university not only realized, but extended and glorified," and resolved to "do something" for American education.[25] Three decades later, Nicholas Murray Butler savored the matchless knowledge of German scholars at the same institution, and acknowledged that it "left an ineffaceable impression of what scholarship meant, of what a university was and of what a long road higher education in America had to travel before it could hope to reach a place of equal elevation." [26] James Burrill Angell, Charles W. Eliot, Daniel Coit Gilman, and Charles Kendall Adams were also in this company of future college presidents who admired Germany.[27] In America's continual rediscovery of her cultural inferiority, the German paradigm played a conspicuous part.

Before the 1850s, those who turned to German universities for inspiration were more impressed by the advancement and specialization of their teaching than by their commitment to scholarly research.[28] It was the elementary quality of American collegiate education that discouraged Joseph Green Cogswell at Harvard and made him leave to found his little *Landschule* at Northampton, Massachusetts.[29] It was the thorough-

[24] "The Higher Education in America," *Galaxy*, XI (March, 1871), 373.

[25] Andrew Dickson White, *Autobiography* (New York, 1922), I, 291.

[26] Nicholas Murray Butler, *Across the Busy Years* (New York, 1935), I, 126.

[27] See James Burrill Angell, *Reminiscences* (New York, 1912), p. 102; Henry James, *Charles W. Eliot*, I, 136–37; Gilman, *Launching of a University*, p. 275; Charles Foster Smith, *Charles Kendall Adams, A Life-Sketch* (Madison, Wis., 1924), pp. 12–13. See also, S. Willis Rudy, "The 'Revolution' in American Higher Education, 1865–1900," *Harvard Educational Review*, XXI (Summer, 1951), 165–69.

[28] For example, the primary object of George Ticknor's projected reforms at Harvard in 1825 was to provide for a wider range of subjects, an elective choice of subjects, lectures instead of recitations. This admirer of the German universities did not try to make Harvard over into an institution of research. See George S. Hilliard, *Life, Letters and Journals of George Ticknor* (Boston, 1877), I, 358; George Ticknor, *Remarks on Changes Lately Proposed or Adopted at Harvard University* (Boston, 1825). The early attempts to found graduate schools envisioned advanced studies, but rarely the deliberate encouragement of research. Richard F. Storr, "Academic Overture," unpublished Ph.D. dissertation (Harvard University, 1949).

[29] *Life of Joseph Green Cogswell* (Cambridge, Mass., 1874), p. 134; Joseph Green Cogswell, "University Education," *New York Review*, VII (1840), 109–36.

ness of the German system that drew high encomiums from the Reverend Henry E. Dwight, son of the Yale president, who wrote a widely reviewed book about Germany in 1829.[30] Not until after the middle of the century was the German ideal of academic research approved for emulation. Henry P. Tappan's *University Education* (1850), perhaps the first full-length book by an American author dealing exclusively with advanced studies, was one of the earliest attempts to define a university as a place where, among other things, "provision is made for carrying forward all scientific investigation." [31] The tendency to regard the university from the point of view of the scholar as well as of the student became marked in the next few decades. The object of the German university, wrote James Morgan Hart, in the first extensive study of the German university published in this country, is the "ardent, methodical, independent search after truth in any and all its forms, but wholly irrespective of utilitarian applications." [32] Research, under academic auspices, he argued, breathed life into the university. It attracted men of outstanding abilities, not pedagogues and disciplinarians. It gave students a genuine concern for matters of the mind.[33] This belated recognition of Germany's real glory points up the factor of cultural selection. Cultural goods can only be imported into friendly markets, and before 1850 our canons of education were not receptive to the idea of academic research.[34]

[30] Henry E. Dwight, *Travels in the North of Germany* (New York, 1829), p. 175 and *passim*.

[31] Henry P. Tappan, *University Education* (New York, 1850), pp. 43–45, 68. See, also, Alexander D. Bache, "A National University," *American Journal of Education*, I (May, 1856), 478.

[32] James Morgan Hart, *German Universities: A Narrative of Personal Experience* (New York, 1878), p. 264.

[33] *Ibid.*, pp. 257, 338–55.

[34] Without attempting the almost impossible task of providing a full bibliography, the following arguments for research as an academic function are worthy of mention: George S. Morris, "University Education," in *Philosophical Papers of the University of Michigan* (Ann Arbor, 1886–1888), Series 1–2, pp. 8–9; many addresses by Daniel C. Gilman, including his "Inaugural Address" (1876), in *University Problems in the United States* (New York, 1898), pp. 18–19; David Starr Jordan, "The Building of a University" in *The Voice of the Scholar* (San Francisco, 1901), p. 28; Jordan, "Inaugural Address" (1891) in David Weaver, ed., *Builders of American Universities* (Alton, Ill., 1950), p. 356; F. W. Clarke, "American Colleges versus American Science," *Popular Science Monthly*, IX (August, 1876), pp. 467–74; Charles Phelps Taft, *The German University and the American College* (Cincinnati, 1871), p. 23; Francis A. March, "The Scholar of Today," in Northrup, Lane, Schwab, eds., *Representative Phi Beta Kappa Addresses* (New York, 1915), pp. 112–23; John W. Hoyt, "Address on University Progress," delivered before the National Teachers' Association, 1869, in *National University Pamphlets*, (Columbia University Library), pp. 6–79. Opposition to the idea of searching as an academic function was voiced by many traditionalists; they did not, however,

In time, however, the old assumptions were challenged and were cast aside. In the centennial year of the nation's independence, Johns Hopkins University, the first university in America based on the German model, opened its doors. The aim of this university, said Daniel Coit Gilman when he assumed the duties of the presidency, was "the encouragement of research; the promotion of young men; and the advancement of individual scholars, who by their excellence will advance the sciences they pursue, and the society where they dwell." [35] Suiting action to his words, he appointed a small but eminent faculty, giving it time and freedom for research, and assembled a small but remarkable group of graduate students, giving them incentives for scholarly work; and the names of these men —James J. Sylvester, Henry A. Rowland, Herbert B. Adams, Henry C. Adams, Josiah Royce, Thorstein Veblen, Woodrow Wilson, Richard T. Ely, John Dewey—are the best testimonials of his success.[36] Aptly was this university called the Göttingen at Baltimore. Of fifty-three professors and lecturers on the roster in 1884, nearly all had studied at German universities, and thirteen had been awarded the doctoral degree.[37] Johns Hopkins adopted the lecture, the seminar, and the laboratory, and brought teachers and students together in close and congenial association. What it called the graduate school was the equivalent of the German faculty of philosophy—broad in its range of specialties, nonutilitarian in its objectives, devoted to the tasks of research. And the spirit was German too: "One longed," wrote Josiah Royce, "to be a doer of the word, and not a hearer only, a creator of his own infinitesimal fraction of a product, bound in God's name to produce it when the time came." [38]

Inspired by Johns Hopkins, fifteen major graduate schools or departments were established by the end of the nineteenth century.[39] Decade by

unite on any one argument. Some opposed the German emphasis on self-discipline and argued for the older notion of mental discipline, see "The American Colleges versus the European Universities," *Nation*, XXXIV (Feb. 16, 1882), 142–43, 143–44. Some continued to fear the irreligion of German education, see L. H. Atwater, "Proposed Reforms in Collegiate Education," *Princeton Review*, X (July, 1882), 100–120. Others defended the classical subjects and the prescribed curriculum; see Andrew F. West, *A Review of President Eliot's Report on Elective Studies* (New York, 1886).

[35] Gilman, *University Problems*, p. 35.

[36] John C. French, *A History of the University Founded by Johns Hopkins* (Baltimore, 1946), p. 41 and *passim*.

[37] Thwing, *The American and the German University*, p. 43.

[38] Josiah Royce, "Present Ideals of American University Life," *Scribner's Magazine*, X (September, 1891), 383.

[39] W. Carson Ryan, *Studies in Early Graduate Education* (New York, 1939), pp. 3–14.

decade, the output of American degrees of doctor of philosophy increased almost geometrically. Before 1861 not a single doctorate had been awarded by an American institution; in 1890, 164 such degrees were conferred; in 1900, more than twice that number.[40] In 1871, the total number of postgraduate students in American institutions was 198; by 1890, the number had risen to 2,872.[41] Whatever these figures reveal as to the crowding of the graduate schools and the lowering of standards and results, their chief import is the evidence they give of the thorough domestication of the ideal of academic research.

Rarely, however, does an ideal undergo a drastic change of scene and remain intact in form or spirit. Original meanings are lost in new ideological surroundings; new implications are acquired in strange institutional settings. In practice, America transformed, even as she borrowed, the notion of academic research. Americans did not approach the task of building universities as did the French: no minister of education, like Jules Ferry, could cast our institutions into one comprehensive system: the molding forces were public and private, local and national, lay and professional. Americans did not build their universities with the logical consistency of the Germans: for various reasons no sharp lines separated colleges from graduate schools, or technical from intellectual concerns. In answering the question: "What should the new university be?" every need clamored for satisfaction, every craft hoped for inclusion. Our postwar institutions of higher learning were therefore not merely motley, but mongrel; not only different from each other in size, quality, independence, and sophistication (which was a familiar American pattern), but eclectic in their character and purposes (which on the whole was something new). In calling attention to this fact we do not imply, as do certain critics of the American university, that consistency is a supreme educational good.[42] It may well be that diversity is a sign of effectiveness, that consistency can only be bought at the price of real vitality. But it does appear that our eclecticism was responsible for a confusion and ambivalence in the rela-

[40] Walton C. John, *Graduate Study in Universities and Colleges in the United States* (Washington, D.C., 1935), pp. 9, 19.

[41] *Report of the Commissioner of Education*, 1872, pp. 772–81; *Report of the Commissioner of Education*, 1890–1891, II, 1398–1413.

[42] Critics of American higher education have made much of its hodge-podge character. See, particularly, Abraham Flexner, *Universities: American, English and German* (New York and London, 1930); Robert Maynard Hutchins, *The Higher Learning in America* (New Haven, 1936); Jacques Barzun, *Teacher in America* (Boston, 1945), pp. 253–319; Carnegie Foundation for the Advancement of Teaching, *Second Annual Report of the President and Treasurer* (1907), pp. 76–97.

tion of the university to its publics which affected in turn the spirit and goals of academic research.

It was apparent to certain reformers that colleges and universities were not only different, but essentially incompatible, institutions. In a famous manifesto of the university movement, John W. Burgess, the Columbia political scientist, argued that the college was an educational anomaly, unable to become a university and unwilling to become a *Gymnasium;* and that therefore it should cease to exist.[43] G. Stanley Hall wanted to make Clark University into a "school for professors," designed for original research and instruction of the highest grade, without the encumbrance of an undergraduate department.[44] But this drastic excision of the college did not and indeed could not take place. Sentiment overruled logic, and sentiment is always the main conduit of academic financial support. The alumni and friends of the older colleges were willing to pay to see them exalted, not destroyed, by graduate schools. The state universities would not take so "undemocratic" a step as to differentiate intellectual interests. Even the brand-new universities—Johns Hopkins, Clark, Chicago, Stanford—retained, or (as in the case of Clark) in time acquired, an undergraduate division, either out of deference to local sentiment, or because of a lack of qualified graduate students, or out of a sheer obsession with size. As a consequence the parental assumptions of higher education were never dispelled. Comparing the aims of college educators in 1843–76 with those in 1909–21, one writer has demonstrated the persistence of "morality and character" as basic collegiate values, while the greater attention given in the later period to "civic and social responsibility" was a kind of secular substitute for piety.[45] The existence of the college on university grounds perpetuated a residual belief in the immaturity of academic students, and as their age at the time of entry mounted, their putative age of in-

---

[43] John W. Burgess, *The American University: When Shall It Be? Where Shall It Be? What Shall It Be?* (Boston, 1884), p. 18. Burgess had returned from the seminars of Droysen and Von Gneist to teach survey courses in history at Amherst College. Amherst in the 1870s was still a denominational college of the parental type, and Burgess' attempt to introduce a graduate seminar along German lines met with severe opposition. With higher hopes, he had then turned to Columbia University, only to find that this richer and less pious institution, located in a center of American sophistication, was also opposed to research. Though eventually he was able to establish a graduate school in political science, the lesson he learned was that the collegiate spirit was antipathetic to graduate research. John W. Burgess, *Reminiscences of an American Scholar* (New York, 1934), pp. 138–90.

[44] Ryan, *Studies in Early Graduate Education*, p. 48.

[45] Leonard V. Koos, "College Aims Past and Present," *School and Society*, XIV (Dec. 3, 1921), 500.

nocence was increased. In the public mind, the American university was not clearly defined as a center of independent thought, an agent of intellectual progress; it was also, perhaps primarily, a school of preparation for minors, a substitute parent for the young.[46]

The combination of technical and intellectual interests in each university was also a wedlock of incompatibles. The emergence of the university coincided with the growth of industrialism, urbanism, agricultural commercialism, and corporate enterprise. Dynamic and growing, the machine society needed technical skill to run it, scientific knowledge to improve it, managerial experience to organize it, engineering competence to give it cost advantages. The land-grant colleges were the most famous product of the industrial movement in education. Set up under the terms of the Morrill Act (1862), they reflected the activities of leaders of scientific agriculture, of advocates of a free public education, of politicians free with public lands.[47] As teaching organizations, the land-grant colleges purveyed the abundant and complicated "know-how" that American industry was acquiring. As research organizations, they emphasized the applied sciences—the "better-ways-of-doing"—that American culture was geared to accept. The significant point, however, is not that land-grant colleges and graduate schools coexisted, for each served its own area of need; the significant thing is that they coexisted in the same institutions. In the original disposition of the land-grant fund, agricultural and mechanical arts colleges were added to ten existing universities; ultimately some of the independent land-grant colleges increased their size and added to their purposes by taking on graduate schools.[48] Cornell University, the perfect example of the academic crossbreed, was a land-grant college, a Germanized graduate school, a private university, a liberal arts college.[49] Eclecticism could be achieved, however, in institutions which did not include a land-grant

[46] See Richard H. Shryock's interesting discussion of this point in "The Academic Profession in the United States," *Bulletin*, AAUP, XXXVIII (Spring, 1952), 37 ff.

[47] The best analysis of the industrial movement in education is provided by Earle D. Ross, *Democracy's College: The Land-Grant Movement in the Formative Stage* (Ames, Iowa, 1942), pp. 1–45; Merle Curti and Vernon Carstensen, *The University of Wisconsin, 1848–1925* (Madison, Wis., 1949), Vol. I, Chap. I; Frank T. Carlton, *Education and Industrial Evolution* (New York, 1913); Philip R. V. Curoe, *Education and Attitudes and Policies of Organized Labor in the United States* (New York, 1926), pp. 61, 88, 95–98.

[48] Ross, *Democracy's College*, pp. 68–86.

[49] Walter P. Rogers, *Andrew Dickson White and the Modern University* (Ithaca, N.Y., 1942), pp. 90–123 and *passim*.

college. The University of Chicago, sharing the imperious spirit of the Standard Oil tycoon who was its patron, served both practical and intellectual interests from the outset: it was a community center for the popular diffusion of knowledge, a great institution for scientific and scholarly research, a workshop of practical engineering, a center for professional training, and an undergraduate college.[50]

As a result, the American university united two divergent conceptions of research. In the one view, research was an activity to be initiated and directed from within the university. The searcher was to be independent, not only with respect to his conclusions, but to his choice of an area of work. To fill the gaps in knowledge that continuing inquiry revealed, to conduct investigations as the logic of a discipline directed—these were to be the functions of academic inquiry. Practical results might be forthcoming, but inquiry should be allowed to push against any of the frontiers of knowledge, and not merely along that border where material benefits were promised. Fundamentally, this was the graduate school's conception of research.[51] Adopting the methods of the German seminar and laboratory, it favored an unremitting quest for facts, a strenuous objectivity, the reconstruction of past events "as they actually happened." [52] With the constant development of new specialties, the graduate-school scholar tended to submit his work to a small group of the *cognoscenti* upon whose recognition and approval his professional advancement depended. Moreover, like the German faculty of philosophy, the graduate school preserved its cultural independence by training its own personnel. Not entirely by design,[53] the Ph.D. in America

[50] Thomas W. Goodspeed, *A History of the University of Chicago* (Chicago, 1916), p. 26.

[51] See Daniel C. Gilman, "The Future of American Colleges and Universities," *Atlantic Monthly*, LXXVIII (August, 1896), 175–79; G. Stanley Hall's statement in *Clark University, 1890–1899, Decennial Celebration* (Worcester, Mass., 1899), p. iii, for contemporary expressions of this view of graduate research.

[52] For the German influence on this version of research, see Herbert B. Adams, "New Methods of Study in History," *Johns Hopkins University Studies in Historical and Political Science*, II (1884), 94; Adams, *The Study of History in American Colleges and Universities* (Washington, D.C., 1887); Edward A. Ross, *Seventy Years of It* (New York, 1936), pp. 37–38; Ray Stannard Baker, ed., *Woodrow Wilson: Life and Letters* (New York, 1927), I, 174–75; Carl Murchison, ed., *A History of Psychology in Autobiography* (Worcester, Mass., 1930), I, 2–4, 102–7, 301–10, 450–52; II, 214–20. Paul Shorey, "American Scholarship," *The Nation*, LCII (May 11, 1911), 466–69; C. M. Andrews, "These Forty Years," *American Historical Review*, XXX (January, 1925), 225–50.

[53] The hope of some of the founders of the graduate school that it would also train men for the higher ranks of government was disappointed by the slow development

turned out to be marketable mostly in the type of institution that conferred it, or in the colleges ranking immediately below. But unlike the German faculty of philosophy, which was *primus inter pares* and spiritual leader of the other faculties, the graduate school in the American university was only one of a heterogeneous group of divisions. In the other schools and departments, research was often geared to external and ulterior purposes. The Agricultural College, for example, took its cues for research from the problems of the agricultural community, often from the requests of the Dairyman's Association or the local horticultural society.[54] The departments of commerce, the schools of engineering, the schools of business administration, tended to perfect the skills required by the industrial and business community. In this second view, research was a public service that originated in a client's need and ended in a client's satisfaction.

It would be a mistake to conclude that, compared with the German university, our hybrid university possessed and offered no advantages. From the standpoint of science there was much to be said for keeping open the channels between pure and applied research. From the standpoint of social policy it could be argued that there was something intrinsically good about a system that did not draw tight distinctions between one kind of interest and another, one kind of student and another, one kind of inquiry and another. And we shall see that, from the standpoint of academic freedom, one of the cues taken from the workaday world by university scholars was a bolder demand for civil liberty. Yet it is no less true that our eclecticism carried penalties. It blurred the public's picture of what a university was and ought to be. Like Hamlet's cloud, it appeared in the shape of a camel, or a weasel, or a whale. Some saw in that indistinct image a refuge for recondite thought; others perceived a public station, catering to all comers. Each delineation of the university carried a different interpretation of its rights. As a culturally autonomous gild, the university was independent of all social groups and stood above the clash of their in-

---

of the civil service and the superiority of the study of law as a threshold to political careers. Nor, as originally planned, did the graduate schools fill the higher echelons of journalism, business, and secondary education, once these functions were taken over by special graduate institutions after the turn of the century. See Richard Hofstadter and C. De Witt Hardy, *The Development and Scope of Higher Education in the United States* (New York, 1952), pp. 57–100.

[54] An excellent analysis of community initiative in the research projects of the "Ag" college can be found in W. H. Glover, *Farm and College: The College of Agriculture of the University of Wisconsin* (Madison, Wis., 1952).

terests; as a serviceable folk institution, it was the instrument of all social groups and dared not rasp the interests of constituents. The members of the university did not relieve this confusion. In undertaking to perform a variety of services, the university engaged many teachers to whom unqualified freedom of inquiry was not desirable or not germane. In the university, searchers, the seekers for truth wherever it led, hobnobbed with technicians, who were the purveyors of *ad hoc* techniques, and craftsmen, who were the executors of someone else's designs. In a faculty composed of accountants, home economists, sociologists, military scientists, physicists, physicians, physical educationalists, fashion designers, marketing experts, and mining engineers, there could be no unified sense of the need for academic freedom, no united front against attacks on university independence, no sure definition of the university.

LEHRFREIHEIT AND LERNFREIHEIT

All through the nineteenth century, but particularly after the establishment of the Empire, German scholars boasted of their academic freedom and brought it to the attention of the scholarly world. And the scholarly world, in the habit of paying homage to the German universities, agreed that freedom was triumphant there, the proof and cause of their superiority. In recent times, it is worth noting, the reality of this vaunted freedom has been sharply questioned. With the recent capitulation of the German universities to pseudo-science and the totalitarian state, doubt has arisen as to whether, at any time in the pre-Hitler period, they had ever truly been free. It is pointed out that professors as civil servants had been subject to a special disciplinary code; that under the Kaisers, Social Democrats, Jews, and other minorities had been discriminated against in appointments; that on most questions of national honor and interest (witness the performance of the German professors during the First World War), the academic corps had docilely taken its place in the chauvinistic chorus.[55] It is also pointed out that the German universities were state universities in an undemocratic state,

[55] See E. Y. Hartshorne, "The German Universities and the Government," *Annals of the American Academy of Political and Social Science,* CC (November, 1938), 210–12; Louis Snyder, "German Universities Are on the March Again," *Prevent World War III,* XIV (April–May, 1946), 28–30; R. H. Samuel and R. H. Thomas, *Education and Society in Modern Germany* (London, 1949), pp. 114–15; Frank Smith, "Presidential Address, Association of University Teachers," *Bulletin,* AAUP, XX (October, 1934), 383–84; Paul R. Neureiter, "Hitlerism and the German Universities," *Journal of Higher Education,* V (May, 1934), 264–70.

dependent upon the uncertain good will of the minister of education and on a dynasty far more autocratic than the constitutional forms reveal.[56] Granting all this to be true, however, there remains the question of what was the basis of the boast that the German universities were free.

Two factors point to the answer. The first is the greater independence enjoyed by the universities under the Empire than at any time before. The Reformation had fixed the universities in the theology of the territorial ruler. Though test oaths for students had been abolished in the Protestant universities during the eighteenth century, and speculative philosophy and theological skepticism had flourished at the expense of orthodoxy, it was not until complete separation of church and state was achieved under the Hohenzollerns that the universities were finally free from church control.[57] Likewise punitive action by the state became comparatively rare after unification. The German states lost much of their cameralistic urge to regulate everything directly. The territorial oaths and religious tests in force in the seventeenth century, such as the official resolution of the University of Marburg in 1653 to ban Cartesian philosophy,[58] the capricious absolutism of the eighteenth century, revealed in Frederick William I's expulsion of Christian Wolff and the

[56] For the activities of the high-handed Friedrich Althoff, head of the Prussian Ministry of Education (1897–1907), see Friedrich Paulsen, *An Autobiography* (New York, 1938), pp. 361–69; Ulrich Wilamowitz-Moellendorff, *My Recollections, 1848–1914* (London, 1930), pp. 300–303. The case of the Berlin *Privatdocent* Leo Arons, who was deprived of the *venia legendi* by the Prussian authorities over the pointed objections of the Berlin philosophical faculty, suggests the power that could be exercised by the throne. *Die Aktenstücke des Disziplinarverfahrens gegen den Privatdocenten Dr. Arons* (Berlin, 1900), gives the essential documents in the case. For late 19th century infringements of the faculty's control over *Privatdocenten*, see William C. Dreher, "A Letter from Germany," *Atlantic Monthly,* LXXXV (March, 1900), 305.

[57] Except for the seven Roman Catholic theological faculties, where the appointment of professors, under the religious compromise, had to receive the sanction of the bishop of the diocese.

[58] Similarly at Jena in 1696, the unanimous consent of the faculty was required before a teacher might point out Aristotle's mistakes. Frequently, it was the sovereign who gave distinguished scholars protection against the gild oaths and narrowmindedness of professors. For example, Karl Ludwig, Elector Palatine, invited Spinoza in 1673 to his University of Heidelberg, where the latter was guaranteed every freedom of philosophical instruction, hedged only by the Elector's expectation that he would not disturb the established religion. The Great Elector, Frederick William of Brandenburg, proposed that all scholars oppressed in their homelands assemble in one of his cities—a plan that did not materialize. See G. Kaufmann, *Die Lehrfreiheit an den deutschen Universitäten im neunzehnten Jahrhundert* (Leipzig, 1898).

reprimand of Kant by Prime Minister Wollner,[59] and the repressive censorship of the early and middle nineteenth century, exemplified by the Carlsbad Decrees and the dismissal of the Göttingen Seven,[60] all seemed part of an inglorious but forever finished past. The provision in the Prussian Constitution of 1850 that "science and its teaching shall be free" epitomized the more permissive attitude of the new order. Finally, the German universities were not directly affected by public opinion under the Empire. Public opinion in general never reached the degree of crystallization, organization, and articulation that it achieved in England, France, or the United States. Like the army, the universities belonged to the state, which protected them against local and sectarian pressures.

The German system of control allowed the universities considerable corporate autonomy. The states drew up the budgets, created new chairs, appointed professors, and framed the general scheme of instruction. But the election of academic officials, the appointment of lecturers or *Privatdocenten,* and the nomination of professors were powers enjoyed by the faculty.[61] No lay board of control was interposed between

[59] On the charge that he was encouraging desertion in the army with his fatalistic philosophy, Christian Wolff was run out of Halle on forty-eight hours' notice under pain of the halter (1723). Frederick the Great (1740–86) had no real sympathy for German scholarship, though he reinstated Christian Wolff and was tolerant in religious and intellectual matters. After his death, there was a sharp reaction. A royal decree restricted freedom of teaching and publication in 1788; it was under the authority of this edict that Kant was reprimanded by Prussian Minister Wollner for having used his philosophy "for the purpose of distorting and deprecating several basic teachings of the Holy Bible and of Christianity." Lilge, *The Abuse of Learning,* p. 7.

[60] Military defeat and the great spiritual revival of Prussia in the early nineteenth century brought the brief flowering of German liberal humanism. As Secretary of the Department of Education and Religion in the Prussian Ministry of Education, Humboldt secured the abolition of censorship for scholarly, scientific, and literary works in 1809–10. But with the general reaction that came with the Congress of Vienna, a system of espionage and repressive control was established over the universities. The Carlsbad Resolutions of 1819 provided for strict censorship and a curatorial system to control the universities. During this period of reaction, seven professors at Göttingen, led by Dahlmann, refused to swear allegiance to a new and less liberal constitution in 1837 and were dismissed. There were other dismissals: Mommsen from Leipzig, David Strauss from Tübingen, Maleschott and Kuno Fischer from Heidelberg. See Robert B. Sutton, "European and American Concepts of Academic Freedom, 1500–1914," unpublished Ph.D. dissertation (University of Missouri, 1950), pp. 177 ff.

[61] The federal nature of the German Empire allowed for a certain amount of variation in the forms of state control. In Prussia, the faculty submitted the names of three men to the king to fill vacancies in professorial chairs; the king

the ultimate authority of the state and the plenary powers of the professors. No elaborate administrative structure was required; no office of the president was established. Each faculty was presided over by a dean elected by and chosen from that faculty; each university was represented by a rector chosen from and elected by the whole professorial corps. The German universities were state institutions, but the combination of governmental restraint, cultural isolation, limited professorial co-option, and elected administrators gave them the appearance of self-governing bodies.[62]

The German definition of academic freedom offers the second clue. When the German professor spoke of academic freedom,[63] he referred to a condition summed up by two words: *Lernfreiheit* and *Lehrfreiheit*. By *Lernfreiheit* he meant the absence of administrative coercions in the learning situation. He referred to the fact that German students were free to roam from place to place, sampling academic wares; that wherever they lighted, they were free to determine the choice and sequence of courses, and were responsible to no one for regular attendance; that they were exempted from all tests save the final examination; that they lived in private quarters and controlled their private lives.[64] This freedom was deemed essential to the main purposes of the German university: to forward research and to train researchers. By *Lehrfreiheit*, the German educator meant two things. He meant that the university professor was free to examine bodies of evidence and to report his findings in lecture or pub-

---

usually, but not invariably, chose one of them for the position. On the other hand, Prussia granted the faculty full right to appoint *Privatdocenten* (until the passage of the *Lex Arons*, 1898, which made the minister of education the final court in the disciplining of lecturers). In Bavaria, the king granted the *venia legendi* to all university teachers; in Saxony, Württemburg, and Mecklenburg-Schwerin, the consent of the minister of instruction was necessary.

[62] See, for a good short résumé in English of the structure of university control in Germany, "The Financial Status of the Professor in America and in Germany," *Bulletin,* Carnegie Foundation for the Advancement of Teaching, II (1908), 66.

[63] Actually, the literal translation of academic freedom, *akademische Freiheit,* usually denoted *Lernfreiheit* alone. See J. G. Fichte, "Ueber die einzig mögliche Störung der akademischen Freiheit," in *Sämtliche Werke,* VI, 449–76; Hermann von Helmholtz, "Ueber die akademische Freiheit der deutschen Universitäten," in *Vorträge und Reden* (2 vols.; Braunschweig, 1884), II, 195–216. When the Germans referred to freedom of teaching, or what in current American usage is called academic freedom, they used the term *Lehrfreiheit* or *akademische Lehrfreiheit.* Viz., Friedrich Paulsen, "Die akademische Lehrfreiheit und ihre Grenzen: eine Rede *pro domo,*" *Preussische Jahrbücher,* XCI (January–April, 1898), pp. 515–31.

[64] See Helmholtz, "Ueber die akademische Freiheit," pp. 195–216.

lished form—that he enjoyed freedom of teaching and freedom of inquiry. This, too, was thought to follow from the searching function, from the presumption that knowledge was not fixed or final, from the belief, as Paulsen put it, that *Wissenschaft* knew no "statute of limitation," no authoritative "law of prescription," no "absolute property right." [65] This freedom was not, as the Germans conceived it, an inalienable endowment of all men, nor was it a superadded attraction of certain universities and not of others; rather, it was the distinctive prerogative of the academic profession, and the essential condition of all universities. Without it, no institution had the right to call itself a "university." [66] In addition, *Lehrfreiheit*, like *Lernfreiheit*, also denoted the paucity of administrative rules within the teaching situation: the absence of a prescribed syllabus, the freedom from tutorial duties, the opportunity to lecture on any subject according to the teacher's interest. Thus, academic freedom, as the Germans defined it, was not simply the right of professors to speak without fear or favor, but the atmosphere of consent that surrounded the whole process of research and instruction.

The German's pride in these two freedoms can be attributed in part to the status they conferred and to their significance as patriotic symbols. To the university student, coming from the strict and formal *Gymnasium*, *Lernfreiheit* was a precious privilege, a recognition of his arrival at man's estate. To the university professor, extremely sensitive to considerations of social esteem, *Lehrfreiheit* was a dispensation that set him apart from the ordinary civil servant. In a nation still aristocratic and feudalistic in its mores, caste considerations thus underlay the loyalty to academic freedom.[67] In addition, *Lern-* and *Lehrfreiheit* had patriotic associations. They were identified with the national revival. The renewal of student peregrinations in the eighteenth century symbolized the breakdown of territorial exclusiveness and the growth of national consciousness. The University of Berlin, dedicated to academic freedom, was a phoenix that had arisen from the ashes of military defeat. The denial of academic freedom in the Metternich era had been the work of Catholic dogmatism, Protestant particularism, petty absolutism—all enemies of a united Reich.[68] Moreover, after unification, academic free-

[65] Paulsen, *The German Universities and University Study,* p. 228.
[66] Paulsen, "Die akademische Lehrfreiheit," pp. 515–31.
[67] For analysis of social structure in nineteenth-century Germany, see Ernst Kohn-Bramstedt, *Aristocracy and the Middle Classes in Germany* (London, 1937).
[68] See Paulsen, *German Universities and University Study,* pp. 36–67, 227–62;

dom was thought to atone for the lack of political freedoms and to prove the special virtue of the Fatherland.[69] The romantic nineteenth century was given to equating freedom and nationality, but it was a peculiarity of German thought that it made academic freedom one of the major terms in this equation.

The German conception of academic freedom, reflecting the philosophical temper of German academic thought, distinguished sharply between freedom *within* and freedom *outside* the university. Within the walls of academe, a wide latitude of utterance was allowed, even expected. With Fichte's heroic scholar as their model, university professors saw themselves, not as neutral observers of life, but as the diviners and spokesmen of absolutes, as oracles of transcendent truths. In the normative sciences particularly, "professing" in Germany tended to be the presentation with aggressive finality of deep subjective convictions. Among certain professors, to be sure, there were proponents of a more restrained and cautious conception. In 1877, in the heat of the Darwinian controversy, Rudolph Virchow, the great German pathologist, argued that unproved hypotheses should never be taught as true, that professors should stay within their spheres of competence, that they should consult the *consensus gentium* before expressing possibly dangerous beliefs.[70] But in a famous reply to Virchow, Ernst Haeckel, the biologist, contended that no line between objective and subjective knowledge could or ought to be drawn, that science advances only through the open clash of wrong and correct opinions, that the obligation of the professor to adhere to indubitable facts or to defer to existing opinion would relinquish the field of education to the religious infallibilists.[71] The leading theorists [72] of academic freedom in this period adhered to the latter position—Max Müller of St. Gallen, Georg Kaufmann, von Helmholtz, Friedrich Paulsen. Reasoning from ration-

---

Virchow, "The Founding of Berlin University," p. 685; Fichte, "Ueber die einzig mögliche Störung der akademischen Freiheit," *Sämtliche Werke,* VI, 451–76.

[69] Helmholtz, "Ueber die akademische Freiheit," p. 214.

[70] R. Virchow, *Freedom of Science in the Modern State.* Discourse at the Third Meeting of the 50th Conference of the German Association of Naturalists and Physicists, Munich, 1877 (London, 1878), pp. 8, 22–24, 41, 49–50.

[71] Ernst Haeckel, *Freedom of Science and Teaching* (New York, 1889; first printing 1878), pp. 63 ff.

[72] Max Weber was an exception. See "Die Lehrfreiheit der Universitäten," *Hochschul-Nachrichten,* XIX (January, 1909), 89–91. Weber argued for neutrality on normative issues, insisting, however, that the professor be the judge of his own transgressions.

alistic or idealistic premises, they believed that the only alternative to
the presentation of personal convictions was the prescription of authoritative dogma, that the only alternative to polemical controversy was
the stoppage of academic inquiry. Recognizing that there were dangers
in subjective and polemical teaching, they thought there were adequate
safeguards in the freedom and maturity of the student, who was neither
captive nor unprimed. As Paulsen put it:

The content of instruction is not prescribed for the academic teacher; he is,
as searcher as well as teacher, attached to no authority; he himself answers
for his own instruction and is responsible to no one else. Opposite him is his
student with complete freedom to accept or to reject; he is not a pupil but
has the privilege of the critic or the improver. There is only one aim for both:
the truth; only one yardstick: the agreement of thought with reality and with
no other outside authority.[73]

To Helmholtz,

Whoever wants to give his students complete conviction about the accuracy
of his statements must first of all know from his own experience how one wins
conviction, and how one does not. Thus he must have had to know how to
struggle for this by himself when no predecessor had yet come to his aid; this
means that he must have worked on the boundaries of human knowledge and
conquered new realms for it. A teacher who imparts convictions that are not
his own is sufficient for students who are to be directed by authority as the
source of their knowledge, but it is not for such as those who demand a foundation for their conviction down to the very last fundamentals. . . . The free
conviction of scholars is only to be won if the free expression of conviction
on the part of the teacher, freedom of teaching, is assured.[74]

But outside the university, the same degree of freedom was not condoned. Though quite a few German professors played prominent political roles in the nineteenth century, and a number of these—notably
Mommsen and Virchow—were outspoken critics of Bismarck, it was
not generally assumed that *Lehrfreiheit* condoned or protected such activities. Rather, it was generally assumed that professors as civil servants
were bound to be circumspect and loyal, and that participation in partisan politics spoiled the habits of scholarship. Even so firm a libertarian
as Paulsen held that

the scholars cannot and should not engage in politics. They cannot do it if
they have developed their capacities in accordance with the demands of their
calling. Scientific research is their business, and scientific research calls for

[73] Paulsen, "Die akademische Freiheit," p. 517.
[74] Helmholtz, "Ueber die akademische Freiheit," pp. 208–9.

constant examination of thoughts and theories to the end of harmonizing them with the facts. Hence those thinkers are bound to develop a habit of *theoretical indifference* with respect to the opposing sides, a readiness to pursue any other path in case it promises to lead to a theory more in accordance with the facts. Now every form of practical activity, and practical politics particularly, demands above everything else a determination to follow *one* path that one has chosen. . . . Political activity . . . produces a habit that would prove fatal to the theorist, the habit of *opportunism*.[75]

A university teacher who violated this canon by working for the Social Democratic Party (a legal party after 1890) might find the temporal power rigid and severe. The removal of Dr. Leo Arons, *Privatdocent* at the University of Berlin, for having delivered speeches for the Social Democratic Party is a case in point. The Prussian Minister of Education declared, in removing him, that every teacher "must defend the existing order against all attacks." [76] The philosophical faculty of Berlin had admonished Arons some years before "to cease from such agitation . . . as may bring . . . the good name of the university into obloquy." [77] When, however, their power to discipline the *Privatdocenten* was infringed upon by the Prussian Minister, they defended Arons and demanded that he be retained. Their verdict, which was overruled, contained the statement that university professors "were not strictly comparable to other officials" and that they should enjoy "a wider realm of utterance." But they did concede that professors were not "free and independent citizens," and that professors were obliged, as members of state institutions, to adhere to a special code of decorum.[78] What was noticeably missing from their statement was any assertion that professors, as citizens, enjoyed an uninfringeable right to freedom of extramural speech. The issue was debated on the ground of prerogative, not on the ground of civil liberty.

In this dichotomy between freedom within and freedom without, we perceive, in transmuted form, some of the classic dualities in German philosophy. The assumption that there were two realms of professorial existence—the one, within the university, the realm of freedom; the other, outside the university, the realm of legal compulsion—suggests Kant's division of the noumena and the phenomena, of the world of

---

[75] Paulsen, *German Universities and University Study*, pp. 255–56.
[76] *Die Aktenstücke . . . gegen den Privatdocenten Dr. Arons*, p. 12.
[77] *Ibid.*, pp. 18–19.   [78] *Ibid.*, pp. 16–17.

free will and the world of causal necessity. The limitation of freedom to the inner realm suggests Luther's formula of spiritual freedom combined with temporal obedience. And the injunction that the scholar withdraw from the sphere of practical matters to the anchorite's world of contemplation suggests Fichte's distinction between the true student and the false one, between him who is dedicated to truth and him who seeks selfish advantage.

The American reaction to the German universities' concept of academic freedom again shows striking evidences of dependence, selectivity, and modification.[79] Dependence appeared from the days of the first expatriates, when the freedom of the German professor in theological affairs gripped the attention and won the admiration of Americans. Ticknor wrote from Göttingen:

No matter what a man thinks, he may teach it and print it; not only without molestation from the government but also without molestation from publick opinion. . . . The same freedom in France produced the revolution and the same freedom in England would now shake the deep foundations of the British throne—but here it passes as a matter of course. . . . If truth is to be attained by freedom of inquiry, as I doubt not it is, the German professors and literati are certainly on the high road, and have the way quietly open before them.[80]

Considerably cooler to the skepticism and impiety of the Göttingen theologians, George Bancroft also marveled at the fact that

the German literary world is a perfect democracy. No man acknowledges the supremacy of another, and everyone feels himself perfectly at liberty to

[79] We have uncovered only one article that deals with this aspect of the impact of German ideals: Leo L. Rockwell, "Academic Freedom—German Origin and American Development," in *Bulletin*, AAUP, XXXVI (Summer, 1950), 225–36. Scattered references to *Lehrfreiheit* and *Lernfreiheit* abound, but no attempt has been made to follow their career in American thought, and sometimes the one is confused with the other, as for example by Morison in his *Three Centuries of Harvard* (p. 254), when he gives the false impression that it was freedom of teaching and not the freedom of learning that first appealed to the Harvard reformers. The bulk of the material bearing on this question must be sought in autobiographical statements. Autobiographical information is unreliable, however, first on the general ground that it is subject to faulty memory and prejudiced interest, and second on the particular ground that during and after the First World War, American academic opinion changed from admiration of to hostility toward the freedoms of the German university, so that an opinion expressed at the later date may be a distortion of the author's first impression.

[80] Ticknor to Jefferson, October 14, 1815, quoted in Orie W. Long, *Thomas Jefferson and George Ticknor: A Chapter in American Scholarship* (Williamstown, Mass., 1933), pp. 13–15.

follow his own inclinations in his style of writing and in his subject. . . . No laws are acknowledged as limiting the field of investigation or experiment.[81]

Decades later, William Graham Sumner, no Germanophile, paid tribute to the freedom and courage of the German scholar in an area designated as sacrosanct in America:

I have heard men elsewhere talk about the nobility of that spirit [the seeking of truth]; but the only *body* of men whom I have ever known who really lived by it, sacrificing wealth, political distinction, church preferment, popularity, or anything else for the truth of science, were the professors of biblical science in Germany. That was precisely the range of subjects which in this country was then treated with a reserve in favor of tradition which was prejudicial to everything which a scholar should value.[82]

After the Civil War, when theological freedom under university auspices no longer occasioned surprise, American economists, psychologists, and philosophers sang the praises of German freedom. "The German University is to-day the freest spot on earth," wrote G. Stanley Hall, the psychologist; [83] the German university made him "free intellectually, free spiritually," attested Paul Russell Pope, professor of German at Cornell; [84] "we were impressed in the German university by a certain largeness and freedom of thought," said Richard T. Ely, speaking for himself and for other founders of the American Economic Association.[85]

Since the propensity of Americans to acknowledge that others are free is not usually great, we are led to seek the reason for the lavishness of this praise. As far as the earlier enthusiasts are concerned, the reason may lie in the fact that most of them attended the freest of the German universities, Göttingen and Berlin. This was not by chance: at these universities they did not have to take the religious oaths that would have

[81] Bancroft's journal and notebook, March, 1819, in Long, *Literary Pioneers,* p. 122.

[82] "Sketch of William Graham Sumner," *Popular Science Monthly,* XXXV (June, 1889), 263. See also Philip Schaff, *Germany: Its Universities, Theology and Religion* (Philadelphia, 1857), pp. 48, 146–51.

[83] G. Stanley Hall, "Educational Reforms," *Pedagogical Seminary,* I (1891), 6–7.

[84] Thwing, *The American and the German University,* p. 63.

[85] Ely, "Anniversary Meeting Address," *Publications,* American Economic Association, XI (1910), 77. "The American Economic Association took a stand at its organization for entire freedom of discussion. We were thoroughly devoted to the ideal of the German university—*Lehrfreiheit* and *Lernfreiheit;* and we have not hesitated to enter the lists vigorously in favor of freedom when we have considered it endangered" (p. 78).

tried their consciences at the South German Catholic universities or at the universities of Oxford and Cambridge.[86] In addition, it should be recalled that most of the Americans who went to Germany throughout the century were young men who were suddenly projected into an older and more permissive culture than their own. Temperament decided how this situation would be used, but we can assume that it would be an American in whom the asceticism of Calvin and the prudishness of Victoria were deeply and ineradicably ingrained who would resist the blandishments of the carefree German Sabbath, the *Kneipe* in the afternoon, and perhaps an innocent, initiating love affair. Biography and autobiography are not very revealing on this score, but it is not unlikely that many an American small-town boy shared, with G. Stanley Hall, a sense of deliverance from "the narrow, inflexible orthodoxy, the settled lifeless *mores,* the Puritan eviction of joy." "Germany almost remade me," the president of Clark University wrote in his candid autobiography. "It gave me a new attitude toward life . . . I fairly revelled in a freedom unknown before." [87] To an unmeasurable degree, the German university's reputation rested on the remembrance of freedoms enjoyed that were not in any narrow sense academic. Needless to say, this did not diminish its reputation.

"To the German mind," wrote James Morgan Hart, "if either freedom of teaching or freedom of learning is wanting, that institution, no matter how richly endowed, no matter how numerous its students, no matter how imposing its buildings, is not . . . a *University.*" [88] If one were to single out the chief German contribution to the American conception of academic freedom, it would be the assumption that academic freedom, like academic searching, *defined* the true university. This simple though signally important idea fastened itself upon American academic thought. It became an idea to which fealty had to be expressed. It took hold in the rhetoric of academic ceremonials, a rhetoric that,

---

[86] See Goldwin Smith, *A Plea for the Abolition of Tests* (Oxford, 1864). Not until 1854 was the requirement of the student's submission to the Thirty-nine Articles of the established church remitted for the degrees of Bachelor of Arts, Law, and Medicine at Oxford; not until 1856 was it remitted at Cambridge. Test oaths for fellowships were not removed until 1871 and other religious restrictions not until 1882. See John William Adamson, *English Education, 1789–1902* (Cambridge, 1930), Chaps. III, VII, XV.

[87] G. Stanley Hall, *Life and Confessions of a Psychologist* (New York, 1923), pp. 219, 223.

[88] Hart, *German Universities,* p. 250.

for all its flamboyance, tells much about underlying assumptions. Charles W. Eliot in his 1869 inaugural address decked this idea with memorable words:

A university must be indigenous; it must be rich; and above all, it must be free. The winnowing breeze of freedom must blow through all its chambers. It takes a hurricane to blow wheat away. An atmosphere of intellectual freedom is the native air of literature and science. This university aspires to serve the nation by training men to intellectual honesty and independence of mind. The Corporation demands of all its teachers that they be grave, reverent and high-minded; but it leaves them, like their pupils, free.[89]

Not since Jefferson had an academic leader acclaimed academic freedom so aphoristically and from so high a tribunal. But where Jefferson's tribute to the "illimitable freedom of the human mind" spoke for a waning hope, Eliot's words were harbingers of a mood that would thoroughly conquer. Again and again, high-placed figures in the academic world gave this idea their support. Gilman, at his inauguration, asserted that freedom for teachers and students was essential to a true university.[90] Andrew Dickson White, commenting on the Winchell case, declared that "an institution calling itself a university thus violated the fundamental principles on which any institution worthy of the name must be based." [91] William Rainey Harper of Chicago spoke these glowing words:

When for any reason, in a university on private foundation or in a university supported by public money, the administration of the institution or the instruction in any one of its departments is changed by an influence from without, when an effort is made to dislodge an officer or a professor because the political sentiment or the religious sentiment of the majority has undergone a change, at that moment the institution has ceased to be a university, and it cannot again take its place in the rank of universities so long as there continues to exist to any appreciable extent the factor of coercion. . . . Individuals or the state or the church may found schools for propagating certain special kinds of instruction, but such schools are not universities, and may not be so denominated.[92]

Nor did these hosannas swell from the throats of reformers alone: a president of a small church-related college, a trustee to whom Ricardo

[89] Charles W. Eliot, "Inaugural Address," *Educational Reform* (New York, 1898), pp. 30–31.

[90] Gilman, "Inaugural Address," *University Problems*, p. 31.

[91] Andrew Dickson White, *History of the Warfare of Science with Theology* (New York, 1896), I, 315.

[92] University of Chicago, *President's Reports,* 1892–1902, p. xxiii.

was the last word in economics, an alumnus proud of his university's achievement at games, were also willing choristers.[93]

It need hardly be said that a gap existed between these words and their implementation. Early in his regime, Charles W. Eliot told a professor to omit a doctrine offensive to Boston businessmen from his projected book, or else erase any reference to his Harvard connection from the title page: the Harvard president was to regret his arbitrary imposition.[94] Andrew Dickson White's understanding of the principle of tenure was so underdeveloped when he took office that he proposed an annual scrutiny of the performance of each professor by the trustees, with dismissal to follow upon a sufficient number of unsatisfactory ballots.[95] White's discreditable role in the Adler case has already been recounted. William Rainey Harper's statement on behalf of academic freedom was preceded some years before by the dismissal of the economist Edward W. Bemis on what appeared to be ideological grounds.[96] And many a eulogy to academic freedom was followed by a contradictory recitative proclaiming the absolute right of trustees to hire and fire whomsoever they pleased.[97] Nevertheless, the idea that academic freedom was part of the definition of a university was new and consequential. It was a norm from which the distance to practice could be measured. It was a belief which, in entering the ambit of good form, more easily won advocates and an audience. It was an ideal that elevated academic freedom from an undefined and unconscious yearning to a conscious and declared necessity of academic existence.

[93] See Julius Hawley Seelye, "The Relation of Learning and Religion," Inaugural Address as President of Amherst College, 1877, in Weaver, ed., *Builders of American Universities,* pp. 181–82; Judge Alton B. Parker, "The Rights of Donors," *Educational Review,* XXIII (January, 1902), 19–21; Thomas Elmer Will, "A Menace to Freedom: the College Trust," *Arena,* XXVI (September, 1901), 255.

[94] Charles W. Eliot, *Academic Freedom,* Address, Phi Beta Kappa Society (Ithaca, N.Y., 1907), p. 13. This address also appeared in *Science,* XXVI (July 5, 1907), 1–12, and *Journal of Pedagogy,* XX (September–December, 1907), 9–28.

[95] "Report of a Committee on Appointment of Faculty" (1867), in Rogers, *Andrew Dickson White,* pp. 161–64. The plan was never put into effect.

[96] For discussion of this case, see Chap. IX.

[97] Thus D. B. Purinton: "It is the business of any board of trustees to see that every instructor under its charge has absolute freedom to investigate truth in his department and to promulgate the results of his careful and deliberate investigation." BUT: "In case the published doctrines of an instructor in a state institution are plainly subversive of the state, of society or good morals, the trustees cannot sustain the instructor in such doctrines. . . . Whether a given doctrine is or is not thus subversive in character, is a question to be decided by the trustees themselves." "Academic Freedom from the Trustees' Point of View," *Transactions and Proceedings,* National Association of State Universities, VII (1909), 181–82.

The contribution to the development of academic freedom in America made by German-trained scholars was more than oratorical. From the nineties to the First World War, a good proportion of the leaders and targets in academic-freedom cases had studied in Germany: Richard T. Ely, E. Benjamin Andrews, Edward A. Ross, John Mecklin, J. McKeen Cattell.[98] Others—E. R. A. Seligman, Arthur O. Lovejoy, and Henry W. Farnam—worked on behalf of embattled colleagues.[99] Eight of the thirteen signers of the 1915 "Report on Academic Freedom" of the American Association of University Professors had studied in Germany: Seligman, Farnam, Ely, Lovejoy, U. G. Weatherly, Charles E. Bennett, Howard Crosby Warren, Frank A. Fetter.[100] Some of the leaders in the fight for professorial self-government were German university alumni: Cattell, Joseph Jastrow, and George T. Ladd.[101] That the attitudes of these prominent professors were formed solely by their sojourn abroad is not, of course, certain. It is possible that their very prominence, combined with their interest in the threatened social sciences, placed them in the forefront of battle. But it is not too fanciful to see also in their remarkable showing a pattern of withdrawal-and-return wherein American scholars, temporarily abandoning their world and drawing courage from alien springs, returned to dispense their inspiration.

This much we take to be the direct German contribution. But evidence of selection and modification can also be perceived. The 1915 "Report on Academic Freedom" of the AAUP opened with the statement that " 'academic freedom' has traditionally had two applications—to the freedom of the teacher and to that of the student, to *Lehrfreiheit* and *Lernfreiheit*." [102] This was a gracious acknowledgment of the influence the Germans exerted. When, however, one reads further in that classic

[98] See Chaps. IX and X for discussions of these cases.

[99] Seligman supported Ely when the latter was attacked at Wisconsin, was the chairman of the committee of the American Economic Association that investigated the Ross dismissal, and took a leading part in the formation of the AAUP. Arthur O. Lovejoy was one of those who resigned from the Stanford faculty in protest against the dismissal of Ross and Howard, and was a leading theorist on the subject of academic freedom. Henry W. Farnam was one of the economists who investigated the Ross case. All three, as noted, took part in the framing of the 1915 Report.

[100] See Chap. X for a discussion of the founding of the AAUP.

[101] See J. McKeen Cattell, *University Control* (New York and Garrison, N.Y., 1913), pp. 6–8; Joseph Jastrow, "The Administrative Peril in Education," *ibid.*, p. 321; George T. Ladd, *ibid.*, p. 31.

[102] *Bulletin,* AAUP, I (December, 1915), 20.

document, it soon becomes apparent that the American conception was no literal translation from the German. The idea had changed its color, its arguments, and its qualifications in the process of domestication. All the peculiarities of the American university—its inclusion of a college, its eclectic purposes, its close ties to the community—and all the peculiarities of American culture—its constitutional provision for free speech, its empiricist traditions, its abundant pragmatic spirit—contributed to a theory of academic freedom that was characteristically American.

One obvious difference was the dissociation of *Lernfreiheit* and *Lehrfreiheit* in the American pattern of argument. "It need scarcely be pointed out," wrote the authors of the 1915 report, "that the freedom which is the subject of this report is that of the teacher." [103] The frame of reference had not always been so limited. Indeed, before the nineties, "academic freedom" had alluded primarily to student freedoms, particularly the freedom to elect courses. In 1885, when Dean Andrew F. West of Princeton wrote an article asking "What Is Academic Freedom?" he answered: the elective system, scientific courses, voluntary chapel attendance.[104] But once the battle for elective courses had been won, and attention came to be focused on the collision of social ideologies that was leading to faculty dismissals, the phrase came to be applied to professorial freedoms, to the producer rather than the consumer in education. The new reference became fixed in the nineties, when, at the nearest hint of a violation of professorial freedom, "academic freedom" and *Lehrfreiheit* were invoked, as though merely to sound the phrases had a certain incantational value.[105] In 1899, when Professor Albion W. Small of Chicago wrote an article entitled "Academic Freedom," he made no mention of student freedoms.[106] After that date, only one of

[103] *Ibid.*

[104] Andrew F. West, "What Is Academic Freedom?" *North American Review,* CXL (1885), 432–44.

[105] Seligman wrote Ely: "I was very much disturbed reading in the papers that they have appointed a committee at Madison to investigate your teaching. I had thought that in our State Universities, if anywhere, 'Lehrfreiheit' would be respected." (August 13, 1894; Ely Papers, Wisconsin State Historical Society). H. H. Powers wrote to Ely: "Our 'Lehrfreiheit' [is] sharply challenged." (Oct. 4, 1892; Ely Papers). H. P. Judson offered his congratulations to Ely on the successful outcome of his trial, "in the interest of 'lehrfreiheit' of which every university should be jealously regardful." (Sept. 3, 1894; Ely Papers).

[106] Albion W. Small, "Academic Freedom," *Arena,* XXII (October, 1899), 463–72.

the important documents of academic freedom linked *Lernfreiheit* with *Lehrfreiheit;* this was Charles W. Eliot's 1907 Phi Beta Kappa address. Under the heading of "Academic Freedom," the septuagenarian Harvard president included the student's freedom to choose his studies, to refuse to attend chapel, to compete on even terms for scholarships, and to choose his own friends, as well as the professor's freedom to teach in the manner most congenial to him, to be free from harassing routines, to enjoy a secure tenure, and to receive a fixed salary and a retirement allowance.[107] But this catholic approach was exceptional.

A close reading of Eliot's Phi Beta Kappa address provides the reason for the subordination or exclusion of student freedoms in later definitions. Eliot's discussion of *Lehrfreiheit* was almost entirely given over to administrative issues: to the hazardous relations of professors with nonprofessional boards of trustees, to the friction between professors and dictatorial presidents. He made a point of the fact that "so long as . . . boards of trustees of colleges and universities claim the right to dismiss at pleasure all the officers of the institutions in their charge, there will be no security for the teachers' proper freedom," that "it is easy for a department to become despotic, particularly if there be one dominant personage in it." [108] The status of the American professor in the university organization presented a unique set of problems. He was an employee of a lay board of control; he was not, as in Germany, a civil servant of the state or, as in England, a director in a self-governing corporation. Further, he was governed by an administrative hierarchy which possessed the power to make important decisions; not by officials elected from the professors' ranks, as in Germany and England, or by a Ministry of Education removed from the scene, as in Germany. To resolve the anomaly of being at one and the same time an employee and a scientific researcher, to cope with the problem of maintaining spontaneity in a highly bureaucratized system—these problems absorbed the interest of American theorists. Faced with the task of adorning, democratizing, and protecting the academic job, they lost sight of the goal of *Lernfreiheit*. The focus of the problem of academic freedom in this country became institutional, not primarily educational.

Another difference between the American and the German theories of academic freedom lay in their arguments for the defense of the independence of the university. German theorists leaned on the protective

---

[107] Eliot, *Academic Freedom.*   [108] *Ibid.*, pp. 2, 4.

power of the state and on traditional gild prerogatives. Neither of these was meaningful on the American scene. Here government by trustees not only prevented professorial independence, but encouraged the widespread notion that professors were incapable of self-government. The state was an unreliable mainstay. The tradition of local sponsorship in American education made federal intervention—assuming that it might have improved the position of the university—impossible. The courts were unwilling to upset decisions of the administrative authorities save when these clearly conflicted with the university's charter. To appeal to state legislatures was hazardous, since their members were so often no better disposed toward intellectual freedom or academic independence than were trustees or private pressure groups. Thus, American theorists, unable to appeal with practical effect to the lawmakers or the courts, yet searching for some authority which could be used to check continual encroachments, appealed to the will of the whole community. They asserted that all universities, private or state, belonged to the people as a whole; that the trustees were merely public servants, the professors public functionaries, the universities public properties. Hence, regardless of legal provisions for control, to treat the universities as though they were private possessions, to tie them to a particular faith or ideology, to bend them to the interest of a class or sect or party, was to violate a public trust. At this point, American theorists faced a further problem. What if, as so often happened, the public should consent to the violation of that trust? What if crusading newspapers or patriotic groups, presuming to speak for the whole community, should try to warp the university toward their particular goals? American theorists had to maintain that the real public interest was not the same as the public opinion of the moment. Indeed, from Tocqueville to Lippmann, no group was more critical of the workings of public opinion in democracy than the theorists of academic freedom.[109] In America, where the university presented such diverse and irreconcilable aspects, academic freedom was too new an idea to arouse patriotic feelings, too exclusive to prompt mass support. In sponsoring the public interest, therefore, American theorists were sponsoring something that transcended all the current and ephemeral forms of its expression. Like Rousseau, they found the true will and need of the public to lie not in

[109] See Eliot, *Academic Freedom*, p. 2; Arthur T. Hadley, "Academic Freedom in Theory and Practice," *Atlantic Monthly*, XCI (March, 1903), 344.

the public's own transient notions, but in something more nebulous and abstract. They fell back in the last resort upon a *mystique* of the general will.[110]

We come to the heart of the difference when we compare the American and German conceptions of inner and outer freedom. We need not assume that the lines of each were exactly drawn in order to assert that the areas they covered were incongruous. The German idea of "convincing" one's students, of winning them over to the personal system and philosophical views of the professor, was not condoned by American academic opinion. Rather, as far as classroom actions were concerned, the proper stance for American professors was thought to be one of neutrality on controversial issues, and silence on substantive issues that lay outside the scope of their competence. Innumerable statements affirmed these limitations. Eliot, in the very address that so eloquently declared that the university must be free, made neutrality an aspect of that freedom:

Philosophical subjects should never be taught with authority. They are not established sciences; they are full of disputed matters, open questions, and bottomless speculations. It is not the function of the teacher to settle philosophical and political controversies for the pupil, or even to recommend to him any one set of opinions as better than any other. Exposition, not imposition, of opinions is the professor's part. The student should be made acquainted with all sides of these controversies, with the salient points of each system; he should be shown what is still in force of institutions or philosophies mainly outgrown, and what is new in those now in vogue. The very word "education" is a standing protest against dogmatic teaching. The notion that education consists in the authoritative inculcation of what the teacher deems true may be logical and appropriate in a convent, but it is intolerable in universities and the public schools, from primary to professional.[111]

The norm of competence was neatly summarized in President Harper's convocation address, cited above:

A professor is guilty of an abuse of his privilege who promulgates as truth ideas or opinions which have not been tested scientifically by his colleagues in the same department of research or investigation. . . .

A professor abuses his privilege who takes advantage of a classroom ex-

[110] Cf. "Preliminary Report of the Joint Committee on Academic Freedom and Academic Tenure," *American Economic Review,* Supplement, V (March, 1915), 316; Thorstein Veblen, *The Higher Learning in America* (New York, 1918), *passim;* and Arthur O. Lovejoy, "Anti-Evolution Laws and the Principle of Religious Neutrality," *School and Society,* XXIX (Feb. 2, 1929), 137–38, for different approaches to this argument.

[111] Eliot, "Inaugural Address," *Educational Reform,* pp. 7–8.

ercise to propagate the partisan views of one or another of the political parties.

A professor abuses his privilege who in any way seeks to influence his pupils or the public by sensational methods.

A professor abuses his privilege of expression of opinion when, although a student and perhaps an authority in one department or group of departments, he undertakes to speak authoritatively on subjects which have no relationship to the department in which he was appointed to give instruction.

A professor abuses his privilege in many cases when, altho shut off in large measure from the world and engaged within a narrow field of investigation, he undertakes to instruct his colleagues or the public concerning matters in the world at large in connection with which he has had little or no experience.[112]

These were not merely the cautious constructions of conservative elements in education. If they were narrowly interpreted by certain members of boards of trustees to prevent professors from criticizing the social order,[113] if they were invoked by university presidents to justify disciplinary action against nonconformist professors,[114] they were also upheld by liberal professors like Howard Crosby Warren and John Dewey,[115] and by progressive college presidents like Alexander Meiklejohn of Amherst.[116] The liberal wing of the academic community, like

[112] University of Chicago, *President's Report* (December, 1900), p. xxiii.

[113] For an example of how conservative trustees interpreted these limitations, see Judge Alton B. Parker, "The Rights of Donors": "With the indoctrination in the minds of students of such social, political, economical or religious ideals as tend to subvert the purpose of the founders or directors of the chair he occupies, or which can have reference only to a more or less distant, revolutionary future, the professor and university should have nothing to do" (p. 21).

[114] For statements of conservative university presidents making use of the narrow code of propriety for this purpose, cf. William Oxley Thompson, "In What Sense and to What Extent Is Freedom of Teaching in State Colleges and Universities Expedient and Permissible," *Transactions and Proceedings,* National Association of State Universities, VIII (1910), 64–78; D. B. Purinton, "Academic Freedom from the Trustees' Point of View," pp. 177–86; Nicholas Murray Butler, "Is Academic Freedom Desirable?" *Educational Review,* LX (December, 1920), 419–21; Butler, "Concerning Some Matters Academic," *Educational Review,* XLIX (April, 1915), 397; Herbert Welch, "Academic Freedom and Tenure of Office," *Bulletin,* Association of American Colleges, II (April, 1916), 163–66.

[115] John Dewey, "Academic Freedom," *Educational Review,* XXIII (January, 1902), 1–9; Howard Crosby Warren, "Academic Freedom," *Atlantic Monthly,* CXIV (November, 1914), 691. One article has been uncovered which expresses the spirit of German academic freedom in the classroom: Josiah Royce's "The Freedom of Teaching," *The Overland Monthly,* Vol. II, New Series (September, 1883), pp. 237–38. "Advanced instruction aims to teach the opinions of an honest and competent man upon more or less doubtful questions. . . . Honesty . . . requires that as a teacher of doctrines the instructor should be free to teach what doctrines he has been led freely to accept." Compare with the statements of Eliot and Harper above.

[116] Alexander Meiklejohn, "Freedom of the College," *The Atlantic Monthly,* CXXI (January, 1918), 88–89.

every other, still believed that college students were in constant danger of mental seduction by their teachers. The old fear that students were easy prey to heretical doctrine became the new fear that students had but fragile defenses against subtle insinuation of "propaganda." [17] The norms of "neutrality" and "competence" constituted a code of fair practices in ideas, and as such won assent from all sides.

Of course, the roots of these norms went deeper still. "Neutrality" and "competence" describe not only the limits of American academic freedom, but the very temper of American academic thought. They reflect, in the first place, the empiricist bias of that thought. Even in the ante-bellum period the main accent of American philosophy, sounded by the Scottish school, was empirical, realistic, commonsensical.[118] No invading Napoleon in that period forced our professors to seek refuge in thought against disturbing realities. The transcendental philosophy, the American version of German idealism, generally could not breach the academic barrier. Its intuitionism was opposed by our clerics, lest each man disclose his own religion and become unto himself a church; its idealism was resisted by our philosophers, lest mind or nature be deified, and atheism or pantheism result.[119] With the advent of the university, the triumph of science-oriented philosophies deepened the commitment to empiricism. Kant and Hegel had a brilliant revival, yet their luster was dimmed somewhat by the more effulgent light of evolutionary pragmatism and positivism. Most Americans who went to study in Germany in this period took home the methods of her seminars and laboratories, but left the *Anschauung* of idealism behind. To this empiricist heritage, one must add the influence of Darwinism on American academic thought. In Germany, the first success in the attack upon religious authority was achieved by philosophy; in America, as we have seen, the hold of religious authority was broken by the advocates of science. The empiricist heritage fostered the belief that facts must be the

---

[117] An interesting contemporary analysis of the norm of neutrality can be found in Paul S. Reinsch, "The Inner Freedom of American Intellectual Life," *North American Review,* CCI (May, 1915), 733–42.

[118] James McCosh, "The Scottish Philosophy as Contrasted with the German," *Princeton Review,* LVIII (November, 1882), pp. 326–44.

[119] See Ronald Vale Wells, *Three Christian Transcendentalists: James Marsh, Caleb Sprague Henry, Frederick Henry Hedge* (New York, 1943), for an analysis of the limited appeal of transcendentalism in the ante-bellum colleges; for orthodox expressions of hostility to transcendentalism, see Francis Bowen, "Transcendentalism," *Christian Examiner,* XXI (January, 1837), 371–85, and "Locke and the Transcendentalists," *Christian Examiner,* XXIII (November, 1837), 170–94.

arbiters between competing notions of truth, thus strengthening the standard of neutrality; that universal and synthetic speculation must give way to specialized knowledge, thus promoting the standard of competence. The Darwinian influence, as we have noted, fostered the belief that certainty was as alien to inquiry as immutability was to the processes of life (neutrality); that the right to pass judgment on scientific questions was reserved to those who possessed special credentials (competence). The German and American theories of intramural freedom thus reflected different philosophical traditions.[120]

These theories, it should be emphasized, were concerned with norms for intramural utterance, for the utterances of professors in their role as teachers. Outside the university, for professors in their civil roles, the American norm was more permissive than the German, because it reflected a stronger social and constitutional commitment to the idea of freedom of speech. The connections between free speech and academic freedom are many and subtle. One thing is clear as far as their historical linkages are concerned: the advance of the one has not automatically produced a comparable advance of the other.[121] We have seen, for example, that academic freedom scored victories in which freedom of speech did not share. The masters of the North European medieval uni-

[120] One notes that the partisanship, dogmatism, and metaphysics of German professors frequently repelled the American student; often this was the single stain of disapproval in his otherwise generous endorsement. Ticknor reacted unfavorably to the "spirit of philosophical vehemence" that he observed among German professors. (Hilliard, *Life, Letters, and Journals of George Ticknor,* p. 97). G. Stanley Hall observed that the professors of philosophy in Germany "seemed to be almost mouthpieces of the Divine. Some of them claimed to ignore all other authors and to lecture only upon their own ideas or discoveries, to demonstrate God—as though He had been waiting all these years to have the honor of this proof conferred upon Him—or they established the reality of the world as though it depended upon their ratiocination" (*Life and Confessions,* p. 212). Nicholas Murray Butler condemned von Treitschke for giving "scant attention to the teaching of the history of Europe and Germany, altho his chair was supposed to deal with these subjects. What von Treitschke really did was to make lectures on the history of Europe and of Germany the vehicle for the very effective and emphatic expression of his own personal opinions on men and things in the world about him. . . . There is something to be said for the policy of making academic teaching effective by relating it to present-day interests and problems, but there is nothing to be said for turning academic teaching into an exercise in contemporary journalism." "Concerning Some Matters Academic," *Educational Review,* XLIX (April, 1915), 397.

[121] This point does not appear often in the literature of academic freedom, probably because it is strategic to identify academic freedom, a comparative stranger to our loyalties, with reverenced constitutional rights. For one of the earliest clearcut distinctions between the two, see Arthur T. Hadley, "Academic Freedom in Theory and Practice," p. 157.

versities won a measure of philosophical freedom without like benefits being conferred on the laity; Halle and Göttingen in the eighteenth century were islands of intellectual freedom amid seas of petty despotism; Imperial Germany was far less free in the political sphere than in the sphere of academic education. Conversely, freedom of speech has made gains while academic freedom stood still. Thus, the abolition of the Alien and Sedition laws coincided with the expansion of denominational colleges and the sectarianizing of the state universities. One may therefore conclude that the two freedoms develop independently for different reasons, or that they are causally related to a common long-term factor, such as the diffusion of political power or the growth of the habit of tolerance.[122]

Nevertheless, it can also be demonstrated that, under certain favorable conditions, these two freedoms do affect one another directly, and that the secure position of the one may improve the position of the other and deepen and broaden its meaning and potency. Free speech was protected in America; the post-bellum university presented the favorable conditions. First, the university granted its teachers the time to engage in outside activities: it removed the old residence requirement, it ended the boarding-house vigil. Secondly, the university appointed men whose interests were not engrossed by campus duties. It brought in the professional scholar, whose works were appraised by other specialists; it brought in the new-style president, a man of wide affairs; it brought in the technical expert, available for outside consultation. Thirdly, the university professor began to give up the quiet retreat of moral philosophy for the more worldly concerns of social science. This movement was accelerated by a fourth development, the rise of the philosophy of pragmatism, which sanctioned the application of the trained intelligence to the varied problems of life. For these reasons, the American university professor, much more than his German counterpart, functioned in the arena of social and political action.[123] In that arena, he demanded the prerogative of free speech that was given to other citizens. There he felt that he had the right to express his opinion even on controversial subjects, even on matters outside his scholarly

[122] Thus, the universities of France lost their autonomy when the Crown asserted its unqualified authority, and the fate of both freedoms under the totalitarian system is well known.

[123] See the report of Committee G, "Extra-collegiate Intellectual Service," *Bulletin, AAUP*, X (May, 1934), 272–86. Surveying 42 articles and books, the report showed overwhelming approval of professors who engaged in extramural activities.

competence. There academic freedom became an aspect of the struggle for civil liberty.

And it was precisely in that arena that the greatest amount of academic friction was generated. The attempt to assimilate the doctrine of free speech into the doctrine of academic freedom aroused hostility in certain quarters. It seemed to demand a special protection for professors when they engaged in the rough give-and-take of politics. To argue that the institutional position of professors should not be affected by what they said as citizens was to urge immunity for them from the economic penalties that may repay unpopular utterances— the dwindling of clients, the boycott of subscribers, the loss of a job. Such a demand for immunity, exceeding anything provided by the constitutional safeguard of free speech, going even further than the "free-market" conceptions of the great philosophers of intellectual liberty,[124] was bound to strain the less tensile tolerance of American trustees and administrators. A barrage of argument was touched off by this demand. In its favor, professors and certain presidents mustered methodological arguments: "ideas must be tested in action," [125] the function of philosophy "is to clarify men's ideas as to the social and moral strifes of their own day"; [126] administrative arguments: "If a university or college censors what its professors may say . . . it thereby assumes responsibility for that which it permits them to say . . . a responsibility which an institution of learning would be very unwise in assuming"; [127] pedagogi-

---

[124] Thus Milton, in fighting for free speech and publication against public censorship, did not argue that social penalties were inadmissible. There is, moreover, in his picture of free intellectual competition the suggestion that ostracism or worse will ultimately repay the purveyor of falsehood. "And though all the winds of doctrine were let loose to play upon the earth, so Truth being in the field, we do injuriously, by licensing and prohibiting, to misdoubt her strength. Let her and Falsehood grapple; who ever knew Truth put to the worse in a free and open encounter: Her confuting is the best and surest suppressing. . . ." *Areopagitica* (Regnery edition, pp. 58–59). John Stuart Mill's *On Liberty* addressed itself to the tyranny of the majority rather than the tyranny of the state, and in it the pregnant statement occurs that "in respect to all persons but those whose pecuniary circumstances make them independent of the good will of other people, opinion, on this subject, is as efficacious as law; men might as well be imprisoned, as excluded from the means of earning their bread" (Regnery edition, p. 39). But Mill did not say that this immunity belonged to any particular body of men, but to all men, or to a minority of one, against the despotism of numbers.

[125] See John Dewey, *Democracy and Education* (New York, 1916), pp. 76–77 and *passim*.

[126] John Dewey, *Reconstruction in Philosophy* (New York, 1920), p. 26.

[127] A. Lawrence Lowell, "Report for 1916–17," in Henry Aaron Yeomans, *Abbott Lawrence Lowell* (Cambridge, Mass., 1948), p. 311.

cal arguments: what young men need "are not hermit scholars, but active zealous citizens, with opinions to express upon public questions, and power to express them." [128] The answering volleys were usually, but not exclusively, returned by presidents and trustees. They too used methodological arguments: when a teacher enters politics, he acts "as a partisan and [loses his] place as a judge and an unbiased individual"; [129] administrative arguments: "to use this institution and the funds so contributed for a purpose foreign and contrary to the ideas both of the contributors and of the whole community, and appropriate them to the propaganda of the exceptional ideas of a single individual, is a perversion of public trust"; [130] pedagogical arguments: the professor who uses his university position as "an object of political purpose" destroys his educational effectiveness.[131] And the salvos resound to this day.

The second source of friction was the closely allied problem of professional ethics in the public forum. Despite the invocation of the right of free speech, it was generally conceded by the academic fraternity that professors reached a limiting line of professional propriety long before they approached the boundary of libel, slander, or sedition. But where was that line to be drawn? Was it proper for a professor to run for political office or to work actively for a political party? The academic community spoke with two voices on this point.[132] Was it proper for a professor publicly to criticize the actions of a colleague or a superior? In this most bureaucratically controlled of all the professions, it was not easy to decide where free speech left off and insubordination began. Was the professor's relation to his trustees analogous to the relation of the judiciary to the executive power? The analogy was useful in suggesting that the trustees could not remove their appointee at will, but it was a two-edged sword, for it also suggested that professors were

[128] Editor's Table, *New England Magazine*, XVII, New Series (September, 1897), 126; cf. Edward P. Cheyney, "Trustees and Faculties," *School and Society*, II (Dec. 14, 1915), 795. Also, W. H. Carpenter, "Public Service of University Officers," *Columbia University Quarterly*, XVI (March, 1914), 169–82.

[129] Letter of President Frank L. McVey of the University of North Dakota to Professor Joseph L. Lewinsohn, in "The Participation of University Professors in Politics," *Science*, Vol. XXXIX, New Series (1914), pp. 425–26.

[130] "Free Thought in College Economics," *Gunton's Magazine*, XVII (December, 1899), 456.

[131] Letter of President McVey, in "The Participation of University Professors in Politics," p. 426.

[132] See U. G. Weatherly, "Academic Freedom and Tenure of Office," *Bulletin*, Association of American Colleges, II (April, 1916), 175–77.

bound by the staid public ethics of judges.[133] Again, the conflict between free speech and professional ethics created a storm center which has never lifted.

AN AMERICAN CODE

We can best summarize what has preceded by quoting more extensively from the classic 1915 Report of the Committee on Academic Freedom and Tenure of the American Association of University Professors. How representative of faculty opinion this report may have been is an open question. It was strictly a product of professorial thinking; college and university presidents and deans were explicitly banned from membership in the AAUP in its early years. The authors, being among the most illustrious, were perhaps not the most representative members of the profession. Seven of the thirteen members were social scientists, and may have reflected the bias of their disciplines. Still, the report has great value for synopsis and reference. It was not the product of haste or improvisation, nor was it an angry answer to some galvanic injustice. Many of the ideas contained in the report had been adumbrated by its authors in previous articles or can be traced back to a preliminary report of a joint conclave of economists, political scientists, and sociologists which was written a year before.[134] It created a widely favorable impression. One comment in the press hailed it as "the most comprehensive, general declaration of principles regarding academic freedom that has ever appeared in this country." [135] The United States Commissioner of Education called it "one of the most valuable contributions of the year to the discussion of educational policy," and the Bureau of Education distributed thousands of copies.[136] It was the basis for the statement of the principles of academic freedom and tenure endorsed

[133] For the academic debate over the use and limitations of the analogy of the judiciary, cf. John H. Wigmore, "An Analogy Drawn from Judicial Immunity," *The Nation,* CIII (Dec. 7, 1916), 539–40; Arthur O. Lovejoy's rejoinder, "Academic Freedom," *The Nation,* CIII (Dec. 14, 1916), 561; Wigmore's counter-reply, in *The Nation,* CIII (Dec. 14, 1916), 561–62. The debate was waged intensively in the succeeding decades. Cf. Raymond Buell, Letter to the New York *Herald Tribune* (June 17, 1936); Lippmann's rejoinder, Letter to the New York *Herald Tribune* (June 20, 1936); Walter E. Spahr in defense of Buell's position, Letter to the New York *Herald Tribune* (June 29, 1936).

[134] "Prefatory Note," 1915 Report, *Bulletin,* AAUP, I (December, 1915), 17.

[135] *Current Opinion,* LX (March, 1916), 192–93.

[136] *Report of the Commissioner of Education* (1916), I, 138.

in subsequent years by the Association of American Colleges, representing college administrative officers, and the American Association of University Professors.[137] One modern commentator has properly called it "a landmark in the development of the teaching profession." [138]

ACADEMIC FREEDOM AS AN INDISPENSABLE ATTRIBUTE OF A UNIVERSITY

The Committee tied academic freedom to three requirements—the needs for academic research, adequate instruction, and the development of experts for public service. Some of their arguments closely resembled those of the Germans. "In the earlier stages of a nation's intellectual development, the chief concern of educational institutions is to train the growing generation and to diffuse the already accepted knowledge." It was only slowly that the purpose of conservation gave way to that of searching. More and more, "the modern university is becoming . . . the home of scientific research." Now, in all the domains of knowledge, in natural science, in social science, in religion and philosophy, the chief condition of progress "is complete and unlimited freedom to pursue inquiry and publish its results. Such freedom is the breath in the nostrils of all scientific activity." [139]

Such freedom is no less important to the teacher. No man can be a successful teacher, wrote the framers of the report, who does not enjoy the respect of his students, and this respect will not be forthcoming if the confidence of students in his intellectual integrity and courage is impaired. Helmholtz would have endorsed the following:

It is not only the character of the instruction but also the character of the instructor that counts; and if the student has reason to believe that the instructor is not true to himself, the virtue of the instruction as an educative force is incalculably diminished. There must be in the mind of the teacher no mental reservation. He must give the student the best of what he has and what he is.[140]

The third justification for academic freedom was more originally American. Reflecting the mood of Progressivism, the authors also believed that the modern university should aim to develop experts to help solve the complex problems of society. The professor can only be of use

---

[137] Robert P. Ludlum, "Academic Freedom and Tenure," *Antioch Review,* X (Spring, 1950), 25.
[138] *Ibid.,* p. 19.   [139] *Bulletin,* AAUP, I (December, 1915), 27–28.
[140] *Ibid.,* p. 28.

to the legislator and the administrator if his conclusions are disinterested and his own.[141]

UNIVERSITY INDEPENDENCE AND THE GENERAL WILL

With the *legal* supremacy of the boards of trustees the professors who wrote the report did not quarrel: but legal power, to them, was not equivalent to moral duty. As they saw it, the moral obligations of university trustees were two. Where trustees were bound by their charters to propagate specific doctrines, they should be completely candid about it. The public should not be misled into thinking that the school is searching for truth when in fact it is communicating dogma. In all other cases, the trustees were trustees for the public, and "they cannot be permitted to assume the proprietary attitude and privilege, if they are appealing to the general public for support." If the basis of academic authority was public, the nature of the professor's calling was no less so. Any assumption that the professors were employees of the governing board was gratuitous and insupportable.

The responsibility of the university teacher is primarily to the public itself, and to the judgment of his own profession; and while, with respect to certain external conditions of his vocation, he accepts a responsibility to the authorities of the institution in which he serves, in the essentials of his professional activity his duty is to the wider public to which the institution itself is morally amenable.[142]

To nail down this point, the Committee used the analogy of the relationship between the executive and the judiciary, albeit (one gathers from the text) with some trepidation lest the analogy be misused.

So far as the university teacher's independence of thought and utterance is concerned—*though not in other regards*—the relationship of professor to trustees may be compared to that between judges of the Federal courts and the Executive who appoints them. University teachers should be understood to be, with respect to the conclusions reached and expressed by them, no more subject to the control of the trustees, than are judges subject to the control of the President, with respect to their decisions.[143]

But the authors of the report did not confuse the public with its political representatives, or the public will with contemporary opinion. To rely wholly on the government was dangerous:

[141] *Ibid.*, pp. 21–22.   [142] *Ibid.*, pp. 22–23, 26.
[143] *Ibid.*, p. 26. Italics supplied.

Where the university is dependent for funds upon legislative favor, it has sometimes happened that the conduct of the institution has been affected by political considerations; and where there is a definite governmental policy or a strong public feeling on economic, social, or political questions, the menace to academic freedom may consist in the repression of opinions.[144]

Similarly, public opinion, which was apt to regard any departure from convention with suspicion, was a weak staff on which to lean. Rather, the university

should be an intellectual experiment station, where new ideas may germinate and where their fruit, though still distasteful to the community as a whole, may be allowed to ripen until finally, perchance, it may become a part of the accepted intellectual food of the nation or of the world.[145]

The public for which the trustees acted and to whom the professors were responsible was an abstraction called "posterity."

THE NORMS OF NEUTRALITY AND COMPETENCE

On the assumption that freedom is never absolute and unqualified, but entails limits and obligations, the Committee gave its clear approval to the norms of neutrality and competence.

The liberty of the scholar within the university to set forth his conclusions, be they what they may, is conditioned by their being conclusions gained by a scholar's method and held in a scholar's spirit; that is to say, they must be the fruits of competent and patient and sincere inquiry, and they should be set forth with dignity, courtesy and temperateness of language.

This did not mean that the teacher had to hide his opinions under a mountain of equivocal verbiage. But he should

be a person of fair and judicial mind; he should, in dealing with such [controversial] subjects, set forth justly, without suppression or innuendo, the divergent opinions of other investigators; he should cause his students to become familiar with the best published expressions of the great historic types of doctrine upon the questions at issue; and he should, above all, remember that his business is not to provide his students with ready-made conclusions but to train them to think for themselves.[146]

The committee's opposition to oracular and dogmatic teaching rested in large part on the supposed immaturity of students:

In many of our American colleges, and especially in the first two years of the course, the student's character is not yet fully formed, his mind is still rela-

[144] *Ibid.*, p. 31. [145] *Ibid.*, p. 32. [146] *Ibid.*, pp. 33–34.

tively immature. In these circumstances it may reasonably be expected that the instructor will present scientific truth with discretion, that he will introduce the student to new conceptions gradually, with some consideration for the student's preconceptions and traditions, and with due regard to character-building.

The teacher must especially be on guard against

taking unfair advantage of the student's immaturity by indoctrinating him with the teacher's own opinions before the student has had an opportunity fairly to examine other opinions upon the matters in question, and before he has sufficient knowledge and ripeness of judgment to be entitled to form any definitive opinion of his own.[147]

Again, the assumption was that university education is adolescent education, and that the young mind yields to the imprint of ideas as easily and uncritically as wax.

FREEDOM OF SPEECH FOR EXTRAMURAL UTTERANCE

The Committee spoke boldly on the general principle of free extramural utterance. In their extramural utterances, the Committee contended, it is not desirable that scholars should be bound by the norms of neutrality and competence. It is not desirable that they be debarred "from giving expression to their judgments upon controversial questions, or that their freedom of speech outside the university should be limited to questions falling within their own specialties." Nor is it proper that they be prohibited "from lending their active support to organized movements which they believe to be in the public interest." [148] But the Committee also recognized that professors were saddled with the obligation of discretion incumbent upon professional persons. "It is obvious that academic teachers are under a peculiar obligation to avoid hasty or unverified or exaggerated statements, and to refrain from intemperate or sensational modes of expression." And this led to the vexing question of whether professors should be allowed to work for a political party or run for political office. As one of its members later revealed, the Committee was divided between those who took the view that scholarship and partisan action were not antipathetic, and those who held to the German position that political partisanship was incompatible with objective inquiry.[149] The Committee could only express its indecision. On the one hand, it wrote,

[147] *Ibid.*, p. 35.   [148] *Ibid.*, p. 37.
[149] See the statement of U. G. Weatherly in "Academic Freedom and Tenure of Office," pp. 175–77.

it is manifestly desirable that . . . teachers have minds untrammeled by party loyalties, unexcited by party enthusiasms, and unbiased by personal political ambitions; and that universities should remain uninvolved in party antagonisms.

On the other hand,

it is equally manifest that the material available for the service of the State would be restricted in a highly undesirable way, if it were understood that no member of the academic profession should ever be called upon to assume the responsibilities of public office.[150]

On this inconclusive note, the 1915 report closed.

The scheme of the 1915 report, like that of this chapter, was analytical rather than historical. But it did make one historical reference which leads us back to a sequential treatment of our subject. The authors of the report noted that the character of the infringements of academic freedom had changed in the last few decades:

In the early period of university development in America the chief menace to academic freedom was ecclesiastical, and the disciplines chiefly affected were philosophy and the natural sciences. In more recent times the danger zone has been shifted to the political and social sciences.

The present problem, as the Committee saw it, was that every question in the political, social, and economic fields affected the private interests of class, and that,

as the governing body of a university is naturally made up of men who through their standing and ability are personally interested in great private enterprises, the points of possible conflict are numberless. When to this is added the consideration that benefactors, as well as most of the parents who send their children to privately endowed institutions, themselves belong to the more prosperous and therefore usually to the more conservative classes, it is apparent that . . . pressure from vested interests may . . . be brought to bear upon academic authorities.[151]

More calmly and judiciously than some of their professorial contemporaries, the members of the Committee gave support to the thesis that wealth was an academic malefactor, and that a particular class was opposed to academic freedom. This is the thesis we must now evaluate, and we shall do so by turning to the Populist period in which the thesis was born.

[150] *Bulletin*, AAUP, I (December, 1915), 38.   [151] *Ibid.*, pp. 29–31.

IV: ACADEMIC FREEDOM AND
BIG BUSINESS

CONFRONTATION

IN THE FINAL DECADES of the last century, the leaders of American business began to support our universities on a completely unprecedented scale. Before that period, old mercantile wealth, with its tradition of patronage, had had only modest resources for philanthropy, while new industrial wealth, with ever-growing resources, had been bent on unceasing acquisition and had not learned the great virtue of giving. Thus it is recorded that the largest single gift to an American college before the Civil War was Abbott Lawrence's $50,000 to Harvard.[1] An institution like Amherst College, to take another example, had been founded on $50,000, assembled from small contributions.[2] Weighed in the scale of big-business philanthropy, these sums seem almost negligible. Johns Hopkins University received $3,500,000 from a Baltimore merchant and capitalist; Leland Stanford Junior University received $24,000,000 from the estate of the California railroad king; the University of Chicago received $34,000,000 from the founder of the Standard Oil Company.[3] The foundation came to supplement the endowment as a method of bestowing gifts. Among the early foundations assisting the colleges and universities in some way were the General Education Board, founded in 1902 by John D. Rockefeller, with assets of $46,000,000; the Carnegie Corporation, founded in 1911, with assets of $151,000,000; the Commonwealth Fund, founded in 1918 by Mrs. Stephen V. Hark-

---

[1] Charles F. Thwing, "The Endowment of Colleges," *International Review,* XI (September, 1881), 259.

[2] *Ibid.,* p. 260.

[3] Daniel Coit Gilman, *The Launching of a University* (New York, 1906), p. 28; Orrin L. Elliott, *Stanford University, the First Twenty-five Years* (Stanford, 1937), p. 251; Thomas W. Goodspeed, *A History of the University of Chicago* (Chicago, 1916), Appendix I, p. 487.

ness, with assets of $43,000,000.[4] Truly, the new men of wealth organized their philanthropies as grandiosely as they organized their businesses.

Inevitably, the increase in the size of gifts changed the relations of donor to recipient. Borrowing a term from economic history, one may say that the givers became entrepreneurs in the field of higher education. They took the initiative in providing funds and in deciding their general purposes. William Rainey Harper wrote in 1905 that "in the case of 90 percent of the money given to a large institution the initiative is taken by the donor, and not by the university concerned." [5] This was a reversal of the procedure that had been in effect before the Civil War, when college presidents sued for alms on the basis of needs which they determined. But passive roles did not suit the new men of wealth. It was Jonas Gilman Clark, not G. Stanley Hall, who made the decision to found a new university at Worcester; Clark hired Hall to carry out his ideas.[6] It was Leland Stanford, not David Starr Jordan, who conceived the project at Palo Alto.[7] It was (to take a crowning example) Andrew Carnegie who decided to give retirement pensions to professors, and this without their prior solicitation.[8] Sometimes, depending upon inclination, these donors were also active in determining educational policies. Before the Civil War, businessmen did not usually earmark their gifts for specific educational projects. Abbott Lawrence's gift for an engineering school at Harvard was an exception, but it is interesting to note that President Everett thwarted the intention of the donor by converting the school into a department of natural science.[9] To compare Everett's treatment of Lawrence with Clark's treatment of Hall is to compare the power of $50,000 with the power of several millions of dollars, and to compare the independence of a well-established college with the servility of a young university dependent on the benevolence of one man. In Hall's autobiography we find that the president

[4] Ernest V. Hollis, *Philanthropic Foundations and Higher Education* (New York, 1938), pp. 303–6.

[5] William R. Harper, *The Trend in Higher Education* (Chicago, 1905), p. 178.

[6] Calvin Stubbins, "Biography of J. G. Clark," *Publications of the Clark University Library*, I (April, 1906), 138–76.

[7] David Starr Jordan, *The Days of a Man* (New York, 1922), pp. 268–69.

[8] See letter of Andrew Carnegie to the trustees of the Carnegie Foundation (April 16, 1905). In *Annual Report of the Carnegie Foundation for the Advancement of Teaching* (Washington, D.C., 1906), pp. 7–8.

[9] Samuel Eliot Morison, *Three Centuries of Harvard* (Cambridge, Mass., 1936), p. 279.

was forced to break contracts at the orders of the founder, to reduce the scale of salaries because the founder wished to economize, to add an undergraduate college to what he had hoped would be a graduate institution, because the founder willed it so.[10] The antagonisms between Hall and Clark were not in any sense typical. More common was a harmonious association like that of Andrew D. White and Ezra Cornell, and more common still was an obsequious attitude like that of David Starr Jordan toward Mrs. Jane Stanford.[11] But Hall's story does exemplify the passage of academic initiative to the great providers who had come upon the scene.

The change in the occupational background of trustees measures the growing power of the business element in education. Whereas wealth and a talent for business had once been considered virtues in trustees, now they were thought to be prerequisites. The increase in income and endowment brought new problems of balances and budgets, of property investment and management, of the husbanding and parceling of resources, with which businessmen were presumed to be familiar. As a result, a trusteeship in a large university became, along with a listing in the Social Register, a token of business prominence and of pecuniary qualification. Charles and Mary Beard did not exaggerate when they wrote that "at the end of the century the roster of American trustees of higher learning read like a corporation directory." [12] In 1865, Ezra Cornell could boast of the representative composition of the board of the university that bore his name. Aside from ex-officio members representing the locality and the state, it included, he said, three mechanics, three farmers, one manufacturer, one merchant, one lawyer, one engineer, and one "literary gentleman." [13] By 1884, the Cornell Board of Trustees included five bankers, three lawyers, two manufacturers, two judges, and one editor.[14] Among the new arrivals was Henry W. Sage, the owner of the largest lumber business in the world at that time.[15] By 1918, new prizes had been added: Andrew Carnegie;

[10] G. Stanley Hall, *Life and Confessions of a Psychologist* (New York, 1923), pp. 225–57.

[11] Carl L. Becker, *Cornell University: Founders and the Founding* (Ithaca, N.Y., 1943), p. 118.

[12] Charles A. Beard and Mary R. Beard, *The Rise of American Civilization* (New York, 1927), II, 470.

[13] Becker, *Cornell University,* Document 11.

[14] In several cases, the occupations of trustees fall into more than one category.

[15] "Henry W. Sage," *National Cyclopedia of American Biography,* IV, 478.

Charles W. Schwab, president of Bethlehem Steel; H. H. Westinghouse, chairman of the board of the Westinghouse Company; and others of the top business elite.[16] This trend was observable elsewhere. In a study of twenty private and state universities, McGrath found that 48 percent of the members of the boards of trustees were businessmen, bankers, and lawyers in 1860; in 1900, 64 percent belonged to those occupational categories.[17] The great anomaly of American higher education—that laymen dominate the domain of professionals—had become more patent than ever.

But the line between business and scholarship was not crossed from one side alone. Under the stimulus of a newly awakened interest in the workaday world and its problems, professors in the social sciences began to focus on the institutions by which society was organized and its activities maintained. The trend in the field of economics was toward historical and statistical analysis, and away from the speculative search for logically consistent systems. This was the period when E. R. A. Seligman wrote his studies of public finance; when Taussig wrote his *Tariff History;* when Henry Carter Adams wrote "The Relation of the State to Industrial Action"—all of them evidence of their authors' departure from the belief that life could be deduced from first principles.[18] This was the period when Ely wrote about labor and socialism and actually took these subjects seriously, proving that economics could be something more than conventional conservative apologetics.[19] Moreover, this was the period when the American Economic Association, in defiance of the edicts of Manchester, took its stand against *laissez faire,* and called upon the nation's economists to play a part in the shaping of public policy. In sociology, no less than in economics, the desire to take hold of realities was apparent and pervasive. "Pure" sociology—both Ward's and Sumner's—gave support to social programs; "applied" sociology—the other large division of the field—was little more than the art of social betterment.[20] By 1901,

[16] *Register of Cornell University, 1918–19*, p. 8.

[17] Earl McGrath, "The Control of Higher Education in America," *Educational Record*, XVII (April, 1936), 264.

[18] Joseph Dorfman, *The Economic Mind in American Civilization* (New York, 1949), III, 167, 245–57, 264–71.

[19] Richard T. Ely, *Ground under Our Feet* (New York, 1938), pp. 309–23.

[20] In announcing that a chair in sociology had been established, the Columbia Faculty of Political Science justified it by proclaiming: "it is becoming more and more apparent that industrial and social progress is bringing the modern commu-

hardly a college did not promise, under the heading of "sociology," a course on "the city and its problems," or "defectives, delinquents and dependents," or "socialism, its history and philosophy," or "the methods of social reform." [21] Finally, in the newest of the new social sciences—political science—the attention of scholars was given to political and administrative reform.[22] Throughout the field of the social sciences, the concern with public problems sought legitimation and expression.

More than anything else, it was the sense that the world was out of joint that gave rise to this new academic worldliness. By long habituation, Americans had become accustomed to social change: to the movement of rootless populations, to an economy permanently in flux. But the changes that came late in the nineteenth century were changes in the rhythm of change, upheavals in social relations, and they challenged settled assumptions. The traditional morality of individualism and the traditional injunction to get rich had produced an undisciplined wealthy elite that thought itself mightier than the laws and threatened democratic institutions. The classical world of small business and the classical law of competition had given birth to gargantuan trusts that were ruining or enveloping their rivals and were rigging the machinery of the market. Worst of all, the appearance of persistent poverty—hunger in the granary of the world, class war in the classless society, despair in the land of opportunity—put all our social shibboleths on trial.

This discomfiture of old ideologies helped vitalize American social science. It was not that our social scientists agreed on policies and programs. But there was one identifying bias that social Darwinists like Sumner and Darwinian socialists like Veblen, that gold-standard partisans like Laughlin and silver-standard partisans like Ross, that high-tariff advocates like Patten and low-tariff advocates like Walker, all

nity face to face with social questions of the greatest magnitude, the solution of which will demand the best scientific study and the most honest practical endeavor." Frank L. Tolman, "The Study of Sociology in Institutions of Higher Learning in the United States," *American Journal of Sociology,* VIII (July, 1902), 85; see, also, Albion W. Small, "Fifty Years of Sociology in the United States (1865–1915)," reprinted in the *American Journal of Sociology,* Index to Vols. I–LII (1947), pp. 187 ff.

[21] Tolman, "The Study of Sociology," pp. 88–104.

[22] Anna Haddow, *History of the Teaching of Political Science in the Colleges and Universities of the United States, 1636–1900* (New York, 1939).

significantly shared. This was the fundamental belief, of ancient lineage but of new allure, that science applied to society could alleviate social crises and remedy social problems. A number of invidious comparisons were used in support of this belief. It was thought that other groups were bound to ideology, but that social scientists were ideology-free. Other panaceas were looked upon as fanciful; the prescriptions of social science were presumably based on facts and social laws.[23] The distinguishing badge of competence that natural scientists wore was claimed by social scientists by right of direct descent.[24]

Thus big businessmen and professors came into fateful contact. The former supported the university and took command of its organ of government, the latter surveyed society and tried to sway its course: two spheres of action and interest, formerly far apart, drew close and overlapped. It was not immediately apparent, nor was it at any time inevitable, that this confrontation would be hostile. If there is truth in the popular antithesis between the "doers" and the "thinkers" of the world, there were also, in this case at least, substantial reasons for friendship. For one thing, some of the more articulate big businessmen, even of that parvenu generation, were fond of expressing admiration for the life of study and research. The contrary notion notwithstanding, the large contributors to the universities were usually not of that philistine crowd that undervalued the wisdom in books, or thought it far more edifying to meet a payroll than to meet a class. A philanthropist like Andrew Carnegie romanticized the life of intellectuals. He held up their "higher satisfactions" and "indifference to material possessions" as examples for the wealthy to follow; he consorted with writers and philosophers. Not every philanthropist was a Carnegie, yet the theme in his "Gospel of Wealth"—that the province and office of wealth was the diffusion and advancement of culture—proved strangely attractive to men whose one goal had been accumulation and who were themselves extravagantly uncultivated.[25] For all

[23] Cf. Lester F. Ward, *Applied Sociology* (Boston, 1906), pp. 5–6, 28–29; *Glimpses of the Cosmos* (New York, 1913–18), III, 172; IV, 11; Albion W. Small, *General Sociology* (Chicago, 1905), pp. 36–37.

[24] John Lewis Gillin, "The Development of Sociology in the United States," *Papers and Proceedings of the American Sociological Society*, XXI (1926), 1–6.

[25] Andrew Carnegie, "Individualism and Socialism," in *Problems of Today* (New York, 1908), pp. 121–39; "Wealth," *ibid.*, p. 35; "Variety and Uniformity," *ibid.*, p. 145. Cf. John D. Rockefeller, *Random Reminiscences of Men and Events* (New York, 1909), p. 166; Sarah K. Bolton, *Famous Givers and Their Gifts* (New York, 1896), pp. 108–28.

their quirks and vulgarities, the tycoons of Fifth Avenue and New-
port were closer to the patricians of Beacon Street than to the business gentry of Main Street. Besides, the patrons of the university received from the academic world the ornate courtesies of gratitude.
They did not enter academe as intruders; they were welcomed into
the realm and escorted to its high places by its very grateful inhabit-
ants. Within the academic fraternity, to cultivate the good will of
donors was a highly approved activity, betokening fine public spirit. To
offend the bearer of gifts was an action sometimes defined as the deep-
est disloyalty and treachery. Cordiality was thus demanded of professors by the most compelling of motives—self-interest and the desire for social approval.

In the light of these reasons for friendship, it is particularly surpris-
ing that sharp antagonisms developed over the issue of academic freedom. Yet almost from the moment of confrontation, the picture of
the business patron as an enemy of academic freedom took form in the
minds of professors. This began in the middle eighties, when Professor Henry Carter Adams was dismissed from Cornell for having
delivered a pro-labor speech that annoyed a powerful benefactor.[26]
The picture acquired lurid colors in the nineties, when such cases occurred in profusion, and when the victims, unlike Adams, would not
suffer the blow in silence. In this period, it derived a certain plausibility
from the Populist suspicion that big business supported the universities only to further its own interests, and that the attacks upon academic freedom were part of a plutocratic plot. In the Progressive
period and beyond, the picture was colored and defined by another belief—that the values of the factory and the counting house were injurious to the values of research, and that the attacks upon academic freedom were the results of this basic disaccord. We have no way of
measuring the popularity of the theses of "conspiracy" and "cultural incompatibility" among professors. It is probable that professors of social
science were generally more hostile to businessmen than were professors
of business administration. Undoubtedly, in every department, there was
a minority of critics and crusaders who were more outspoken than the

[26] See E. R. A. Seligman, "Memorial to Former President Henry Carter Adams,"
American Economic Review, XII (September, 1922), 405; R. M. Wenley, Lawrence
Bigelow, and Leo Sharfman, "Henry Carter Adams," *Journal of Political Economy,*
XXX (April, 1922), 201–11. Letter of Henry C. Adams to E. R. A. Seligman,
February 27, 1901, in Seligman Papers, Columbia University.

rest. But there can be no doubt that the image of the businessman as a malefactor became a potent academic stereotype. In the martyrology of wronged professors and the demonology of oppressive trustees, the businessman acquired, in the space of a few short decades, a conspicuous and infamous place.

A reappraisal of these beliefs is in order. How valid were the theses of conspiracy and cultural incompatibility? This question, we are aware, impinges on current ideological controversies. But we shall try to abstain from the present contest between "neo-conservatives" and "New Dealers," and from the provocative use of such terms as "Robber Barons" and "free enterprise." Our reasons for holding aloof are several. For one thing, it is doubtful whether high-order generalizations about the social role of big business can be deduced from these materials. Attitudes toward academic freedom are too specific for broad extrapolation. In this very circumscribed play, many facets of behavior are discrete: a man can give and give and be a villain, or be ungenerous with his purse and still a saint. Then, again, we deface the meaning of history by interlineating it with current knowledge. How the third generation of Rockefellers comports itself should not place a lien on our judgment as to how the founder of that house behaved. But most of all, we must let the evidence speak for itself, a difficult thing at best, yet hardly possible if we defend inclusive theories. Hence, in the following sections, we shall examine certain pre-World War academic freedom cases and certain trends in academic government with the modest ambition of putting two specific theses to a test.

THE THESIS OF CONSPIRACY

In 1901, Thomas Elmer Will, erstwhile professor and president of Kansas State Agricultural College, listed the academic-freedom cases that had occurred during the preceding decade. As he described them, they were all of the same ugly pattern: a professor had espoused reform, or had criticized the social order, and had thereupon been summarily dismissed. This, he wrote, was the story behind the dismissal of Dr. George M. Steele, president of Lawrence College, for leanings "toward free trade and greenbacks" (1892); the dismissal of President H. E. Stockbridge of North Dakota Agricultural College for "political" reasons (1893); the trial of Richard T. Ely, professor of economics at

Wisconsin, for heretical social and economic writings (1894); the dismissal of Docent I. A. Hourwich of the University of Chicago for participating in a Populist convention (1894); the dismissal of Edward W. Bemis, economist, from the University of Chicago, for championing antimonopoly views (1895); the dismissal of James Allen Smith, political scientist, from Marietta College for "antimonopoly teaching" (1897); the attack upon President E. Benjamin Andrews of Brown University for having promulgated views favorable to free silver, and his eventual resignation (1897); the dismissal of John R. Commons, economist, from Indiana University because of his economic views (1896), and the withdrawal of support from his chair at Syracuse University for the same reason (1899); the removal of Frank Parsons and Bemis from the Kansas State Agricultural College because of their "positions on economic questions" (1899); the forced resignation of President Henry Wade Rogers from Northwestern University for his opposition to imperialism (1900); the dismissal of Edward A. Ross from Stanford University for his opinions on silver and coolie immigration.[27] With this list, Will called the role of most of the well-known liberals in academic life at that time.

To Will, the cause of these attacks upon academic freedom was entirely self-evident. All academic-freedom cases were, he believed, the results of inevitable clashes between free disinterested inquiry and self-seeking vested interest. Formerly, this conflict had taken the form of a war between science and theology; now it was openly displayed as a war between science and wealth. Science is bent on telling the truth without favor. But the truth, dispassionately told, was what "the industrial monarchy" dared not and would not tolerate. It knows that "free investigation is all that is necessary to expose the rottenness of the existing economic system." Accordingly, "with the arrogance equalling that of the slave power, our plutocracy has issued its edict that the colleges and universities must fall into line." "Hence the inevitable conflict." [28] In the folklore of Populism, the three assumptions in this argument—that free inquiry exposes social evils and is therefore inherently reformistic, that big business dreads such exposure and is therefore incorrigibly intolerant, and that therein lies the cause of

[27] Thomas Elmer Will, "A Menace to Freedom: The College Trust," *Arena,* XXVI (September, 1901), 254–56.
[28] *Ibid.,* pp. 246–47.

infringements of academic freedom—gained wide acceptance.[29] And many later historians, pondering the cases that arose in the nineties, have also accepted these assumptions, though often not in their Populist frame.[30]

The first step in a reappraisal of this thesis is to ask: Was Will's catalogue of the cases accurate, was it complete and inclusive? In one case—that of George Steele—it is very likely that Will was in error, for Steele resigned in 1879, and his last presidential report suggests that he did so voluntarily.[31] In three other cases—those of Stockbridge, Hourwich, and Rogers [32]—the desolate wastes of the trustees' minutes reveal nothing that supports Will's contention, and without a statement from the participants there is nothing to go on, save the contention itself.[33] In another case—that of Commons—the evidence is entirely

[29] Charles A. Towne, "The New Ostracism," *Arena*, XVIII (October, 1897), 433–51; Edward W. Bemis, "Academic Freedom," *The Independent*, LI (August 17, 1899), 2196–97; Edward A. Ross, *Seventy Years of It* (New York, 1936), p. 64.

[30] Cf. Russel B. Nye, *Midwestern Progressive Politics* (East Lansing, Mich., 1951), pp. 154–55; Eric F. Goldman, *Rendezvous with Destiny* (New York, 1952), pp. 100–104; Arthur M. Schlesinger, *The Rise of the City* (History of American Life Series, X, 1933), pp. 227–29; Howard K. Beale, *A History of Freedom of Teaching in American Schools* (New York, 1941), pp. 227–34.

[31] Steele's last annual report, dated April 7, 1879, reviewed the course of his presidency which had lasted fourteen years, and referred to his onerous duties as financial agent which had cost him a considerable sum of money. "The reasons for my resignation are implied in the present situation of the College. I feel that the time has come for a movement which I do not feel that I have the ability or energy to conduct with any assurance of success. I am confident that someone else can, and that it is my duty, as well as yours, to heed the indications of God's providence in the premises." Letter of H. A. Brubaker, Librarian, Lawrence College, to the author, October 7, 1953.

[32] The librarian of North Dakota Agricultural College reports that many of the records of the trustees and of the president's office have been destroyed, and those that are available are not informative. Letter of H. D. Stallings to the author, January 13, 1954.
The University of Chicago archives reveal nothing about Hourwich or his dismissal: his name was simply dropped from the *Annual Register*. The trustees' minutes merely record the resignation of I. A. Hourwich, Docent, on February 1, 1895.
The only published material on Rogers' resignation in the Northwestern University archives is a letter of resignation, dated June 12, 1900. Whatever antagonism there might have been between Rogers and his board was masked by conventional politeness: "The time has come when in my judgment it is best for me to retire. . . . In thus terminating our official relations, I desire to express my grateful appreciation of the kindness you have always shown me in all our personal and official relations."

[33] The inference that Rogers was dismissed for his opposition to American policy in the Philippines was drawn from the bitter attack upon him in the press. See "The Menace to Free Discussion," *The Dial*, XXVI (May 16, 1899), 327. An article in

ex parte.[34] In the remaining six cases, however, there is a good deal of evidence to support Will's basic charges. Materials that have since come to light—the Ely correspondence, the Seligman letters, the Jameson papers [35]—show that in each of these cases the expression of personal opinion which was repugnant to officious conservatives led to the professor's undoing. It is true that Ely, compelled to defend his opinions, was vindicated and retained,[36] and that Andrews, asked to withhold his views, was not dismissed when he refused to do so.[37] Nevertheless, these six authenticated cases make it abundantly clear that the decade of the nineties— so curiously and inappropriately called "gay"—had seen the rise of a new kind of heresy defined as economic nonconformity.

But there are other genuine cases, not listed on Will's famous roster, in which the demand for economic conformity arose from the Populist "left." The career of J. Allen Smith provides an example of the bipartisan nature of intolerance. The author of a liberal dissertation on the money problem and a supporter of William Jennings Bryan

---

the Elgin (Ill.) *News,* November 8, 1895, may give some basis for assuming that Hourwich was dismissed for his opinions. "Chicago University seems to be singularly unfortunate in its professors of political economy. Following the lead of the old school writers of free trade, they not only teach their heresies but go a step further and champion the pernicious doctrines of socialism and populism. Prof. Bemis was 'resigned' for that cause, and now Dr. Isaac Hourwich is debarred from teaching because he is an 'avowed socialist, an infidel, and a sympathizer with the people's party.' The last count is not so bad, because every man has a right to his political convictions, but no self-respecting institution should retain for an hour among its lecturers one who holds such dangerous opinions as Dr. Hourwich. While the prompt action of President Harper saved the university from serious harm, he should be warned against nominating men to professorships till their fitness is fully ascertained." Mr. George Kennan Hourwich, the son, conveyed to the author his impression that President Harper had warned his father to give up politics or his post, but another member of the family denies that this had ever happened.

[34] John R. Commons, *Myself* (New York, 1934), pp. 50–68. To an earlier request to examine the Syracuse material, the librarian of Syracuse reported that the material could not be made available. S. R. Rolnick, "The Development of the Idea of Academic Freedom in American Higher Education," unpublished Ph.D. dissertation (University of Wisconsin, 1951), p. 169. To this writer the author of the forthcoming history of Syracuse University, reports that he was unable to discover "ground for assuming he was dismissed." Letter of Professor W. F. Galpin to author, November 20, 1953.

[35] The Ely papers are in the Wisconsin State Historical Society, Madison, Wisconsin. A microfilm of the letters bearing on academic freedom cases is in the Columbia University Special Collections. The Seligman letters are in the Columbia University Special Collections. The Jameson papers are in the possession of Dr. Leo Stock, Research Historian, Carnegie Institution, Washington, D.C.

[36] A discussion of the Ely case may be found on pp. 425–36.

[37] The best discussion of the Andrews case is Elizabeth Donnan's "A Nineteenth-Century Cause Célèbre," *New England Quarterly,* XXV (March, 1952), 23–46

in the election of 1896, Smith was fired from Marietta College by a board of trustees dominated by Charles G. Dawes, a wealthy partisan conservative.[38] When, however, Smith applied for a university position in the West, he discovered that there monometallism was the heresy and free silver the orthodox creed. The Populist president of the University of Missouri proposed to make room for a true believer by firing a gold-standard professor; Smith saw the moral equivalence between this and Marietta's action, and would not accept the offer. Ideological considerations figured in his next appointment nevertheless. The Populist presidents of Kansas State Agricultural College and the University of Washington offered Smith jobs; he accepted the Washington offer.[39] The tendency in both parties was for like to seek out like.

The vicissitudes of the Kansas State Agricultural College are further proof that the conservatives did not sin alone. In 1894, the Board of Regents, then under the control of a Populist majority, decreed that "the principles maintained by the advocates of land nationalization, public control of utilities, and reform of the financial or monetary system shall be fairly stated and candidly examined . . . without bias or prejudice." [40] For this purpose, Thomas Elmer Will, a doughty champion of reform causes, was appointed professor of economics, thus insuring an "unprejudiced" examination in behalf of Populism, an "unbiased" statement against Republicanism. In 1896, the state-wide victory of Democrats and Populists resulted in a thorough reorganization of the college. All contracts with the faculty were at once terminated, and the president was forced to resign. Many of the professors were rehired, but the presidency and the department of economics were taken as Populist prizes.[41] Will was elevated to the presidency; Edward W. Bemis, expelled from Rockefeller's Eden in Chicago, was made professor of economics; Frank Parsons, reform crusader, was made professor of

[38] See "The Case of Professor James Allen Smith," *The Industrialist*, XXIII (September, 1897), 180, which effectively scotches the argument of the Marietta authorities that they were moved by financial considerations. It was the nation's, rather than the college's, finances that were uppermost in their minds, for the places of the dismissed professors were very quickly filled.

[39] Eric F. Goldman, "J. Allen Smith: The Reformer and His Dilemma," *Pacific Northwest Quarterly*, XXXV (July, 1944), 198 ff.

[40] Julius T. Willard, *History of the Kansas State College of Agriculture and Applied Science* (Manhattan, Kansas, 1940), p. 96. Willard gives most of the documents relevant to this case.

[41] George T. Fairchild, "Populism in a State Educational Institution, the Kansas State Agricultural College," *American Journal of Sociology*, III (November, 1897), 392–404.

history and political science.[42] A faculty organ, *The Industrialist,* became the spokesman for the party of reform.[43] The Populization of the college lasted for only three years. In 1899, by another turn of the wheel of politics, the Republicans returned to power. This was the occasion for partisan reprisal from the "Right." Abruptly, Will, Bemis, and Parsons were dismissed, and Kansas State was once more restored to sound conservative economics. In judging the actions of the Populist board, Bemis had written to his friend Ely that the Regents "were not really violating academic freedom." When he reflected upon the Republicans' purge, however, Bemis wrote that "there can be no doubt whatever that the present dismissals . . . were entirely for political reasons in order to prevent the possible development among the students and in the state at large of a point of view different from that usually favored by the donors to private universities and colleges." [44] The beam was always in the other's eye.

According to the thesis of conspiracy, there were certain essential conditions for and one effective cause of the curtailment of academic freedom. A liberal professor, pursuing his science; a conservative board, dominated by business—these were the necessary conditions. An antagonistic trustee or an imperious patron—this was the efficient cause. A closer look at two of Will's cases offers a test of this theory of causation. Richard T. Ely and Edward W. Bemis were economic infidels to about the same degree. Both subscribed to the "new" economics and rejected the immutability that had been claimed for laissez-faire doctrines. Both looked to the power of the state as the guardian of the general welfare; both looked upon the study of economics as a way of defending public interests.[45] And both were meliorists in social reform and gradualists in social action, rejecting the anarchist's method

---

[42] The course of events at Kansas State Agricultural College can be traced in notices of *The Outlook.* See LVI (May 15, 1897), 144, and (May 29, 1897), 240–41; LVII (September 4, 1897), 10, and (September 25, 1897), 209. On Parsons, see Arthur Mann, "Frank Parsons, The Professor as Crusader," *Mississippi Valley Historical Review,* XXXVII (December, 1950), 471–90; Benjamin O. Flower, "An Economist with Twentieth Century Ideals," *Arena,* XXVI (August, 1901), 157–60.

[43] *The Industrialist,* in the years of Will's presidency, gives an excellent picture of the one-sidedness of the faculty's point of view. See Vols. XXIV–XXV.

[44] Letter of Bemis to Ely, October 3, 1897, in Ely Papers: Bemis' statement, June 10, 1899, in Ely Papers.

[45] Cf. Sidney Fine, "Richard T. Ely, Forerunner of Progressivism, 1880–1901," *Mississippi Valley Historical Review,* XXXVII (March, 1951), 599–624; Edward W. Bemis, "A Point of View," *Biblotheca Sacra,* LIII (January, 1896), 145–51.

and the socialist's total panacea.[46] Yet each, when taken to task, was treated and judged very differently. Ely, attacked for his heterodox views, was tried, acquitted, and vindicated; Bemis, attacked for his heterodox views, was dismissed without formality. The comparison automatically suggests that there existed a greater variety of factors, and more complex initial conditions, than were dreamed of in Populist philosophy.

In 1894 Ely, director of the University of Wisconsin School of Economics, Politics and History, was tried by a committee of the Regents for believing in "strikes and boycotts, justifying and encouraging the one while practicing the other." His accuser was Oliver E. Wells, superintendent of public instruction and an ex-officio member of the board. Ely was alleged to have threatened to boycott a local firm whose workers were on strike; to have said that a union man, no matter how dirty and dissipated, was always to be employed in preference to a nonunion man, no matter how industrious and trustworthy; to have entertained and advised a union delegate in his home. Ely's books, Regent Wells went on to charge, contained "essentially the same principles," provided a "moral justification of attack upon life and property," and were "utopian, impracticable or pernicious." [47] Given the hysteria of the times, the authority of the Regent, and the public nature of the charges, Ely's position was gravely jeopardized. With conservative lawyers and businessmen sitting on the board and on the trial committee, Ely and his supporters feared the very worst. Their fears, however, proved to be unfounded. The trial resulted not only in Ely's exoneration, but in a declaration in favor of academic freedom that

[46] Ely's conservativism appears in his "Fundamental Beliefs in My Social Philosophy," *Forum*, XVIII (October, 1894), 173–83. Bemis presented his views in a letter to President Harper, which he wrote when he learned that he was suspect. "Having been informed today on second hand but apparently trustworthy authority that some of the authorities (trustees, I assume) of our University are displeased with what they suppose has been my attitude in this great RR strike, I write to correct any possible false reports. I wrote a letter to Mr. Debs, just before the strike, urging him, for I knew him slightly, not to have the strike. Then when all the trade unions were considering the propriety of a general strike in the city, I spent several hours in trying to dissuade the leaders of some of the unions. . . . In every way have I tried to calm the troubled waters while making use of the opportunity to urge upon employers a conciliatory Christ-like attitude." Letter of Bemis to Harper, July 23, 1894, in Harper Papers, University of Chicago Archives.
[47] Letter of Oliver E. Wells to *The Nation*, LIX (July 12, 1894), 27. Theodore Herfurth, *Sifting and Winnowing: A Chapter in the History of Academic Freedom at the University of Wisconsin* (Madison, Wisconsin, 1949), p. 8.

one historian of the University has called the "Wisconsin Magna Charta" [48] and that Ely hailed as "the strongest defense of freedom of instruction which was ever issued authoritatively from an American University." [49]

As Regents of a university with over a hundred instructors supported by nearly two millions of people who hold a vast diversity of views regarding the great questions which at present agitate the human mind, we could not for a moment think of recommending the dismissal or even the criticism of a teacher even if some of his opinions should, in some quarters, be regarded as visionary. Such a course would be equivalent to saying that no professor should teach anything which is not accepted by everybody as true. This would cut our curriculum down to very small proportions. We cannot for a moment believe that knowledge has reached its final goal, or that the present condition of society is perfect. We must therefore welcome from our teachers such discussions as shall suggest the means and prepare the way by which knowledge may be extended, present evils be removed and others prevented. We feel we would be unworthy of the position we hold if we did not believe in progress in all departments of knowledge. In all lines of academic investigation it is of the utmost importance that the investigator should be absolutely free to follow the indications of truth wherever they may lead. Whatever may be the limitations which trammel inquiry elsewhere we believe the great State University of Wisconsin should ever encourage that continual and fearless sifting and winnowing by which alone the truth can be found.[50]

At the very same time, Edward W. Bemis, one of Ely's former students, ran afoul of the authorities at the University of Chicago. He had delivered a speech against the railroad companies while the Pullman strike was going on, and had declared:

If the railroads would expect their men to be law-abiding, they must set the example. Let their open violation of the inter-state commerce law and the relations to corrupt legislatures and assessors testify as to their past in this regard. . . . Let there be some equality in the treatment of these things.[51]

The speech was reported in the press, and in certain Chicago circles it was considered nothing short of seditious. The president of the University, William Rainey Harper, was quick to express his displeasure.

Your speech . . . has caused me a great deal of annoyance. It is hardly safe for me to venture into any of the Chicago clubs. I am pounced upon from

[48] J. F. A. Pyre, Wisconsin (American College and University series, New York, 1920), p. 292.
[49] Letter of Ely to Henry D. Lloyd, December 24, 1894, in Ely Papers.
[50] Herfurth, Sifting and Winnowing, p. 11.
[51] Letter of Bemis to Ely, August 13, 1894, in Ely Papers.

all sides. I propose that during the remainder of your connection with the University you exercise very great care in public utterance about questions that are agitating the minds of the people.[52]

But it was already too late for repentance. At the end of the academic year, Bemis was dropped without a trial or an open specification of charges.

Contemporary opinion was greatly divided as to the causes of Bemis's dismissal. Ely, Ross, and Commons had no doubt that Bemis had been sacrificed on the bloody altar of Mammon.[53] Harper and Albion W. Small, head of the Sociology Department, were just as insistent that Bemis had been removed for incompetence.[54] One cannot judge motives from so far a remove, or take sides with complete assurance. But the timing of the dismissal and the self-incriminating letter of the President make the assumption highly plausible that a quiet or conservative Bemis would not have lost his position.

[52] *Ibid.*

[53] Ross wrote to Bemis: "I see that the issue between you and the Gas Trust University has become a national affair. I feel certain that the storm of public indignation while it may come too late to benefit you this year will react in your favor and ultimately more than compensate you for the treatment received by the University. I have known the tendencies there but have always tried to treat the University in a liberal spirit, but from now on I vow that I shall never recommend the economic, political or sociological departments of the University of Chicago to any student. . . . The Chicago concern has forfeited all right to the name and dignity of a University till it falls under other control." September 5, 1895, in Ely Papers. Ely wrote to Hamilton Mabie, the editor of *The Outlook:* "I will say, at once, that it is my firm conviction that Professor Bemis who is stronger than any man they now have in the department of economics, would be a member of the faculty of the University of Chicago in good standing had he not held the views which he entertains." August 24, 1895, in Ely Papers. However, Allan Nevins reports, in his biography of Rockefeller, that Ely in later years changed his mind and told him in 1939 that this was not a *bona fide* academic freedom case. *John D. Rockefeller* (New York, 1940), II, 263–65.

[54] Small insisted in letters and in articles that Bemis's dismissal had nothing to do with the doctrines he espoused. He attempted to explain away Harper's letter as follows: "It should be noted that President Harper's request that Mr. Bemis should exercise care in his statements was not made with reference to any utterances which Mr. Bemis was making in university work or in a university extension lecture, but in an outside capacity before a promiscuous audience. This was, as already intimated, at a time when agitation of any kind was universally regarded as imprudent. It should also be noted that President Harper did not even then take issue with Mr. Bemis on any 'doctrine' but that he requested him to be careful about making untimely and immature statements." Small's press statement on Bemis, October 18, 1895, in Ely Papers. The explanation is almost as damning as the action it seeks to explain. Small's exclusion of extramural utterance from the meaning of academic freedom was a truncated view of that principle and represented surrender on what to the pro-Bemis group was precisely the vital issue. His failure to grasp the intimidating overtones of Harper's letter was a quibble or a deliberate evasion.

Puzzled by the discrepancy in their treatment, Ely and Bemis searched for the key to explain it. Their conclusion, colored by the suspicion of conspiracy, was that the crucial factor in each case was the degree of big-business domination that existed in their respective institutions. Ely believed that state control of the University of Wisconsin minimized the influence of wealth. "Some of the Germans have a theory that society is tyrannical and that the state is an organ of freedom. This was illustrated in my case; the state protected me from the attacks of private persons." By contrast, he thought, a private university must pay court to its sources of support and need not publicly account for its actions.[55] Bemis believed that the pressure of local corporations was particularly strong at Chicago because of the University's crass commercial spirit. Pointing to the conservative Laughlin and the timorous Albion W. Small as key examples, he asserted that Chicago had established a "line" agreeable to those business interests; from this no professor could ever deviate and hope to keep his position.[56]

None of these interpretations adequately covers the facts. In the light of current and subsequent attacks on academic freedom in state universities, Ely's diagnosis was not perceptive, certainly not pro-phetic. The shaky tenure of faculties in the state universities was exemplified by the mass dismissals that occurred at Kansas State.[57] Even at Wisconsin, practice lagged behind principle, as Edward A. Ross discovered when he was reprimanded by the Board of Regents in 1910 for having announced to a class that the anarchist Emma Goldman would give a public lecture in Madison.[58] Ely's diagnosis is also refuted by later evidence compiled by Committee A of the American Associa-tion of University Professors from 1915, the year of its founding, to

[55] Letter of Ely to Henry D. Lloyd, December 24, 1895, in Ely Papers.

[56] At first Bemis blamed Rockefeller for his dismissal, but later thought that the manager of the Gas Trust of Chicago was the really sinister influence. Letter of Bemis to Ely, January 12, 1895, in Ely Papers. Nevins offers rather convincing proof that Rockefeller did not impose his economic views on the university, though he did intervene in theological matters. Nevins, *Rockefeller*, II, 259–62. The charge that the Gas Trust opposed Bemis and was responsible for getting him removed was made by George H. Shibley and denied by President Henry P. Judson of the University of Chicago before a House of Representatives Committee in 1914. See Rolnick, "Development of the Idea of Academic Freedom," p. 142.

[57] At the State University of Iowa in 1887, Democratic politicians led a movement to remove 3 Republican professors who were prohibitionists. In 1893 the Regents of West Virginia University dismissed the entire faculty including the President. Rolnick, "Development of the Idea of Academic Freedom," pp. 108, 116.

[58] Herfurth, *Sifting and Winnowing*, pp. 14–31.

1947. In that period, the Committee reported on 73 violations of academic freedom, of which 37, or more than half, occurred at state universities.[59] Bemis's explanation also leaves much to be desired. It does not explain, for example, why Professor Charles Zeublin, a socialist, was retained in the Department of Sociology;[60] how that congenital nonconformist, Thorstein Veblen, managed to survive at Chicago for as long as fourteen years;[61] why Harper put E. J. James, a defender of bimetallism and labor unions, at the head of the Extension Division the year after Bemis departed;[62] and why Bemis had been appointed in the first place, since his views had always been well known.[63] Plainly, one must search for additional factors.

One of these factors was the role of the presidents at Wisconsin and Chicago. From the start, Wisconsin's president, Charles Kendall Adams, supported Ely and his cause. It does not appear that his reasons were primarily ideological, for he was much more conservative than Ely; nor that they were based on administrative principles, for he had often offended professors with tactless and high-handed actions.[64] More likely, his reasons were personal—he happened to be fond of this young

[59] These figures are based on a statistical analysis of the AAUP Bulletins from 1915 to 1947, Vols. I–XXXIII.

[60] Zeublin was appointed in 1892 as instructor, was promoted to the rank of assistant professor in 1895, to the rank of associate professor in 1896, and to the rank of full professor in 1902. He resigned in 1908 to become editor of the *Twentieth Century Magazine. National Cyclopedia of American Biography*, XIV, 454–55.

[61] Oddly enough, J. Laurence Laughlin was Veblen's protector at Chicago. Laughlin had been a thorn in Bemis's side, and Bemis had always attributed his hostility to ideological differences. Yet, in 1903, when Veblen directly contradicted Laughlin's credit theories in an article, Laughlin arranged to have the article published. Largely through Laughlin's offices, Veblen took on most of the duties of managing editor of the *Journal of Political Economy* and was promoted to assistant professor in 1900, though he did not attract undergraduates as a teacher and though Harper was critical of his personal life. Alfred Bornemann, *J. Laurence Laughlin* (Washington, D.C., 1940), pp. 26–28.

[62] "Personal Notes, University of Chicago," *Annals of the American Academy of Political and Social Science*, VII (January, 1896), 78–86; "Personal Notes, University of Chicago," *Annals of the American Academy of Political and Social Science*, XVII (March, 1901), 318–21.

[63] In an exchange of letters with Laughlin, Bemis had made it very clear where he stood on such things as government ownership of telegraph, the tariff, immigration restriction, child labor laws, and the currency question. Laughlin had agreed that he would have the liberty of expression he demanded. Letter of Bemis to Laughlin, February 27, 1892, in Harper Papers.

[64] Waterman T. Hewett, *Cornell University: A History* (New York, 1905), I, 198; Jessica Tyler Austen, *Moses Coit Tyler* (New York, 1911), pp. 249, 250, 253, 264; Merle Curti and Vernon Carstensen, *The University of Wisconsin, 1848–1925* (Madison, Wis., 1949), II, 576–77.

professor and to detest the Regent who accused him. At any rate, all through the hectic summer of 1894, while Ely was preparing his defense, Adams offered him comfort and sage advice. At the trial, he submitted a testimonial in Ely's behalf. There are indications, too, that he wrote the text of the "sifting and winnowing" statement.[65] With the president staunchly at his side, Ely was spared the disconsolate feeling of being forsaken by the parent, of which institutional authority is a symbol. And Adams's word carried weight: a patriarchal figure in the world of scholarship, an intimate of men of affairs, he was an incalculably valuable ally. By the same token, the forceful and domineering Harper was an extremely powerful antagonist. In all his dealings with Bemis, he was uncharitable, curt, and uncandid. Had he so desired, he might have defended the right of professors to speak as freely as other citizens; instead, he accepted the right of other citizens to curb the speech of professors. Had he been scrupulous, he would have given Bemis a chance to answer the charges against him; had he been kind, he would not have hinted to the press that those charges were utterly damning.[66] There is no mistaking Harper's animus, but controversy still beclouds his motives. A generous interpretation would have it that he was confronted with an incompetent professor and handled the problem ineptly. Perhaps the more accurate view would be that he was obsessed with the grandoise dream of a rich and great university, that to make that dream a reality he wished to stay in the good graces of his patrons, and that with this objective in view a talkative professor in the Extension Division was carelessly considered expendable. But it is clear that in both cases—can one not say, in most cases?—the president held the key to the outcome.

Still another differentiating factor was the professional position of

[65] The elder Robert LaFollette assumed that Chynoweth, the chairman of the investigating committee, wrote the text. Robert M. LaFollette, *Autobiography* (Madison, Wis., 1913), p. 29. But Ely was certain that Adams was the author. Letter of Ely to Edwin S. Witte, June 5, 1942, in Ely Papers.

[66] Bemis wrote to Ely: "If I had evidence of Harper's directly attacking me the way would be plain, but he is likely to speak well of my character and work but shrug his shoulders and express the hope to other presidents. 'Try him. I hope you will like him (or get along with him) better than we did.' Such 'damning with faint praise' and the natural action of trustees I now think were what Pr't H. had in mind when he said, 'If we say we did not like you (i.e., he explained, did not like my personality), you cannot get a college place in America.' " September 24, 1895, in Ely Papers. This, however, was exactly what Harper was saying surreptitiously to the press. See letter of Harper to Arthur T. Edwards, editor of the *Northwestern Christian Advocate*, August 1, 1895, in Harper Papers.

the defendants. Before coming to Wisconsin, Ely had taught for eleven years at Johns Hopkins, at a time when its fame was unrivaled. No teacher in America had had a more brilliant group of graduate students, nor could any boast more devoted disciples. Among them were Frederick Jackson Turner, at the time of the trial, professor of history at Wisconsin; David Kinley, professor of political economy at Illinois; Charles Homer Haskins, professor of history at Wisconsin; H. H. Powers, professor of economics and sociology at Smith; William A. Scott, associate professor of political economy at Princeton; Edward A. Ross, professor of economics at Stanford; John R. Commons, professor of economics at Indiana; Albion W. Small; Albert Shaw, editor of the *Review of Reviews;* John H. Finley, president of Knox College; and George P. Morris, associate editor of the *Congregationalist.*[67] "These," said Ely, "are my jewels." [68] They were, indeed, priceless assets. Scott, Turner, and Kinley masterminded Ely's defense; Shaw, Warner, and Morris gave him a sympathetic press; Shaw, Small, Turner, and Kinley were character witnesses at the trial. Their agitation aroused the entire profession; social scientists everywhere rallied to Ely's defense.[69] They made the Regents aware that Ely was not an isolated individual, but a powerful academic force. They made the Regents aware of what the Regents tended to overlook, that the bonds of obligation were mutual, that if the professor was dependent on the institution for a salary and a platform, the institution was indebted to the professor for his popularity and renown.[70] As a factor in the trial and the acquittal, the importance of Ely's status cannot be overestimated.

[67] Many who had not studied formally under Ely expressed their debt to him. Among these were Frederick C. Howe, LaFollette, and Theodore Roosevelt. See Howe, *The Confessions of a Reformer* (New York, 1925), p. 28; Ely, *Ground under Our Feet,* pp. 216, 277–79.

[68] Ely's Chautauqua Statement, August 14, 1894, in Ely Papers.

[69] So confirmed a conservative as the Harvard economist Charles Dunbar, who had refused to join the American Economic Association because it was too radical, became one of Ely's supporters. Letter of W. J. Ashley to Ely, August 23, 1894, in Ely Papers. Albert Bushnell Hart, the Harvard historian, was in Paris when the case broke, and was so out of touch with academic sentiment that, almost alone among the nation's important academic men, he wrote a letter to the press condemning Ely. When he returned and could gauge the situation, he apologized to Ely. Letter of A. B. Hart to Ely, September 7, 1894, in Ely Papers.

[70] Thus, one of Ely's friends, Professor Jerome L. Raymond of the University of Chicago, wrote to a Wisconsin Regent: "I cannot imagine a greater loss to the University of Wisconsin than the loss of his ministrations. His reputation is not only national, but international. While you have him at Madison, you have the foremost department of Economics in this country. Scour the country throughout and you

By contrast, there can be no doubt that Chicago had less need of Bemis than Bemis had of Chicago. Though not an insignificant figure, Bemis was still on a low rung of fame and not yet rich in disciples. Since he was a teacher in the university's Extension Division, his institutional status was not high. Presumably—and this was a commercial consideration that counted at the University of Chicago—he did not attract enough students to cover the cost of his appointment.[71] Largely at Ely's instigation, many members of the profession took an interest in Bemis and his plight—but not with the same enthusiasm that they showed in Ely's behalf and usually with reservations or a certain condescension. Bemis, wrote Hamilton Mabie to Ely,

is a perfectly guileless, straight-forward and honest man,—industrious, conscientious and well up on his work; but . . . he lacks any notable personal power and is devoid of that contagious element which wins people from the platform and often in the classroom. . . . A year ago when your fight came on you had solid ground under your feet. I do not think Bemis has.[72]

Bemis lacked the personal and professional resources that might initially have averted the attack or else might have won the engagement.

A third difference lay in the extent to which Ely and Bemis put their theories into action. For all his talk of the need for concrete reform, Ely's criticisms of the social order tended to be general, not specific; hortatory, not programmatic.[73] For all his warm humanitarianism, he made no intimate contact with the multitude. "Only twice in my life," he once wrote, "have I ever spoken to audiences of working men, and I had always held myself aloof from agitations as something not in my province—something for which I am not adapted."[74] Replying to the charge by Regent Wells that he *had* acted on his sympathies for labor, he issued a categorical denial. This author of a friendly history of the labor movement denied, at his trial, that he had ever entertained a walking delegate in his home, that he had ever counseled workers to strike, that he had ever threatened an anti-union firm with a boycott, or

---

could not get a man who would do so much to attract students of Economics to Madison." Letter of Raymond to H. D. Dale, August 13, 1894, in Ely Papers.

[71] See Small's press statement, October 18, 1895, in Ely Papers.

[72] Letter of Mabie to Ely, October 4, 1895, in Ely Papers.

[73] There were occasional exceptions in his writings. See his attack on the Pullman Company in "Pullman: A Social Study," *Harper's New Monthly Magazine,* LXX (February, 1885), 452–66.

[74] Letter of Ely to Amos P. Wilder, July 22, 1894, in Ely Papers.

that he had ever favored the principle of a closed shop.[75] Were these charges true, Ely wrote, they would "unquestionably unfit me to occupy a responsible position as an instructor of youth in a great University." [76] These were the words of a very academic reformer.

Of all who wrote to congratulate Ely, Bemis alone perceived that he had won the particular case, but had relinquished a vital principle. "That was a glorious victory for you," he wrote. "I was sorry only that you seemed to show a vigor of denial as to entertaining a walking delegate or counseling strikers as if either were wrong, instead of under certain circumstances a *duty*." [77] This was the difference between them: Bemis was not only a partisan of, but an active party to, the fight for underdog causes. Bemis, wrote H. H. Powers to Ely, "is a moderate man in his views but he has unquestionably taken a vigorous stand in favor of 'doing something about it.' It is his very efficiency in this line that has made him so obnoxious to interested parties." [78] "I have no doubt," wrote Ely to Mabie,

[that] Professor Zeublin is quite as brave as Dr. Bemis but the nature of the work is such that he does not feel called upon to deal specially with the gas question, street car corporations, etc. Dr. Bemis is not by any means radical, but he happens to take interest in one or two lines of scientific work which appear to be particularly dangerous.[79]

These comments are very illuminating. They point to the significant fact that, in a secular milieu, professors ran greater risks by threatening concrete interests than by doubting accepted ideologies. Not disbelief alone, but disbelief when applied to gas rates, was what most aggrieved the business community. The subsequent careers of Ely and Bemis bear out the importance of this point. Ely survived (and in good part renounced) his spoken and written heresies.[80] He remained in a full state of academic grace for the rest of his life, taking a post at Northwestern in 1925 and one at Columbia in 1937. Bemis became an aca-

[75] *Transcript of the Ely Trial*, p. 19, in Ely Papers.
[76] Ely's Chautauqua Statement, August 14, 1894, in Ely Papers.
[77] Letter of Bemis to Ely, October 4, 1894, in Ely Papers.
[78] Letter of H. H. Powers to Ely, November 14, 1895, in Ely Papers.
[79] Letter of Ely to Hamilton W. Mabie, August 24, 1895, in Ely Papers.
[80] Ely became increasingly conservative as time went on. He became Director of the so-called Institute for Research in Land Economics and Public Utilities (an organization heavily subsidized by the National Association of Real Estate Boards and the public utilities companies) which was accused by labor organizations of pleading in its sponsors' interest. See Laura P. Morgan, "The Institute of Politics and the Teacher," *American Teacher*, XII (November, 1927), 12–14.

demic Ishmael, with a reputation as a partisan and a malcontent that he never was able to live down. Except for his brief and ill-starred tenure at Kansas State, he received no further academic appointments.[81] The trustees of the republic of learning could inflict on this kind of miscreant the terrible retribution of neglect.

Finally, in listing the factors that differentiate these cases, the personality, power, and standing of Ely's chief accuser must be mentioned. The idea of a trial, it should be noted, originated with the Regents, not with Ely and his friends. The latter had many misgivings about it. They were afraid that a trial in those troubled times would not be conducted with respect for the rights of the defendant.[82] They feared that a trial over matters of belief would mark a return to old inquisitional habits, that Wisconsin would go the way of Andover. "It has been reserved for the University of Wisconsin," wrote a writer in the *Dial*,

to offer the first example, to our knowledge, of a trial for heresy in which theology has no part. To hale a public teacher of science before an investigating committee, for the purpose of examining his opinions . . . is a procedure so novel, and, we may add, so startling, that one may well pause to consider its significance, and the possible consequences of an extension of the principle thus involved.[83]

But the trial was intended to serve a purpose that Ely and his supporters did not suspect. At the start of the proceedings the Committee decided not to consider in evidence any of Ely's writings that did not bear directly on doctrines taught in class. It was reluctant, it declared, to censor books in the library or to indulge in the insidious sport of quoting passages out of context.[84] This decision proved fatal to the case of the accuser, for none of the other charges, as it turned out, could be substantiated. Wells walked out midway through the proceedings, objecting to the limitations that had been placed on the scope of the inquiry. After this, the Committee reversed its decision,

---

[81] From 1901 to 1909, Cleveland's reform mayor, Tom L. Johnson, made use of Bemis's practical talents by appointing him superintendent of the water department. From 1913 to 1923, Bemis was a member of the advisory board of the Valuation Bureau of the Interstate Commerce Commission. "Edward W. Bemis" (obituary), New York *Times*, September 27, 1930.

[82] Letter of William A. Scott to Ely, July 21, 1894. Letter of Frederick Jackson Turner to Ely, August 4, 1894, in Ely Papers.

[83] "The Freedom of Teaching," *The Dial*, XVII (September 1, 1894), 103.

[84] *Transcript of the Ely Trial*, p. 22, in Ely Papers.

and allowed Ely to read from his writings any extract that he chose!
Plainly, the Committee was on the side of the professor, and the reason is not hard to find. Regent Wells was cordially disliked and dis-
trusted. He had tangled with his colleagues before, and had earned a
reputation as a troublemaker. He was a Regent only ex officio, and had
been elected to his office only because of a freakish Democratic victory
in a normally Republican state. And he had completely isolated himself by going over the heads of the Regents, by giving his charges to
the public press, and by implying that the university condoned Ely's
teachings and was an accessory to his sins. Therefore, the ulterior
purpose of the trial was to discredit this enemy of the tribe, who had
infiltrated its high council. In the old theological trials—as in certain
congressional hearings that were to come at a later day—accuser and
investigator were one. In the Ely trial at Wisconsin, the accuser stood
accused.

Thus, in the concrete instance, the professor's fate was decided by
a number of non-ideological factors. Admittedly, however, these two
cases do not shed much light on the role of the business patron. At
Wisconsin, the attack upon academic freedom was undertaken by a
bungling, small-town teacher; the defense of academic freedom was
made by a committee of the Regents composed of a city banker, a
wealthy doctor, and a small-town lawyer. At Chicago, the attack was
probably inspired by certain local big-business men. There are, however,
two other cases that exhibit in a clear and unmistakable way the attitudes of business leaders. One was the case of Edward A. Ross at
Stanford, the other the case of John S. Bassett at Trinity, which occurred
in 1903. Both Ross and Bassett were members of institutions that were
dependent on a single rich sponsor. Both were sharply attacked for
speaking unpopular opinions. Ross was eventually dismissed, the victim of his patron's intolerance; Bassett was retained, the beneficiary of
his patron's indulgence. Again, the comparison suggests complexities
not embraced by the theory of class malevolence.

Under the provisions of the founding grant of Stanford University,
the functions of the trustees were exercised solely by the Founders.[85]
The death of Leland Stanford in 1893, and the assumption of full

---

[85] A board of trustees took over the power of the Founder when the charter was
amended by Mrs. Stanford in 1903. Jane Lathrop Stanford, *Address on the Right
of Free Speech*, April 25, 1903, pp. 3–6.

authority by his wife, converted this unusual oligarchy into a still more unusual matriarchate. Into the university built in memory of her son the strong-willed, emotional Mrs. Stanford poured all of her abundant energy. When, in the infancy of the institution, the Stanford estate was tied up in probate court, she contributed her personal income—even sold her personal possessions—to keep the University alive.[86] So well mothered, the infant institution survived, and very soon waxed strong. But universities must, like children, pay a price for filial dependence. Both kinds of organisms must be independent to mature, and both must be mature to be free. Stanford University became the victim of the commanding meddlesome love which an unbridled maternal instinct thrusts upon an only child.

It was not long before the professors found this motherly embrace oppressive. In 1898, Professor H. H. Powers, a popular teacher in political science, delivered a speech on religion which Mrs. Stanford happened to hear.[87] Intensely devout, the "Mother of the University" was shocked by its heretical sophistication.[88] As imperious as she was generous, she demanded that Powers be removed. The founding grant vested the power of dismissal in the hands of the president, and this power could be exercised at will, since all professors were on annual appointment. In David Starr Jordan, a well-known zoologist, an advocate of evolution, a pioneer in the university movement, the faculty had a president who well understood the danger of permitting lay preconceptions of propriety to interfere with academic expression. Unfortunately, the faculty also had, in David Starr Jordan, a president who was compelled by a sense of obligation and by his own sycophantic personality to defer to the wishes of the Founder. Agreeing with the one side, but subservient to the other, he was completely miscast in the role of mediator between the faculty and Mrs. Stanford. In this instance, he

[86] The story of the crisis of the infant Stanford University is graphically told in Elliott, *Stanford University*, pp. 251–308. The Ross case is discussed in this volume with unusual candor and fullness.

[87] The speech, as far as we know, was not recorded. Powers' version of it is as follows: "I offended Mrs. Stanford by an address of a somewhat philosophical religious character which I delivered at the request of a student organization. Mrs. S. whom I had never seen was there and was much offended by my pessimism and heterodoxy which it is needless to say she did not understand." Letter of H. H. Powers to Ely, January 14, 1898, in Ely Papers.

[88] See Bertha Berner, *Mrs. Leland Stanford, An Intimate Account* (Stanford University, 1935), for a chatty, adulatory biography written by Mrs. Stanford's personal secretary, which gives unintended evidence of the latter's naiveté.

pleaded that Powers should be retained and spoke of his valuable services; but yet, when the Founder refused to be moved, he did not challenge her verdict. In 1898, Powers was forced to resign, the first of a very large brood that soon was to be disinherited.

Edward A. Ross was exactly the man to ignite this situation. Fresh from Ely's seminar, fired by liberal causes, convinced that the aim of big business was to throttle social criticism, Ross had come to Stanford almost spoiling for a fight. "As secretary of the American Economic Association," Ross wrote many years later in his autobiography,

I had gained an inside view of the growing pressure on economists and resolved that I for one would be no party to this fooling of the public. I would test this boasted "academic freedom"; if nothing happened to me others would speak out and economists would again really count for something in the shaping of public opinion. If I got cashiered, as I thought would be the case, the hollowness of our rôle of "independent scholar" would be visible to all.[89]

With bravery that verged on bravado, Ross said and did just those things that would put him in the Founder's eye. At a time when the conservative community thought Eugene V. Debs the incarnate devil, Ross publicly defended him; in a university that had been founded by a railroad Republican whose ventures had depended on free labor, he advocated municipal ownership of utilities and a ban on Oriental immigration. At a time when most economists were for McKinley and gold, he wrote a tract in favor of free silver that was used by the Democratic party. Perhaps Leland Stanford, had he been alive, would have tolerated the iconoclasm of this professor. There was something of the iconoclast in Stanford, too, as witness his bill for fiat money that he proposed while a member of the Senate.[90] But his wife had all the prejudices of her class, and they had been hardened by her ignorance into absolutes. "When I take up a newspaper . . . and read of the utterances of Professor Ross," she wrote to Jordan,

. . . and realize that a professor of the Leland Stanford Junior University, who should prize the opportunities given him to distinguish himself among his students in the high and noble manner of his life and teachings before them, thus steps aside, and out of his sphere, to associate himself with the political demagogues of this city, exciting their evil passions, drawing distinctions between man and man, all laborers and equal in the sight of God, and literally plays into the hands of the lowest and vilest elements of socialism,

[89] Edward A. Ross, *Seventy Years of It* (New York, 1936), pp. 64–65.
[90] George T. Clark, *Leland Stanford* (Stanford, 1931), pp. 459–61.

it brings tears to my eyes. I must confess I am weary of Professor Ross, and I think he ought not to be retained at Stanford University.[91]

For several years, Jordan interceded with the Mother on behalf of the erring child. He argued that Ross's scholarship was impeccable, his teaching in the classroom judicious, his personal life unimpeachable. He called Ross (it was a eulogy he was later to regret) a "wise, learned and noble man, one of the most loyal and devoted of all the band" at the University.[92] At the same time, he entreated Ross to use restraint. To hold him in rein, he transferred him from the Department of Economics to the Department of Sociology.[93] As a desperate last step, he prevailed upon Ross to write the patroness directly and present his side of the case.[94] All of these efforts came to nought. Mrs. Sanford was adamant:

All that I have to say regarding Professor Ross, however brilliant and talented he may be, is that a man cannot entertain such rabid ideas without inculcating them in the minds of the students under his charge. There is a very deep and bitter feeling of indignation throughout the community . . . that Stanford University is lending itself to partisanism and even to dangerous socialism. . . . Professor Ross cannot be trusted, and he should go.[95]

Jordan was aware that his own prerogative was invaded by the implacable stand of the Founder.[96] It can be argued that this awareness made his ultimate capitulation more blameworthy. But cowardice never had better reasons. Had Jordan threatened to resign, Mrs. Stanford would no doubt have held her ground; had Jordan carried out his threat and taken the faculty with him, the University might well have expired. In Jordan's scale of judgment, the institution outweighed the individual: the value of the institution's existence was preponderant over other academic values. In 1900, Ross was forced to resign.

[91] Elliott, *Stanford University*, p. 340–41.   [92] *Ibid.*, pp. 346–47.
[93] Letter of Ross to Frank Lester Ward, April 25, 1897; reprinted in Bernhard J. Stern, "The Ward-Ross Correspondence, 1897–1901," *American Sociological Review*, XI (October, 1936), 594.
[94] Even Ross succumbed to the mood at Stanford and expressed his filial loyalty. "I have completely identified myself with the University you founded. I have devoted my whole soul and strength to the glory of Stanford, trusting that Stanford would look out for me. . . . Mrs. Stanford, I do not want to stay unless you can give me that degree of confidence which I deem my just due for faithful service, and without which I can do no good work here. I am loyal to you, and out of reverence for you as the Mother of this University will conform to your wishes in every way I can. I will do everything but sacrifice my self-respect . . ." Elliott, *Stanford University*, p. 343.
[95] *Ibid.*, pp. 343–44.   [96] *Ibid.*

For Ross a silent retreat was unthinkable; it would have defeated the purpose of his rebellion. Hence, the day after he was dismissed, he issued a statement to the press and made the "Ross Case" public property. The statement was skillfully composed to show that there had been a clear-cut violation of academic freedom. Quoting from Jordan's own letters, Ross depicted the president as a victim unwilling to become a martyr. Playing on the Westerner's fear of the "Oriental menace," he implied that his speech on coolie immigration was the primary cause of his downfall. Appealing to academic opinion, he invoked the argument of scientific competence.

I cannot with self-respect decline to speak on topics to which I have given years of investigation. It is my duty as an economist to impart, on occasion, to sober people, and in a scientific spirit, my conclusions on subjects with which I am expert. . . . It is plain, therefore, that this is no place for me.[97]

By this time, academic-freedom cases, particularly those that involved wealthy donors, had become matters of national interest. Ross's charge was headlined in the newspapers throughout the land. By this time, too, a sizable public had been conditioned to accept such a charge at its face value. A large number and variety of journals took the side of the dismissed professor and condemned the Stanford authorities. Some of these journals, like the *Outlook,* had been schooled by a decade of suspicion to see conspiracy everywhere afoot.[98] Others, like *Gunton's Magazine,* had always defended the right of "academic management" to fire any of its employees, but happened to agree with Ross that Oriental immigration should be checked.[99] Ross's partisans ranged from the New York *Evening Post,* now atoning under a new editor for its illiberal views in the Ely case, to the Republican San Francisco *Chronicle,* which bore a grudge against the Southern Pacific.[100] For all sorts of reasons, protest welled in every section of the country.

When colleges were religious institutions, the expulsion of professors for their opinions often went unextenuated and undisguised. Sophistry and self-deception were not then basic to the art of administration.

[97] Ross, *Seventy Years of It,* pp. 69–72.
[98] Editorial, "Freedom of Teaching Once More," *Outlook,* LXVI (November 24, 1900), 727–28.
[99] *Gunton's Magazine,* XX (April, 1901), 367–69.
[100] New York *Evening Post* (February 23, 1901); San Francisco *Chronicle* (November 15, 16, 17, 21, 24, 25, 27, and 29; December 16 and 23, 1900; February 18, 1901). In Bancroft Library, University of California.

This was not a sign of moral superiority: candor comes easily to those who feel they have committed no wrong and who seek only parochial approval. The Stanford authorities, however, were too committed to academic freedom and too sensitive to public opinion to tell the unvarnished truth. They would not admit to themselves that Ross had been punished for heresy; they could not admit to others that his heresy had been detected by the donor. A sense of guilt and a concern for reputation made them seek their justification in the oldest source of absolution—the imperfections of the victim. The need to do this was not lost even on Mrs. Stanford, whose dim comprehension of what she had done was later tinctured by misgivings. In 1903, in turning over the management of the university to a board of trustees, she denied that her objection to Ross had been based on his political opinions. He had had, she averred, perfect freedom to express his views in class. But he had violated the fundamental canon that no professor should use his position for electioneering or for participation in political campaigns. He had been dismissed because he had compromised the neutral position of the university.[101] Jordan let it be known that Ross had not been "the proper man for the place." Ross had been "slangy and scurrilous" in discussing current issues, and he had revealed an unscrupulous character by appealing to the public and divulging family secrets.[102] It may well be that Mrs. Stanford sincerely believed that she had preserved a precious neutrality, and it may well be that Jordan sincerely expected devotion even from a professor who had been ejected from the clan. But the fact remains that in 1896 fifty members of the Stanford faculty had endorsed McKinley without incurring the charge of "partisanism," and that Jordan had warmly defended Ross's character before the denouement.[103]

The argument of neutrality and the charge of moral turpitude did

---

[101] Stanford, *Address on the Right of Free Speech, passim.*

[102] Ross was also accused of attacking Stanford's business methods. This he completely denied. It is not beyond doubt, however, that he did not use the Southern Pacific Railroad as an illustration of the sharp practices of business. See "Still Deeper in the Mire," San Francisco *Chronicle,* November 17, 1900, in Bancroft Library, University of California.

[103] Among the signers of letters praising McKinley and attacking the Democratic standard-bearer in a two-page advertisement in the San Francisco *Chronicle* were 17 of the 37 professors and associate professors of the Stanford Academic Council who later justified Jordan's dismissal of Ross. See San Francisco *Chronicle,* September 27, 1896, pp. 27–28, in Bancroft Library, University of California. See, also, *Science,* New Series, Vol. XIII (May 10, 1901), p. 751.

not convince several Stanford professors. After Ross resigned, Professor George E. Howard took up the torch of rebellion. He declared, in a signed statement to the press, that

the summary dismissal of Dr. Ross for daring in a frank but thoroughly scientific spirit to speak the simple truth on social questions is . . . a blow aimed directly at academic freedom, and it is, therefore, a deep humiliation to Stanford University and to the cause of American education. The blow does not come directly from the founder. It really proceeds from the sinister spirit of social bigotry and commercial intolerance which is just now the deadliest foe of American democracy.[104]

The addition of Howard to the *dramatis personae* changed the whole tenor of the play. For where Ross was headstrong and brash, Howard, who was twenty years his senior and a member of the first Stanford faculty, was known to be circumspect. When Mrs. Stanford successfully put pressure on Jordan to expel this outspoken professor also, a chain reaction was produced. In all, seven professors presented their resignations in protest: Frank Fetter, professor of economics; Arthur O. Lovejoy, associate professor of philosophy; Morton A. Aldrich, associate professor of economics; William Henry Hudson, professor of English; Henry B. Lathrop, professor of rhetoric; Charles N. Little, professor of mathematics; and David E. Spencer, associate professor of mathematics. Ross was jubilant: "Stunning news from the Pacific Coast, isn't it?" he wrote to Ely. "So far $12,000 of annual salary has been voluntarily renounced in protest against Mrs. Stanford's action. That's vindication!" [105] A socialist organ saw the most individualistic of exploited laborers finally developing class-consciousness.[106] This conclusion was premature, for the majority of the faculty remained loyal to Jordan. But it was true that never before had an American faculty demonstrated so great a sense of internal solidarity and so rebellious and courageous a spirit.

Equally unprecedented—and even more momentous—was the decision taken by economists, at the thirteenth meeting of the American Economic Association in 1900, to launch an investigation of the Ross case. With this decision, the first professorial inquiry into an academic-freedom case was conceived and brought into being—the predecessor,

---

[104] Elliott, *Stanford University*, pp. 361–62.
[105] Letter of Ross to Ely, January 19, 1901, in Ely Papers.
[106] "College Class-Consciousness," *International Socialist Review*, I (1901), 586–87.

if not directly the parent, of the proceedings of Committee A of the AAUP. It is doubtful that the "thirty or forty" economists who met that December in Detroit and appointed a committee of inquiry were conscious of the historical importance of the tactic they were devising. Perhaps there were some who did reason that the secular sophistication of administrators now rendered their explanations unreliable, that the greater complexity of the "cases" made disinterested fact-finding essential, that only independent outsiders could safely undertake such inquiries, that only the professor's peers possessed the competence to evaluate the issues.[107] But doubtless many acted on the spur of the moment and the case, impelled by Ross's personal popularity (he had been secretary of the Association, was the son-in-law of Lester Frank Ward, and was part of Ely's entourage), by the flagrancy of Mrs. Stanford's actions (they alarmed diehard conservatives no less than automatic liberals),[108] and by the flimsy excuses of Jordan (which promised easily to be exposed and to reveal a "case" of unparalleled transparency).[109]

Owing to either their lack of long-run objectives, or to their inexperience in these matters, the organizers of the committee made two serious tactical mistakes. First of all, out of the desire not to involve absent members, they did not use the aegis of the Association, but met as an informal body. This laid them open to the charge of lacking official authority and of not being truly representative. The fact that they constituted a large proportion of the members then attending the Detroit sessions, and the fact that they appointed to the committee of inquiry three highly reputed conservatives, did not erase the public impression that the entire investigation was ex parte.[110] Furthermore, the scope of the inquiry was too narrowly conceived. The committee sought

[107] Professor Sidney Sherwood of Johns Hopkins suggested to Ely at this time that a professional association should seize the opportunity to "investigate and report on the general subject of *Lehrfreiheit*" in order to "challenge public attention and create a method by which the professions might work unitedly." Letter of Sherwood to Ely, December 22, 1900, in Ely Papers.

[108] Even Albion W. Small, who had written an article flatly denying that donors infringed academic freedom, was nettled by Mrs. Stanford: "The Dowager of Palo Alto" he wrote to Ely, "has captured the booby prize, with no competition in sight." Letter of November 24, 1900, in Ely Papers.

[109] Letter of Ely to Seligman, June 7, 1901, in Seligman Papers.

[110] Taking this line, several journals refused to take seriously the conclusions of the committee. See *Science*, New Series Vol. X (March 8, 1901), pp. 361–62; *Dial*, XXX (April 1, 1901), 221–23.

the answer to one question—"What were the reasons which led Mrs. Stanford to force Professor Ross's resignation?" [111] In making this foray into feminine psychology, it lost sight of the significant questions that lay beyond the issue of motives: whether it was healthy for a university to be bound by the wishes of one person, however noble her intentions; whether it was good for the community as a whole for philanthropists to make donations to institutions which they then controlled as though they were private properties; whether it was helpful to the science of economics to shun, under the rubric of nonpartisanship, all subjects on which people were divided; whether it contributed to academic freedom to keep professors on year-to-year appointments.

The attempt to uncover motives encountered formidable difficulties. Powerless to subpoena witnesses, without the standing that would secure cooperation, the committee relied on voluntary testimony, which it acquired mainly through letters. This was not an efficient method for probing the inner recesses of the administrative mind. The committee did not even approach Mrs. Stanford—it did not suppose that she would admit its right to interfere in her affairs. With Jordan, the committee was more hopeful. "May we inquire," asked Seligman, the chairman, "whether there are other reasons than those mentioned for the resignation of Professor Ross, and may we hope that, if such other reasons exist, you may be disposed to communicate them to us." [112] Jordan replied that a faculty committee "in possession of the facts" would answer the committee's questions. But the letter of the faculty committee was as patronizing and laconic as any a college president might have written. "In reply," wrote Professors Branner, Stillman, and Gilbert of the Stanford faculty,

we beg to say that the dissatisfaction of the University management with Professor Ross antedated his utterances on the topics you refer to. His removal was not due primarily to what he published, said or thought in regard to coolie immigration or in regard to municipal ownership. We can assure you furthermore that in our opinion his removal cannot be interpreted as an interference with freedom of speech or thought within the proper and reasonable meaning of that expression. These statements are made with a full knowledge of the facts of the case. [113]

[111] "The Dismissal of Professor Ross," *Report of a Committee of Economists* (1901), p. 3.
[112] Letter of Seligman, Farnam, and Gardner to Jordan, December 30, 1900, in *Report of a Committee of Economists*, Appendix, p. 9.
[113] Letter of J. C. Branner, J. M. Stillman, and C. H. Gilbert to Seligman, Farnam, and Gardner, January 14, 1901, *ibid.*, p. 11.

The economists were not willing to take this judgment on faith, even from a faculty committee. They wrote to Jordan again, and received this pontifical reply:

[I do not] consider it expedient or proper to go into a discussion of extracts from my letters or conversations or my statements or alleged statements, or those of others, as published in the newspapers. . . . It will be necessary for you to assume my knowledge of all the facts.[114]

With this pronunciamento, the correspondence came to a close.

The report of the committee had to disclaim any definite knowledge of motives. But it concluded, nevertheless, that the official explanations of why Ross was dismissed were spurious or unsupported by the evidence. It concluded further that there *was* evidence to show that Mrs. Stanford's objections were based, at least in part, on Ross's utterances and beliefs. As it did not indulge in sweeping generalizations, the report did not explicitly support the theory of the conspiracy of big business.[115] But the indictment of Mrs. Stanford—backed as it was by the signatures of eighteen professors high in the Who's Who of social science—gave those who accepted the theory implicit and impressive confirmation.[116] Because of its narrow focus, the report did not mention the many peculiarities of the case—the incapacities of the university's patroness, the dependence of the university, and the absence of such counteracting forces as an effective, long-standing tradition, a stalwart university president, or a functioning board of trustees. Instead, it gave a picture of capitalist aggression which was unrelieved by the tints of personality and circumstance.

The case of John S. Bassett, which occurred in a different setting, shows the business patron in a different light. In 1894, when Bishop John C. Kilgo became its president, Trinity College in Durham, North Carolina, was an impecunious denominational college; in 1910, when Kilgo retired, it could boast a larger endowment than any other Southern college.[117]

---

[114] Letter of Jordan to Seligman, Farnam, and Gardner, February 7, 1901, *ibid.*, pp. 14–15.

[115] *Ibid.*, p. 6.

[116] Those who joined the authors in signing the document were John Bates Clark, Richard T. Ely, Simon H. Patten, Franklin H. Giddings, Davis R. Dewey, Frank W. Taussig, Henry C. Adams, Richmond Mayo-Smith, William J. Ashley, Charles H. Hull, Henry C. Emery, Henry R. Seager, John C. Schwab, Sidney Sherwood.

[117] The best treatment of Trinity College's history can be found in Paul Neff Garber, *John Carlisle Kilgo* (Durham, N.C., 1937). This may be supplemented by Robert H. Woody's "Biographical Appreciation of William Preston Few," in *The Papers and Addresses of William Preston Few* (Durham, N.C., 1951), and John Franklin Crowell, *Personal Recollections of Trinity College, North Carolina, 1887–1894* (Durham, N.C., 1939).

It owed its growth and good fortune to the generous benefactions of the Duke family, and it was bound, like Stanford, by a silver cord of obligation. President Kilgo, who had once been a Populist, became a defender of gold and the tobacco trust, which led one unfriendly wit to say that the old motto of the college, "Eruditio et Religio," had been extended by the influence of the Dukes to read "Eruditio et Religio et Sugario et Cigarro et Cherooto et Cigaretto et Kilgo." [118] But Durham was not Palo Alto. The Dukes, who were unabashed Republicans and leaders of the industrial "New South," were a suspect minority in the region, despised by social conservatives as the foes of white supremacy, feared by agrarian reformers as monopolistic exploiters of the poor.[119] Moreover, Trinity College, retaining its Methodist identity, was not ruled by a single oligarch, but by a board of ministers and businessmen. There was another difference, too: Kilgo belonged to the school of self-righteous preacher-presidents, and not to the newer tribe of public-relations experts. A champion of unpopular causes (he opposed the state university and took a liberal view of the Negro problem), he, and with him Trinity College, did not seek to be universally beloved.[120]

In 1903, John S. Bassett, the editor of the *South Atlantic Quarterly* and a professor of history at the college, made himself a target of attack by writing an article on the Negro problem. A wave of lynchings, disfranchisements, and Jim Crow laws had come in the wake of Southern Populism, and Bassett tried to calm the troubled waters with an appeal to sense and understanding. The Southerner should realize, wrote Bassett, that there are wide differences among Negroes, and that a man like Booker T. Washington, although atypical of the race, was "all in all the greatest man, save General Lee, born in the South in a hundred years." [121] The Southerner should realize that the Negro was becoming "too intelligent and too refined" to accept an inferior position, and that, to avert costly racial conflict, the white man must adopt "these children of Africa into our American life." The Southerner should realize that unscrupulous

[118] Garber, *John Carlisle Kilgo,* p. 226.

[119] The attack upon the Dukes by local conservatives and reformers is described in Josephus Daniels, *Editor in Politics* (Chapel Hill, N.C., 1941), pp. 116–18, 232–33, 426–38; Aubrey Lee Brooks, *Walter Clark, Fighting Judge* (Chapel Hill, N.C., 1944), pp. 102–28.

[120] See Luther L. Gobbel, *Church-State Relationships in North Carolina since 1776* (Durham, N.C., 1938), pp. 132–71; Garber, *John Carlisle Kilgo,* pp. 43–83.

[121] John S. Bassett, "Stirring Up the Fires of Race Antipathy," *South Atlantic Quarterly,* II (October, 1903), p. 299.

elements had seized upon the Negro issue and had awakened "a demon in the South" merely for political advantage.[122] The Negro problem, Bassett declared, cannot be solved by violent aggression and intimidation, but by the infusion of a spirit of conciliation into the hearts of Southern whites. Himself a son of the South, Bassett thought he could speak these unpleasant truths to his kith and kin with complete impunity.[123]

But he had struck a painful nerve of the sensitive Southern conscience. The article was greeted at once with calumnious abuse. Josephus Daniels, publisher of the Democratic, reform-minded Raleigh *News and Observer,* led the attack. The University of Chicago, he wrote, is not "the only institution which harbors freaks who rush into absurd statements and dangerous doctrines—statements which, if true, damn the State of North Carolina, and doctrines which, if carried out, would destroy the civilization of the South." He trusted that the professor would issue a full retraction; otherwise, he added ominously, "let us not anticipate the feeling that Southern people must entertain for a man who can give utterance to such opinions." Almost every hamlet journal and village gazette, playing to its groundlings, devised some new invective. The Lumberton *Robesonian* called him an utter fool; the Greensboro *Telegram* thought he was insane; the Greenville *Eastern Reflector* considered him subversive and incendiary. The Littleton *News Reporter* thought he aimed at a chair at Tuskegee; the Henderson *Gold Leaf* suggested that he was currying favor in the North.[124] The demand arose that Bassett be summarily dismissed, as though to take the professor's scalp would refute the ideas under it. Though Bassett held a doctorate from Johns Hopkins University and was the leading historian of the state,[125] his article was thought to prove its author unfit for his post.[126] Only because he was unpopular, the argument was advanced that he had lost his usefulness to the college. When local pressures mounted, and a boycott of the college was threatened, Bassett submitted his resignation.

But in the Trinity College situation, counterpressures could be registered. Eminent North Carolinians, sojourning in the North and re-

[122] *Ibid.,* p. 304.

[123] For commentary on the writing of this article, see Wendell H. Stephenson, "The Negro in the History and Writing of John Spencer Bassett," *North Carolina Historical Review,* XXV (October, 1948), pp. 427–41.

[124] Garber, *John Carlisle Kilgo,* pp. 244–60.

[125] Bassett had already published his *Regulators of North Carolina, Slavery and Servitude in the Colony of North Carolina, Anti-Slavery Leaders in North Carolina,* and *Slavery in the State of North Carolina.*

[126] Garber, *John Carlisle Kilgo,* pp. 252–53.

flecting its cultural perspective, were in touch with the Dukes and the trustees. Fifteen alumni, now students at Columbia University, petitioned the trustees not to fire Bassett, lest the "national reputation" of Trinity College be impaired.[127] Walter Hines Page, whose brother was a member of the trustees, saw the issue as one of academic freedom, and so presented it to Benjamin N. Duke:

As to the correctness or incorrectness of the opinion he expressed in his article that has given offense, that is a question of no importance. But it is of the highest importance that a professor from Trinity College should be allowed to hold and express any rational opinion he may have about any subject whatever.[128]

And a powerful counterpressure built up within the college itself. Kilgo put his whole strength behind Bassett's defense. He addressed the board with a sermon on the virtues of Christian tolerance. Using religious rather than scientific rhetoric, he warned the trustees that the dismissal of Bassett would be a terrible blow to the college. It would "enthrone a despotism which the world thought was dead a thousand years ago"; it would commit Trinity to "the policies of the inquisition"; it would repudiate "the spirit and doctrines of the Methodist Episcopal Church, South." [129] He was prepared to resign if the board disregarded his urging. Not only Kilgo but every faculty member on the premises signed a petition for Bassett, and wrote a letter of resignation to be acted upon if the trustees were to fail them.[130] Undoubtedly, this unprecedented unanimity in the Trinity faculty was Kilgo's achievement. He gave them the moral support without which few would have dared to be bold; he urged no strategy of compromise to tempt them with safer options; he spared them the need to conspire, with its accompanying feelings of guilt.

The trustees voted 18 to 7 to keep Bassett on the faculty. Their decision was accompanied by a statement which was written by the Dean of the College. Though they disagreed with Bassett's opinions, the trustees took their stand for vindication on the ground of higher principles. They were, they declared, "unwilling to lend ourselves to any tendency to destroy or limit academic liberty, a tendency which has, within recent

[127] Petition of Bruce R. Payne and 14 others to Southgate, November 21, 1903, in Trinity College Papers, Duke University Library.

[128] Letter of Page to Benjamin N. Duke, November 13, 1903, in Trinity College Papers, Duke University Library.

[129] Garber, *John Carlisle Kilgo*, pp. 269–73.

[130] See "Memorial from the Faculty to the Trustees," December 1, 1903, *South Atlantic Quarterly*, III (January, 1904), 65–68.

years, manifested itself in some conspicuous instances." Extramural freedom of expression was included in their definition of academic freedom:
"We cannot lend countenance to the degrading notion that professors in
American Colleges have not an equal liberty of thought and speech with
all other Americans." They used social, political, and religious arguments
(not, it should be noted, scientific ones) to justify their view. Society
must learn that the evils of intolerance and suppression are infinitely worse
than the evils that folly can cause. "We believe that society in the end
will find a surer benefit by exercising patience than it can secure by yielding
to its resentments." Politically, it was important that "rights which were
bought with blood and suffering must not now be endangered for want
of patience, tolerance and a noble self-restraint." Finally, "Trinity College
is affiliated with a great church whose spirit and doctrines are tolerant
and generous, and a due regard for the teachings and traditions of this
Christian society requires us to exercise our judgment in harmony with
its spirit and doctrines." [131] These were memorable phrases, and they
became notable additions to the *belles-lettres* of academic freedom.

The religious tone of the document would lead one to suppose that
the ministers on the board, rather than the business elements, were the
main supporters of Bassett. But the opposite was true. Five of the seven
voting against Bassett were ministers in the Methodist Church, one was
a United States Senator, and only one was a local businessman—the
banker J. F. Bruton.[132] On the Bassett side, four ministers were aligned
with twelve bankers and industrialists. The businessmen who voted for
Bassett included James H. Southgate, head of the largest insurance firm
in the state and a director in a Durham bank; [133] William G. Bradshaw,
managing director of the largest furniture manufacturing company in
the South at that time; [134] Edmund T. White, president of the Bank of
Granville and a director in the Erwin Cotton Mills; [135] William R. Odell,
owner of one of the largest textile manufacturing plants in the state; [136]
James A. Long, director of the Lynchburg and Durham Railroad and

---

[131] "Trinity College and Academic Liberty: The Statement of the Trustees,"
South Atlantic Quarterly, III (January, 1904), 62–64.
[132] *National Cyclopedia of American Biography,* XXXVI, 129.
[133] Samuel A. Ashe, et al., *Biographical History of North Carolina* (Greensboro,
N.C., 1905), II, 410–16.
[134] *Ibid.,* III, 28–31.
[135] Archibald Henderson, ed., *North Carolina: The Old North State and the New*
(Chicago, 1941), III, 129–30.
[136] Ashe, *Biographical History,* II, 1325–27.

president of the Roxboro Mills.[137] And not least, Benjamin N. Duke, the patron, voted in Bassett's favor. Did he do so because he saw the attack on Bassett as an indirect attack on himself, his interests, and his patronage? Would he have done so had Bassett been accused of favoring silver or socialism? Motives are obscure in this as in every case. What is indisputable is that the patron stood foursquare for tolerance, and refused to pander to prevailing prejudice. Duke was reported to have said to Kilgo:

This man Bassett maybe has played the fool and oughtn't to be on the faculty, but he must not be lynched. There are more ways of lynching a man than by tying a hempen rope around his neck and throwing it over the limb of a tree. Public opinion can lynch a man, and that is what North Carolina is trying to do to Bassett now. Don't allow it. You'll never get over it if you do.[138]

In the Avesta of academic freedom, some patrons wore the cloven hoof, but others, it has clearly been recorded, joined the side of the angels.

Though our samples have been arbitrarily chosen, there is enough in the foregoing cases to indicate some of the flaws in the thesis of conspiracy. First of all, like all simplistic explanations, it lacked the social and psychological dimensions that the complexity of situations calls for. It omitted many significant factors—the disposition of the president, the professional status of the accused, the standing of the accusers—that may decide the fate of professors. It omitted many other significant factors—the geographical location of the college, its particular ideals and traditions, its receptivity to various pressures, the power and personality of the patron—that may determine the role of the businessman. It did not draw basic distinctions between different kinds of professorial heretics, such as theorists and activists; or between different kinds of business patrons, such as those who shared the biases of their community and those who were themselves nonconformists; or between different kinds of pressure from business, such as that which originated from patrons and trustees and that which originated from outside. Secondly, like all highly partisan theories, it falsely ascribed to one faction—in this case, to economic conservatives—a uniquely sinister role. But we have seen from the cases we have examined that virtue was not monopolized by "liberals" and that guilt was very widely distributed. The Wisconsin charter of academic freedom, the Trinity College statement, and the economists' report on

---

[137] *Ibid.*, III, 231–36.
[138] Robert H. Woody, "Biographical Appreciation of William Preston Few," pp. 40–41.

the Ross case, were not framed by liberal reformers, but by men of conservative leanings. Kilgo, Adams, and Seligman, no less than Ely, Ross, and Will, were in the vanguard in the battles for freedom. Indeed, one of the significant aspects of the cases of this period was the blurring of ideological lines within the academic profession, and the mustering of united support for professors under attack. This *tu quoque* theme can be applied to the infringements of academic freedom as well. In the altercations at Kansas State Populists were not morally superior to Republicans. There was little to choose between the attitudes of Mrs. Stanford, conservative, and those of Josephus Daniels, reformer. The weakness in the theory of conspiracy—and perhaps, too, the source of its psychological vitality—is that it projects the foibles of man onto particular men who are few, recognizable, and isolable. The germ of truth in the thesis of conspiracy is that power is conducive to evil. Devil theories of history are rarely categorically false, particularly when the devils they delineate are men who are very rich, who have taken controlling positions, and who are accustomed to being obeyed. But power may be a function of numbers, as well as a function of wealth; and power may be curbed and chastened by the safeguards of tradition and form.

THE THESIS OF CULTURAL INCOMPATIBILITY

The fear of conspiracy usually flourishes in times of social anxiety. When men face social problems too new for settled habits to control and too complex for current knowledge to explain, they will ascribe them to the work of outside agents—to the jealousy and malice of the gods, or to the intrigues of hostile strangers. But men abandon demonic explanations when, having lived with their problems awhile, they have lost their terror of them. In periods of confident reform, they will look upon social problems merely as functional disorders which intelligence is competent to correct; in periods of intellectual alienation, they will consider social problems rather as organic defects which satire best can expose. It was not by chance, therefore, that the thesis of conspiracy was exceedingly popular in the overwrought decade of the nineties. In the Progressive period that followed, and in the decade after the Great Crusade, the thesis of conspiracy lost favor, though it never disappeared from stock. By those devoted to good causes, a more profound analysis was desired on which to base a program of reform; by those who cultivated disillusion, a more sweeping hypothesis was required to give scope to satirical commentary. The thesis of cultural incompatibility was, therefore, more in keeping with the temper of these times. Critics of the period looked to the culture of capitalism, rather than to the machinations of capitalists, as the source of academic evils. They saw the threat to academic freedom arising in certain habits and values, not in wicked intentions; they condemned the businessman's ethos, not his malice prepense.

Thorstein Veblen's *The Higher Learning in America* (published in 1918, but written in the preceding decade) was the prototype and most effective presentation of this thesis. With his penchant for dramatic abstraction, Veblen constructed a polarity between the culture of science on the one hand and the culture of business on the other. At the one pole were the scientists who, under the "impulsion and guidance of idle curiosity," sought the "profitless quest of knowledge." Veblen considered their curiosity "idle" because it ignored considerations of expediency; he considered their knowledge "profitless" because it was unconcerned with self-advantage. At the other pole, and newly arrived, were the businessmen on the governing boards and the businessmen in academic dress assigned to the presidents' chairs. Not intentionally, but owing to habits of thought conditioned by their occupations, they have foisted on American universities their crude, utilitarian outlook; their parasitical, predatory tactics; their ethos of "quietism, caution, compromise, collusion and chicane." [139] Unwittingly, they have turned what should have been mansions of learning into what tend to be ordinary business establishments. Under their dominant aegis, the universities of the nation have adopted the hierarchical gradation of staff common to business management; the techniques of salesmanship and promotion native to competitive enterprises; and they have reduced American professors to the status of business hirelings. To Veblen, each of these businesslike features acted as a subtle restraint on the academic freedom of professors. First of all, the bureaucratization of the university served as a convenient method for controlling the faculty from above. Secondly, the promotional activity of the university put a premium on intellectual acquiescence. Thirdly, the reduction of the scholar to the status of an employee destroyed his self-respect and narrowed his freedom of action.[140]

[139] Thorstein Veblen, *The Higher Learning in America* (New York, 1918), p. 70.
[140] Of the vast literature that gives expression to this kind of anti-business animus, the following may be regarded as a representative sample: Robert C. Angell, *The Campus* (New York, 1928), pp. 215–18; John E. Kirkpatrick, *Academic Organi-*

Each part of Veblen's indictment contained an element of truth and yet conveyed an erroneous impression. Acutely, he discerned that the trend toward bureaucratization was transforming the university's personnel, structure, and behavior. This change was already evidenced in the army of academic functionaries—the deans, directors, registrars and secretaries—who had come upon the scene to manage the affairs of the university. It was evidenced in the organization of the faculty into a graded hierarchy of ranks, within which passage was controlled by a series of official promotions.[141] It was evidenced in the writing of rules that defined the rights and obligations of professors and trustees.[142] It marked, though it did not cause, the end of an academic era in which the college had been a community and the faculty a body of peers. That this bureaucratizing tendency brought with it new problems and new dangers no one can deny. Perceptively, Veblen caught the strain that bureaucracy introduces between the university's interest in efficiency and its interest in creative thought. There was (and continues to be) the danger that the ponderous apparatus of administration would deaden the spirit of the university by burdening it with procedures and tying it to routines. There was (and continues to be) the danger that the standard of efficiency, made the measure of all things, would rate scholarship only by its quantity, personality only by its docility, services only by their cost.[143]

But to ascribe these changes to business was very far from the mark. Certain practices of the business corporations—particularly those of office management and finance—were, it is true, adopted by the universities. But this in turn was a symptom of certain basic conditions that business and education shared. For one thing, the drive toward rational efficiency was stimulated by the problem of size. The modern university

---

zation and Control (Yellow Springs, Ohio, 1931); Scott Nearing, "The Control of Public Opinion in the United States," *School and Society*, XV (April 15, 1922), 421–22; "Report of the Committee on Academic Freedom and Tenure," *Bulletin*, AAUP, IV (February–March, 1918), 20-23; Frank L. McVey, "Presidential Address," National Association of State Universities, as quoted in *Bulletin*, AAUP, X (November, 1924), 87–88; Robert Cooley, "A Primary Culture for Democracy," *Publications*, American Sociological Society, XIII (December, 1918), 9.

[141] See A. B. Hollingshead, "Climbing the Academic Ladder," *American Sociological Review*, V (June, 1940), 384–94.

[142] See C. R. Van Hise, "The Appointment and Tenure of University Professors," as quoted in *Science*, XXXIII (February 17, 1911), 237.

[143] The effects of bureaucratization on academic life have been examined by Logan Wilson, *The Academic Man: A Study in the Sociology of a Profession* (New York, 1942), pp. 60 ff., 80 ff.; Charles H. Page, "Bureaucracy and Higher Education," *Journal of General Education*, V (January, 1951), 91–100.

was complex: the various specializations it embraced, the multiple functions it assumed, could only be joined and coordinated through ganglions of administration. The modern university was large: the multitudes of students it enrolled, the vast numbers of teachers it engaged, rendered relationships impersonal. The modern university, it was said, was too much infatuated with size. But "bigness" in America was not only the businessman's idol: it was worshiped, even while it was cursed, by every social element seeking to improve its position. Size was the key to reputation, size was the emblem of power, in a sharply competitive society strewn across a vast continent. Hence, "Big Business" was matched by "Big Labor"; in time "Big Government" came; it could not have been expected that "Big Education" would tarry.

Moreover, it should not be overlooked that a strong impetus toward bureaucratization arose from the ranks of professors, partly in response to the growing competition for placement. Between 1890 and 1900, the number of college and university teachers in the United States increased by fully 90 per cent.[144] Though the academic market continually expanded, a point of saturation, at least in the more attractive university positions, was close to being reached. At the opening of the University of Chicago, for example, the academic world was treated to the depressing spectacle of thousands of men applying to Harper for a job, most of them without prior introductions.[145] The law of supply and demand did not spare the academic market: as the number of available teachers increased, their bargaining power diminished; as more job-hunters came on the scene, job-holders felt less secure. Under these competitive conditions, the demand for academic tenure became urgent and those who urged it became vociferous. And the demand for academic tenure was, after all, a demand for rules and regulations—for contractual definitions of function, for uniform procedures for dismissal, for definite standards for promotion based on seniority and service—in short, for the definiteness, impersonality, and objectivity that are the essence of bureaucratism. Again, the underlying cause of the coming of bureaucracy was not merely the emulation of business methods, but the desire for security in the job which was also exemplified in the fight for civil service in government and for rules of seniority in industry.

Nor were these bureaucratic features necessarily inimical to academic

---

[144] *Bulletin*, United States Department of Interior, Biennial Survey of Education 1928–30 (Washington, D.C., 1932), number 20, p. 18.
[145] Goodspeed, *The University of Chicago*, pp. 134–36.

freedom. Instinctively, Veblen was repelled by the automatism of bureaucracy; uncritically, he assumed that bureaucracy served the purposes of tyranny. But rule by bureaucratic directive must be judged in the light of its alternative, which is rule by discretionary choice. There can be no doubt that the establishment of tenure by rank instead of by constant ingratiation and the fixing of salaries by schedules instead of by individual negotiation made professors more independent, more confident, and more willing to take risks.[146] As for the despotic uses of bureaucracy, here too judgment must follow an examination of the system that had existed. The decline, with the growth of bureaucracy, in administrative meddling with minutiae and in presidential rule by caprice is not the kind of obsolescence that the lover of freedom should deplore. At the same time, it is perfectly true that, insofar as bureaucratic administration can never be fully achieved, in every opening for discretion there lies also an opening for tyranny. Again, it is perfectly true that the rules are not self-enforcing and that where there is the will to circumvent them, that will can find a way. The rules are not the thing wherein one catches the conscience of the president. Tenure by rank can be negated by overlong periods of probation, by refusal to make promotions, or by that "judicious course of vexation" that compels professors to resign. Salary by schedule can be subverted by a range of salaries within each grade, assigned to the various recipients with a malicious partiality. But this is merely to say that the bureaucratic organization, like other forms, requires implementation by men who are loyal to its standards and spirit.

In theory, the bureaucratic system is adaptable to autocratic or democratic procedures. Given a hierarchical order, policy can still be determined at the lowest bureaucratic level—the level of the department—instead of at the apex.[147] Given a chain of command, the wishes of the faculty can still be effected through representation on the board of trustees or through control of higher appointments.[148] In practice, the academic

---

[146] The idea that eccentricities were better tolerated under the personalistic government of the old college than in the bureaucratized university has had much play in academic circles. Thus John Dewey: "The old-fashioned college faculty was pretty sure to be a thorough-going democracy in its way. Its teachers were selected more often because of their marked individual traits than because of pure scholarship. Each stood on his own. . . . All that is now changed." "Academic Freedom," *Educational Review*, XXIII (January, 1902), 12–13.

[147] "Report of Committee T," *Bulletin*, AAUP, XXIII (March, 1937), 224–28.

[148] See W. A. Ashbrook, "The Organization and Activities of Boards Which Control Institutions of Higher Learning," unpublished Ph.D. dissertation (Ohio State University, 1930).

bureaucracy functions in a situation that combines autocracy and democracy in varying degrees and ways. Cornell University can be cited as an example of a university at the democratic extreme. In 1917–18 Cornell was the only institution out of 100 public and private colleges and universities that allowed for faculty representation on the board of trustees, was one of the 10 institutions that provided for faculty nomination of deans, was one of the 27 institutions that gave professors the formal right to participate in the determination of educational policy.[149] Cornell was atypical, as was the institution where all important decisions were handed down through channels from above and where the faculty whiled away its time voting on academic trivia.[150] In 1940, the typical college or university was one that had no definite system for facilitating exchange of opinion between the faculty and trustees or regents, that did not provide a definite procedure whereby the faculty might consult the board of control in the choice of a president, a dean, or departmental chairman, but that did provide for the consultation of department heads with reference to all departmental budgetary needs. As a group, state universities had more faculty participation in budgetary procedures in 1940 than had the total group; women's colleges had a significantly larger amount of faculty-trustee cooperation and faculty participation in appointments, promotions, and dismissals; while the teachers colleges, in general, were more autocratic in their administrative procedures. Interestingly enough, the large endowed universities with graduate schools, where bureaucratization was most complete, were more democratic in their usages than was the total group.[151]

The emphasis on bureaucratization changed the direction of the struggle for academic freedom in this country. The fight for academic freedom became as a result a fight for precautionary rules, for academic legislation, not merely one in which the battles were *ex post facto* attempts to rectify injustices. For good and for ill, academic freedom and academic tenure have become inseparably joined. The good results are many. Too often, the attempt to achieve vindication after a professor has been dismissed is little more than a posthumous inquest: it is the better part of wisdom to look for and devise preventives. Too often, the issues of an academic-freedom case are obscured by the idle question of motives: tenurial rules provide a standard whose infraction is more easily demon-

[149] "Report of Committee T," *Bulletin*, AAUP, VI (January, 1920), 23–30.
[150] Logan Wilson, *The Academic Man*, p. 76.
[151] "Report of Committee T," *Bulletin*, AAUP, XXVI (April, 1940), 171–86.

strable. The danger, however, is that in fighting on the line of intramural law, professors may tend to abandon the line of social principle. With the emphasis on "firing" rather than on "hiring," the temptation is to make academic freedom coterminous with the security of professors in the gild, rather than with the social necessity of assembling independent men whatever their range of dissent.[152]

At no point did Veblen's irony go more deeply than when it penetrated the promotional zeal of the American university president. His depiction of the university president as a merchandiser of good will, as a "Captain of Erudition," was one of those clever caricatures that succeed by apt exaggeration. The Eliots, Harpers, Whites, and Butlers were indeed a new variety of their species, far more like the Rockefellers of their time than like the clergymen-presidents of the generation that preceded them. White's consolidation of capital to build a large university finds its illuminating parallel in the business activities of Morgan and United States Steel. Harper's piratical raid on the faculty of Clark University was indeed, as David Riesman remarks, an academic "Chapter of Erie." [153] Like their business contemporaries, they were superlative drummers in their trade; by dignified effrontery and persuasive skill they acquired patronage and support, and increased the power of their "firms." They were even more adept than their business contemporaries in drawing favorable publicity—to their universities by periodic celebrations and by conspicuous buildings and grounds, and to themselves by a relentless round of speech-making and ceremonializing. Veblen thought the influence of these presidents on the freedom of the university was harmful in the extreme. Along with their advertiser's skill went, he thought, all of the advertiser's timidities. The aphorism of expedience, that the customer is always right, became, he thought, the cardinal motto of the university. A conformity to current prepossessions, a sedulous attention to amenities, an acceptance of things as they are—these were inescapable by-products when businessmen ran universities and universities were run as businesses.

Yet, though here the shaft of irony in Veblen's work went deep, it also went astray. That the presidents in this era sometimes equivocated and often played it safe, that they seldom inspired their faculties to high courage and bold ventures, may be taken without question as true. But

[152] See, for the relationship of academic tenure to academic freedom, Henry M. Wriston, "Academic Freedom," *The American Scholar,* IX (Summer, 1940), 339 ff.; "Tenure: A Symposium," *ibid.,* IX (Autumn, 1940), 419 ff.
[153] David Riesman, *Thorstein Veblen* (New York, 1953), p. 102.

to blame this on their adoption of business attitudes is to make the dubious assumption that timidity and acquiescence were new in the presidential character. If, however, the liegemen of the Lord were more intrepid than the captains of erudition, if they were more finely attuned to the idea of academic freedom, history has not recorded it. Indeed, it was a romantic and erroneous assumption that gallantry could not accord with a business interest and competence. The peaks of presidential valor reached in the business age exceeded any of the preceding era. Among those in the presidential chair who have sacrificed assets for ideals, none can compare with Lowell, who reputedly turned down a $10,000,000 bequest offered to Harvard in 1914 on condition that a professor be dismissed.[154] In the way of united action, there is nothing to compare with the Andrews case, when Eliot, Gilman, and Seth Low united to defend a colleague who was assailed by his board of trustees.[155] Moreover, it is important to bear in mind that if these modern presidents were "salesmen," by the same token they were also energetic missionaries. In mediating between the two worlds, the leading figures of this group—the Eliots, Harpers, and their like—brought university ideals to business, as well as business ideals to the university. They were, as we have seen, leaders in the fight for evolution and in the promulgation of German ideals; no victory in the record of the educational revolution neglects to record their names. They promoted not merely the externals, but the spirit of the university: not merely its spurious side-shows, but its intrinsic love of knowledge, its interest in research, its concepts of academic freedom. These ideals might well have languished had these academic men of the world not carried the gospel to the Gentiles. Let it be conceded that there were presidents of lesser rank whose minds were more completely Rotarian. Yet even they were an educative force, if only by reiterating simple platitudes in the course of academic rituals. The thesis of cultural incompatibility saw the businessman corrupting academia, never academia enlightening the businessman. But the fact was that these two contrasted cultures, through the mediation of the presidents, passed in a two-way flow.

Veblen's third charge against the business culture—that it reduced professors to the rank of hired hands—is one that bears more extensive examination. The truth at the core of this indictment is that lay academic government is a kind of ink-blot test in the interpretation of which men

---

[154] Henry Aaron Yeomans, *Abbott Lawrence Lowell, 1856–1943* (Cambridge, Mass., 1948), pp. 314–17.

[155] Elizabeth Donnan, "A Nineteenth-Century Academic Cause Célèbre," p. 41.

may project preconceptions. A board of trustees could be likened by churchmen to a vestry, by politicians to a governmental agency, by businessmen to a corporation directorate. It took a certain sophistication not to make these identifications, not to suppose, for example, that a president was but a general manager in charge of operational details, or that a professor, because he was hired and paid by the board of trustees, was therefore its private employee. This sophistication was lacking among many business trustees and many business spokesmen. When President Andrews of Brown University voiced sentiments that affronted the trustees and potential donors, one newspaper was of the opinion that "he was only a servant; and a servant must do as his employers wish, or quit their service." [156] One trustee of Northwestern University, a patent lawyer and an officer of the Western Railroad Association,[157] presented this dictum:

As to what should be taught in political science and social science, they [the professors] should promptly and gracefully submit to the determination of the trustees when the latter find it necessary to act. . . . If the trustees err it is for the patrons and proprietors, not for the employees, to change either the policy or the personnel of the board.[158]

This was not an adventitious or atypical comment: when George H. Shibley in 1900 polled the trustees at Chicago, Columbia, Princeton, Yale, Johns Hopkins, Pennsylvania, and American University, he found that the opinion of the trustees whom he interviewed agreed almost unanimously with that of the Northwestern trustee.[159] Perhaps in the intervening years, trustees have grown so sophisticated that they do not now often express such views; but it will not be maintained that they have also become so wise that they do not, on occasion, act upon them.

Again, however, it is important to point out that the businessmen on boards of trustees did not depart from academic tradition. From earliest times, the assumption of American trustees was that professors were employees, and the only way in which the post-Civil War period differs from what went before was that in the later period the professors were more disposed to question the theory, to use professional pressures to mitigate it, and to seek redress in the courts. To be sure, when professors

[156] St. Louis *Globe-Democrat* (July 30, 1897), quoted in Will, "A Menace to Freedom," p. 251.

[157] Northwestern University, *Alumni Record of the College of Liberal Arts* (Evanston, Ill., 1903), pp. 75, 82, 89–90.

[158] Quoted in George H. Shibley, "University and Social Questions," *Arena,* XXIII (March, 1900), 293.

[159] *Ibid.,* p. 295.

took questions of tenure to court, the decisions were mostly unfavorable. This helped to create the impression that the business ideology had taken control of the bench even as it had captured the university. But that impression was mistaken to this extent—the mood of the courts had not changed on the fundamental issues. Before the Civil War, the argument that professors were officers of the corporation with a permanent right to their positions was twice rebuffed in the courts. On the other hand, in the post-Civil War period, professors themselves pressed the view in the courts that they were mere employees of the trustees. Once more, it is a specious reading of the record to say that American professors fell from a pristine high estate.[160]

A brief review of the cases bearing on the legal status of professors in America may supply the historical depth that was missing from Veblen's analysis. The fate of the argument for the "freehold" provides our most suggestive clue. In 1790, in the case of *The Reverend John Bracken* vs. *The Visitors of William and Mary College,* John Taylor of Caroline argued in the Virginia Court of Appeals that professors had a freehold in their office, in which they had tenure for life, and of which they could not be deprived without a hearing and a show of cause. In English common law, the freehold originally designated a holding in land by a freeman in return for homage and services to the lord; later, it designated a tenure in a saleable office to which there were attached rights to collect fees from the public—e.g., a clerkship of a court.[161] Taylor applied this artifact of the common law to the office of the teacher in several ways. He argued that professors had an interest in the landed estates of the corporation. He pointed to the fact that the masters of William and Mary College voted for the college's representative in the Assembly, and thus had, as it were, a political equity in their jobs. He also spoke ambiguously of the "judicial" complexion of the master's office. If Taylor's reasoning was not altogether clear, the gist of his argument was plain. "The Visitors seem wholly to have mistaken their office. They seem to have considered themselves as the incorporated society; and the president and masters as an appendage upon them"—that is, they believed themselves to be employers and the president and professors mere employees. "But the president and masters

---

[160] We take issue on this point with J. E. Kirkpatrick, who has argued that the contractual, employee status of professors was a phenomenon of the post-Civil War period. See *Academic Organization and Control,* pp. 189–201.

[161] Richard B. Morris, "Freehold," *Encyclopedia of the Social Sciences,* VI, 461–65; W. S. Holdsworth, *A History of English Law* (Boston, 1922), I, 247–49.

were a lay corporation, having rights, privileges and emoluments, of which they could not be deprived; at least, without some form of trial." [162]

John Marshall was the attorney for the Visitors in this case, and his arguments against the freehold doctrine have a very modern ring. Marshall denied, first of all, that professors had any share in the property of the corporation. "This is a private corporation. The persons who compose it have no original property of their own, but it belongs to the corporation. There would seem to be no principle on which this College should be placed in a different class of corporations from all other colleges." The estates of the college

are the gift of the founder. They are his voluntary gift. To this gift he may annex such conditions as his own will or the caprice may dictate. Every individual, to whom it is offered, may accept or reject it; but, if he accepts, he accepts it subject to the conditions annexed by the donor. The condition annexed in private corporations is, that the will of the Visitors is decisive.

Marshall denied, secondly, that professors were appointed for life, pointing out that this was not provided for in the charter or statutes. Thirdly, he denied that the courts had the general right to review the acts of a governing body. "If . . . the Visitors have only legislated on a subject upon which they have the right to legislate, it is not for this court to enquire, whether they had legislated wisely or not." Finally, he denied that the professor who brought suit was entitled to a hearing, though he argued this on the narrow ground that Mr. Bracken had not been arraigned for misconduct (that is, he was not deprived of his office by a judicial act), but had been dismissed because the office was declared nonexistent (that is, he was deprived of his office by a legislative act).[163] The Court, without rendering an opinion, voted in the Visitors' favor on the merits of the case.

The second example of the use of the freehold argument was Webster's plea in the Dartmouth College case (1819). By an interesting historical coincidence, Marshall, then Chief Justice of the United States Supreme Court, was the presiding judge. Here the argument took a somewhat different form than it had taken in the Bracken case, for Webster was not defending the interests of professors against the trustees, but the interest of the trustees against a legislature which had repealed the Dartmouth charter and had changed the composition and powers of the college's board without the latter's consent. Hence, Webster admitted that professors were accountable to the trustees, who could hire and fire them for

[162] 3 *Call* 587. [163] 3 *Call* 592, 595, 598.

good cause. But, he contended, the legislature, by appointing persons other than trustees to exercise this power over professors, had deprived the professors of their "freeholds." "All the authorities," said Webster, "speak of the fellowships in colleges as freeholds, notwithstanding the fellows may be liable to be suspended or removed, for misbehavior, by their constituted visitors." This was rhetoric: if all the authorities said so, Taylor would have won the Bracken case; indeed, if any authority said so, Webster would probably have cited it, something he conspicuously did not do. Instead of legal backing, Webster gave his position strong sentimental support:

No description of private property has been regarded as more sacred than college livings. They are the estates and freeholds of a most deserving class of men; of scholars who have consented to forego the advantage of professional and public employments, and to devote themselves to science and literature, and the instruction of youth, in the quiet retreats of academic life. Whether, to dispossess and oust them; to deprive them of their office, and turn them out of their livings; to do this, not by the power of their legal visitors, or governors, but by acts of the legislature; and to do it without forfeiture and without fault; whether all this be not in the highest degree an indefensible and arbitrary proceeding, is a question of which there would seem to be but one side fit for a lawyer or a scholar to espouse.[164]

Marshall ignored the argument altogether and based his decision in favor of the college on the obligation of contract clause.[165] The freehold argument was rarely heard from again.[166] The argument had never been accepted in an American court of law, and all that can be said for its standing in pre-Civil War legal thought is that it possessed enough plausibility to encourage attorneys to make use of it.

One historic pre-Civil War case set the precedent for judicial restraint in reviewing the actions of trustees that was to prevail in the later period. In 1827, after a trial, the Visitors of Phillips Academy in Andover removed James Murdock from his professorial chair. Murdock claimed that the articles of charge were not sufficiently definite and particular, and he challenged the statutory right of the Visitors to dismiss a professor when-

---

[164] 17 *United States Reports* 584.

[165] As for the relevance of the freehold argument in Webster's brief, compare Albert Beveridge's statement that Webster was "laying the foundation for his . . . reasoning on the main question" with David Loth's opinion that Webster took "the most blatant excursion into subjects not involved." *Life of John Marshall* (New York, 1919), IV, 240; *Chief Justice John Marshall* (New York, 1949), p. 293.

[166] It cropped up again in the minority decision of Judge Dent in *Hartigan* vs. *Board of Regents of West Virginia University*, 49 *West Virginia* 14 (1901).

ever in their judgment there was "sufficient cause." The Supreme Court of Massachusetts, to which appeal was brought as provided for in the statutes, declared that it was for the officers of the institution to decide whether the "gross neglect of duty," which it said had been adequately demonstrated, warranted dismissal. The Court would only review the case to see that the accused had his common-law right to a fair hearing. The Court did imply, on the other hand, that a professor was a good deal more than an employee: "We hold that . . . no man can be deprived of his office, which is valuable property, without having the offense with which he is charged, 'fully and plainly, substantially and formally described to him.' " [167] But this notion did not last out the Civil War period. In the case of *Union County* vs. *James* (1853), the Pennsylvania courts declared that a professor was an employee and not an officer of the corporation, and was subject to taxation as such.[168]

In certain post-Civil War cases, the professors themselves were the ones to claim the status of employees, seeking contractual protections against the abolition or vacation of their offices by legislatures or trustees. When a Missouri law of 1859 declared certain professorial offices vacant in the state university, a professor unsuccessfully challenged its constitutionality on the ground that it impaired the obligation of contract. In support of his case, the professor, B. S. Head, offered the argument that

although the university may be a public corporation, the professors therein are not public officers; that they are mere servants for hire, with whom contracts for service may be made, and which are binding upon the corporation; that they have a vested right and legal property in their salaries and offices, of which they can be divested only by legal proceedings; that a contract for such service, at a fixed salary, and for a stipulated period, is as much within the purview of the constitutional provision which prohibits the violation of contracts by the passage of a law.[169]

Again, in *Butler* vs. *Regents of the University* (1873), a professor sought to establish himself as an employee in order to sue for the recovery of salary which the Regents of the University of Wisconsin had resolved no longer to pay. The judge upheld the professor, if not the larger interests of professordom, by declaring:

[167] *James Murdock, Appellant from a Decree of the Visitors of the Theological Institutions of Phillips Academy, in Andover,* 24 *Mass. Reports* (7 Pick) 303 (1828).

[168] *Union County* vs. *James,* 21 *Penn State Reports* 525 (1853).

[169] *B. S. Head* vs. *The Curators of the University of the State of Missouri,* 47 *Missouri Reports* 220 (1871).

We do not think that a professor in the university is a public officer in any sense that excludes the existence of a contract between himself and the board of regents that employed him. . . . It seems to us that he stands in the same relation to the board that a teacher in a public school stands with respect to the school district by which such teacher is employed; and that is purely in a contract relation.[170]

In another case, the court, holding that the professors *were* public officers, declared that the legislature could pass a law abolishing a professorial office without violating the Constitution.[171] On the other hand, when professors sought *quo warranto* and *mandamus* actions, which are available only to public or private officers, then they were willing to argue that they were *not* employees.[172]

The notion that professors had declined in the law from the status of officers to that of hired hands was fictitious. Where the professors sustained heavy losses was not in the definition of their status, but in the impairment of the protections of contract which came about through judicial

[170] *Butler* vs. *The Regents of the University*, 32 *Wisconsin Reports* 124 (1873).

[171] *Vincenheller* vs. *Reagan*, 69 *Arkansas Reports* 460 (1901).

[172] *Quo warranto* is a proceeding to determine the right to the use or exercise of a franchise or office and to oust the holder from his enjoyment, if his claim is not well founded. Thus, in *C. S. James* vs. *Phillips* (1 *Delaware County Reports* 41 [1880]), a professor of the University of Lewisberg, who had been dismissed by the trustees without a trial, obtained a writ of *quo warranto* against his successor. The Supreme Court of the State of Pennsylvania overruled the issuance of the writ, saying: "No authority is given to issue the writ against a mere servant, employee or agent of the corporation. It was therefore incumbent on the relator [James] to show that the professorship . . . is a corporate office, and that he was unjustly and illegally removed therefrom. . . . The mere creation of a professorship does not endow it with a fixed term of existence or give its incumbent a term either for life or good behavior. Corporate offices are such only as are expressly required by the charter. The professorship in question is manifestly not one of that character." *Phillips* vs. *Commonwealth ex rel. James*, 98 *Penn. State Reports* 394 (1881).

A writ of mandamus may be issued to compel proper authorities to enact or enforce the laws or to perform a specific duty imposed on them by the law. In the absence of other adequate remedies, mandamus is a proper remedy to restore a person to the possession of a public office from which he had been illegally removed. Thus, when Professor Kelsey of the New York Post Graduate Medical School sought to compel the trustees to reinstate him through mandamus, the Appellate Division of the New York State Court denied the writ: "His application, so far as the mandamus is concerned seems to be based upon the notion that the position of a professor in the defendant's college is in the nature of an office, and that it is the province of mandamus to reinduct him into that office and keep him there. This is an erroneous view, both of the relator's true position and of the office of the writ. The college is a private corporation, and its professors and instructors are simply professional men appointed to serve the institution in a particular manner." *The People of the State of New York ex rel. Charles B. Kelsey* vs. *New York Post Graduate Medical School and Hospital*, 29 *Appellate Division* 244 (1898).

interpretation of state statutes and through "escape clauses" in by-laws and contracts. After the Civil War, the courts were called upon to decide whether state statutes vesting discretionary power to dismiss professors in the regents nullified the tenurial protections of contracts.[173] In 1878, in the case of *Kansas State Agricultural College* vs. *Mudge,* the court refused to make the governing board so supreme and irresponsible that it could violate any agreement it entered into with professors. The court then declared:

While the legislature intended to confer upon the board of regents extensive powers, yet it did not intend to confer upon them the irresponsible power of trifling with other men's rights with impunity. And making the regents responsible for their acts does not in the least abridge their powers. It only tends to make them more cautious and circumspect in the exercise of their powers.[174]

In time, however, a different interpretation came to prevail, and the trustees and regents, unless the statutes provided to the contrary, were empowered to dismiss professors at will. In *Gillan* vs. *Board of Regents of Normal Schools* (1894) the court held that a board of regents could remove a professor without a trial of charges.[175] In *Devol* vs. *Board of Regents of the University of Arizona* (1899), the court held that "when the legislative Assembly gave the board of Regents power to hire and dismiss employees . . . they did not grant to the board the power to bind themselves, or to bind others . . . by a contract different from that which was prescribed by statute." [176] In *Hartigan* vs. *Board of Regents of West Virginia University* (1901), the court denied that it had the right to exercise judicial review of the judgment of a board. "Is the Board of Regents to do as it pleases, without control, erroneous as its actions may be? Yes, so far as the courts are concerned." [177] In *Ward* vs. *The Regents of Kansas State Agricultural College* (1905), the court decided that the statute authorizing the regents to remove any professor "whenever the interests of the college required" became a condition for the employment of a professor, overruling all contractual provisions to the contrary.[178] With few exceptions,[179] the sanctioning of arbitrary and unilateral dis-

[173] See Edward C. Elliott and M. M. Chambers, *The Colleges and the Courts* (New York, 1936), p. 81.

[174] 21 *Kansas Reports* 223.   [175] 88 *Wisconsin* 7.

[176] 6 *Arizona Reports* 259.   [177] 49 *West Virginia Reports* 14.

[178] 138 *Federal Reporter* 372.

[179] *State Board of Agriculture* vs. *Meyers,* 20 *Colorado App.* 139 (1904). Also, *Matter of Kay* vs. *Board of Higher Education* (The "Bertrand Russell Case"), 173 *Misc. Reports* 943, 18 *N.Y.S.* (2d) *Sup. Ct.* (1940).

missal came to represent the law. Private institutions were also affected by this animus of the courts. At Drury College, where the by-laws contained an explicit provision against sectarian tests for the faculty, a professor was dismissed for donating a book on theosophy to the library. In *Darrow* vs. *Briggs* (1914), the court held that the action of the trustees was permissible under the contractual clause that allowed it to dismiss professors "when the interest of the college shall require it." [180] It was not to a new status, but to a more helpless state, that the law reduced American professors.

And yet the ineffaceable fact remains that professors did feel that they had been socially and institutionally demoted. If this feeling was not altogether warranted, it was not for that reason less poignant; if it was based on a poor historical judgment, it was still a significant historical fact. It is all very well to point out that, as far as income is a social denominator, professors in 1893 had an average income 75 percent higher than that of clerical workers, 75 percent higher than that of Methodist and Congregationalist ministers, 300 percent higher than that of industrial laborers.[181] Though the inflation that set in after 1900 cost them dearly, even so, in the decade of the 1920s, the income of professors was higher than that of social workers, ministers, journalists, and librarians.[182] It is all very well to point out that at no time in the past had professors been consulted by government so frequently, or for so wide a range of projects, as in the era before the First World War and during the war itself.[183] One can also point to the fact that, of the Ph.D.'s graduated from seventeen major institutions between 1884 and 1904, one out of three was mentioned in *Who's Who* and in *American Men of Science;* [184] that as late as 1910 academic scientists were still mostly recruited from the homes of clergymen, farmers, and well-to-do businessmen of native American or northern European stock—that is, from highly regarded social and ethnic

[180] 261 *Missouri Reports* 244.

[181] John J. Tigert, "Professional Salaries," Address before the Association of American Colleges, in *School and Society,* XV (February, 25, 1922), 208; Paul H. Douglas, *Real Wages in the United States, 1890–1926* (New York, 1930), pp. 382, 386, 392.

[182] Harold F. Clark, *Life Earnings in Selected Occupations in the United States* (New York, 1937), p. 6. Cf. also, Viva Boothe, *Salaries and the Cost of Living in Twenty-seven State Universities and Colleges, 1913–1932* (Columbus, Ohio, 1932).

[183] See Charles McCarthy, *The Wisconsin Idea* (New York, 1912).

[184] Gregory D. Walcott, "Study of Ph.D.'s from American Universities," *School and Society,* I (January 9, 1915), 105.

elements.[185] Yet still there was profound dissatisfaction and the deep-seated feeling among professors that their profession had lost caste. To this, no doubt, the presence of the big businessmen contributed, but not in the manner indicated by the thesis of cultural incompatibility. The addition of a new wealthy extreme to the range of classes in America seemed to depress and demote all the others. Compared with the enormous returns that accrued to business, the professor's emoluments seemed small. Compared with the high adventure of finance and the epics of industrial derring-do, his existence seemed drab. Compared with the honors heaped on the practical men, the distinctions accorded the thinking men seemed grudging and picayune. The illusion of a paradise lost was viewed against a perceptual field of sharp contemporary social contrasts.

[185] J. McKeen Cattell, "Families of American Men of Science," *Popular Science Monthly*, LXXXVI (May, 1915), 504–15.

V: ORGANIZATION, LOYALTY,
AND WAR

THE ESTABLISHMENT of the American Association of University Professors in 1915 is significant both as a culmination and as a beginning. It was the culmination of tendencies toward professorial self-consciousness that had been operating for many decades. It was the beginning of an era in which the principles of academic freedom were codified, and in which violations of academic freedom were systematically investigated and penalized. To analyze the movement that brought about the establishment of the AAUP is to capture the flavor of American academic life in the period between the turn of the century and the First World War. To examine the activities and achievements of the AAUP since its establishment is to view the main outlines of the problems of academic freedom in the twentieth century. Finally, to explore the difficulties that the AAUP encountered during the First World War is to introduce some of the complications and predicaments that academic freedom encounters today.

THE ESTABLISHMENT OF THE AAUP

Why did the AAUP appear so late in the story? Looking back, one can discover several occasions which might have brought it into being but which somehow did not do so. One might suppose that the Darwinian crisis, in challenging the academic patriotism that espouses "my institution, right or wrong," would have given rise to a professorial union. Nevertheless, the 1860s and 1870s passed without a serious attempt at organization. One might suppose that the alarums and excursions of the Populist period would have led to a defensive alliance of professors. But, though several professors suggested united action and the economists set up an investigating committee in the Ross case, no permanent organization was established.[1] The fifteen-year hiatus between the setting up of the econ-

[1] Thomas E. Will had written to Ely that there was a need "to form some kind of association for mutual defense and protection," and Sidney Sherwood of Johns

omists' investigating committee and the constitution of Committee A of the AAUP cannot entirely be explained by a scarcity of academic-freedom cases.[2] While there was a falling off in the number of cases in that period, there were enough of them to whet the anxiety of professors—take, for instance, the several well-publicized cases in the South, particularly the Bassett case; the Peck and Spingarn cases at Columbia University; the rumors of pressure against liberals and radicals at the University of Pennsylvania; and, of the thirty-one cases handled by Committee A in the first two years of its existence, those which had been incubating for a rather long time.[3] The inertia of the professors seems all the more curious when one remembers that other professionals in America, notably the lawyers and the doctors, were banding together in this period to protect their special interests.

One must seek the reason for delay in the factors that divided the professorial community and militated against the development of united opinion and action. One of these factors was the conditions of scholarly work. Factories, offices, and mines are places of socialization; but libraries, laboratories, and classrooms seclude the academic worker and turn him to his own resources. Nevertheless, the doctors and the lawyers were able to overcome the disadvantages of their self-sufficiency. Perhaps more unique and important in delaying professional organization were the institutional and disciplinary barriers that cut across the professorial community. In America, academic matters tended either to be handled parochially by each individual institution (in the absence of a ministry of education or a unifying educational tradition, each institution was a law unto itself), or else nationally by one or another of the learned societies (which often embraced specialists who were not professors). The different

---

Hopkins had suggested to Ely that a professional organization to investigate academic freedom cases was needed. The idea was in the air, but nothing was done to effect it. Letter of Will to Ely, October 15, 1895; letter of Sherwood to Ely, December 22, 1900, in Ely Papers.

[2] Stanley Rolnick makes this assumption in "The Development of the Idea of Academic Freedom and Tenure in the United States, 1870–1920," unpublished Ph.D. dissertation (Wisconsin, 1952), pp. 237, 284.

[3] For cases arising in the South, see Leon Whipple, *The Story of Civil Liberty in the United States* (New York, 1927), p. 320; Carrol Quenzel, "Academic Freedom in Southern Colleges and Universities," unpublished Master's thesis (University of West Virginia, 1933). For the situation at Pennsylvania, see Edward P. Cheyney, *History of the University of Pennsylvania, 1740–1940* (Philadelphia, 1940), pp. 367–69. For the conflicts of Peck and Spingarn with President Butler, see Horace Coon, *Columbia: Colossus on the Hudson* (New York, 1947), pp. 122–25; Columbia *Alumni News*, II (May 18, 1911), 548.

standards and merits of "colleges" and "universities," the medley of abilities and personalities blanketed by the title of "professor," the gradations of experience and repute signified by different academic ranks, all induced caste divisions.[4] Most important, there was a deep aversion among academic men to entering into an organization whose purposes smacked of trade unionism. The idealism of the profession, built on the rhetoric of service and sustained by psychic compensations, eschewed any activity that had material gain as its main object. The ideology of the profession, claiming to transcend all ideology, did not countenance permanent commitments even to an organization for self-help. The dignity of the profession, fashioned on a genteel code of manners, was opposed to the tactics of the pressure group.[5] And over and above all this, there was the fear of administrative reprisal, and a certain inertness and timidity which the academic mind had acquired through years of ivied isolation.

In the decade prior to the establishment of the AAUP, many of these barriers were broken down. Part of the work of demolition was accomplished by a force that had long been active—the appeal to collective effort inspired by the ideals of science. In discussing the aims of the AAUP in his 1922 presidential address, E. R. A. Seligman paid his re-

[4] See Henry Pritchett, "Reasonable Restrictions upon the Scholar's Freedom," *Publications of the American Sociological Society*, IX (April, 1915), 152.

[5] The further problem of whether professors should join labor unions has agitated the profession from that day to this. Against such affiliation, it was maintained that teachers serve the public; that, unlike labor, pecuniary gain is not their main object; that the strike and other labor tactics of intimidation are indefensible for teachers; that traditions must be interpreted and passed on without bias; that the competitive situation which defines the essential function of a trade union does not exist in the academic calling, where teachers and trustees are both custodians of the public interest. Cf. W. C. Ruediger, "Unionism among Teachers," *School and Society*, VIII (November 16, 1918), 589–91. C. E. Myers, "Should Teachers Affiliate with the AFL," *School and Society*, X (November 22, 1919), 594–97; A. O. Lovejoy, "Teachers and Trade Unions," *Educational Review*, LX (September, 1920), 108–19; and more recent comments, Arthur O. Lovejoy, "Professional Association or Trade Union," *Bulletin*, AAUP, XXIV (May, 1938), 410–15; Samuel P. Capen, "The Teaching Profession and Labor Unions," *The Management of Universities* (Buffalo, 1953), pp. 56–63. On the other side, it has been argued that there can be no protection of professional ideals without improvement in the teacher's economic security; that boards of trustees are allied with business; that the conditions of teaching are indeed like those of labor; that the AFL does not have a class ideology; that the unwillingness to join with labor is evidence of academic snobbery; that unions are a democratic force. Cf. Bird Stair, "The Unionizing of Teachers," *School and Society*, X (December 13, 1919), 699–703; Harry A. Overstreet, "Should Teachers' Organizations Affiliate with Organized Labor," *Survey*, XLIII (March 13, 1920), 736–37; John Dewey, "Why I Am a Member of the Teacher's Union," *American Teacher*, XII (January, 1928), 3–6.

spects to those persisting ideals. "Loyalty to our institution is admirable," he declared,

> but if our institution for some unfortunate reason stands athwart the progress of science, or even haltingly follows that path, we must use our best efforts to convince our colleagues and the authorities of the error of their ways. . . . In prosecuting this end we need both individual and collective effort. The leisure of the laboratory and of the study count for much; but almost equally important is the stimulus derived from contact with our colleagues.[6]

"The progress of science"—there was a vibrant tocsin to arouse the most sluggish professors.

Another slow-working factor was the constant tension between administrators and faculties. Of particular importance in building camaraderie among professors was the conflict over the question of who should speak for higher education. Trustees, presidents, and deans assumed that they had the right to act as its spokesmen, and the editors of professional journals did nothing to challenge that assumption. It began to gall professors that the public identified the voice of the presidents of the universities with the voice of the profession itself, that the league of university presidents should call itself the "Association of American Universities." Prior to the establishment of *School and Society* in 1915, which coincided with the publication of the first *Bulletin* of the AAUP, only one of the educational journals—Cattell's *Science*—registered professorial opinion that was critical of the operations of the university. At a time when professors were attacking businessmen in the popular press,[7] *Education* (founded 1881) had published before 1914 only three articles (and those laudatory) on the academic role of businessmen, and *Educational Review* (founded 1891 and under the editorship of Nicholas Murray Butler) did not print a clear-cut attack on the businessman until 1906.[8] Nor was the university a place where professors felt free to criticize their superiors. Evidence of this feeling of constraint can be found in the debate held in

---

[6] E. R. A. Seligman, "Our Association—Its Aims and Accomplishments, *Bulletin*, AAUP, VIII (February, 1922), 106.

[7] Claude C. Bowman, *The College Professor in America* (Philadelphia, 1938), pp. 173–74.

[8] In *Education*, these articles were by Howard A. Bridgman, "Clark University," X (December, 1889), 239; an editorial on the Ross case unfriendly to Ross, XXI (January, 1901), 307; an editorial on the "Peabody Fund," I (March, 1881), 329. William Cranston Lawton's "The Decay of Academic Courage" was the first highly critical article on the businessman to appear in the *Educational Review* (XXXII [November, 1906], 395–404), and it was quickly answered by J. H. Canfield's article of the same title (XXXIII [January, 1907], 1–10).

the early stages of the founding of the AAUP on the question of whether college and university presidents were to be admitted into the organization. In opposing their admittance, Professor Bloomfield of Johns Hopkins University made the suggestive remark that "this is the first opportunity we have had of being ourselves." [9] When it was proposed that presidents be allowed to speak but not to vote, Cattell moved to amend the proposal by asking that the presidents have the right to vote, but not the right to speak.[10] Another professor expressed the fear that professors would be outvoted by administrators because the former could not afford the expense of attending the meetings, whereas administrators would have their expenses paid by the institution.[11] In the end, it was decided that "no administrative officer who does not give a substantial amount of instruction shall be eligible for membership." [12] This was not to be a company union. The professors sought a platform for their own opinions, a journal for their own ideas, an organization that they would control.

The movement toward an association of professors was pushed forward by more immediate factors as well. One of these was the spirit and ideology of Progressivism. Professors, no less than politicians, caught the epidemic fever for reform. Opposition to boss rule in the cities had its counterpart in opposition to trustee rule in universities; certain instruments advocated by political reformers—the initiative, the primary, the referendum—were advocated as well by professors to make academic government more responsible. Cattell used Progressive ideas when he wrote that "no one believes that a city should be owned by a small self-perpetuating board of trustees who would appoint a dictator to run it, to decide what people could live there, what work they must do and what incomes they should receive. Why should a university be conducted in that way?" [13] Several universities took action in response to this kind of criticism. In 1916, on the basis

[9] H. Carrington Lancaster, "Memories and Suggestions," *Bulletin,* AAUP, XXVI (April, 1940), 220.

[10] Letter of Arthur O. Lovejoy to Gaynor Pearson, March 3, 1947, in Gaynor Pearson, "The Decisions of Committee A," unpublished Ed.D. dissertation (Teacher's College, Columbia University, 1948), p. 28.

[11] Lancaster, "Memories and Suggestions," p. 220.

[12] *Bulletin,* AAUP, II (March, 1916), 20. The eligibility rules of the Association did not bar all administrators. If at least half of the work of administrators was in teaching or research, they could be elected to membership. When an active member of the Association accepted an administrative position, he could continue as an associate member. Ralph E. Himstead, "The Association: Its Place in Higher Education," *Bulletin,* AAUP, XXX (Summer, 1944), 464.

[13] J. McKeen Cattell, *University Control* (New York and Garrison, N.Y., 1913), p. 35.

of answers to a questionnaire sent to college administrators, Stephen Duggan concluded that in filling vacancies on boards of private institutions there had been a trend away from co-option toward granting alumni representation (notably at Ohio Wesleyan and Pennsylvania), for presidents to consult heads of departments in matters of appointment, promotion, and tenure (Illinois, Reed, Kansas), for permanent heads of departments to be replaced by temporary chairmen (Harvard, Yale, Chicago, Illinois).[14]

But it was widely believed in this period that reform was too slow and scanty. This is apparent from the reaction to Cattell's plan for university government which he first proposed in 1906. Cattell did not see much point in tinkering with the old machinery; he preferred a new design. He would have had the university corporation include all the professors of the university, all its officers and alumni, and all the members of the community who wished to pay dues to belong. The corporation would elect the trustees, whose primary duty would be to care for the institution's property. The professors would elect the president, whose salary would not be larger, or position more dignified, than their own. The professors would be selected by the department and the university senate, subject to the veto of the trustees.[15] Having invited comment on his plan from American scientists, Cattell received 299 replies. The reaction to his proposal was not unanimous. Some did not agree with the spirit of the changes he advocated; others suggested alterations in details. A few cautioned against the parties and political intrigues that might result from such democratic innovations; a few emphasized the sterility of faculty deliberations and the personal animus and contentiousness that they assumed characterized faculty self-government. But the great majority of Cattell's respondents did agree that the powers of the trustees should be limited and faculty control much increased. Roughly 85 percent were on the side of change: an indication that on this issue a real consensus of opinion had been formed.[16] The logical next step in this Progressive age was a league for better government to realize such schemes for reform.

[14] Stephen P. Duggan, "Present Tendencies in College Administration," *School and Society,* IV (August 12, 1916), 233–34.

[15] Cattell, "University Control," *Science,* XXIII (March 23, 1906), 475–77.

[16] Cattell, *University Control,* pp. 23–24. The questionnaire was sent to Cattell's friends and acquaintances, and the figures may be biased on that account. On the other hand, they were sent to men in the natural sciences who, being generally favored by university governors, were probably not as opposed to the existing system as, say, their colleagues in the social sciences.

Progressivism also abetted the movement to standardize the theory and practice of academic freedom and tenure. Just as economists began to see the social costs of unregulated business enterprise, so professors began to see the liabilities of an uncoordinated academic system. As far as academic freedom was concerned, there was a wide diversity of opinion with respect to its principles and scope, and a wide diversity of practices with respect to its protection and aid. For other ambiguous freedoms, like those of speech and the press, the courts provided clarification. But there were practically no legal dicta on academic freedom as such.[17] In other institutions, custom fostered fixed standards; but the transformation of our universities had been too recent to allow tradition to regulate policy. Hence, in the hope of introducing some semblance of order, three learned societies collaborated in 1913 to formulate general rules of academic freedom and tenure. A joint committee, composed of members of the American Economic Association, the American Sociological Society, and the American Political Science Association, labored for a year to solve the thorny problem of principles.[18] At the end of its deliberations, it was compelled to conclude that the "subject bristled with complexities of such a character that [the committee] feels itself in a position at present to make only a preliminary report." On the issue of academic freedom, the committee was in doubt as to whether universal rules should apply to colleges as well as universities, to the teachers of immature as well as of advanced students, to men who pronounce on matters outside their subjects as well as to those who stay within their competence, to extramural as well as intramural utterances. It also could not decide where the line of propriety should be drawn: "Can freedom of speech be permitted to cover self-exploitation or mere desire for notoriety?" On the subject of tenure, it posed but could not answer such questions as whether a professor should be virtually irremoveable, as in the Continental universities; whether distinctions should be drawn "between a college and a university teacher, between an officer of higher grade and one of low grade, between

[17] To this day, the phrase "Academic Freedom" is not listed separately in the *Legal Digests* or in *Words and Phrases*. A recent survey of academic-freedom cases concludes that "the courts do not appear to have passed upon causes of dismissal raising direct questions of academic freedom at the university level." Thomas I. Emerson and David Haber, eds., *Political and Civil Rights in the United States* (Buffalo, 1952), p. 890.

[18] The members were eight professors and one journalist who were generally recognized as authorities in the field: Seligman, Ely, Fetter, Weatherly, Lichtenberger, Pound, Judson, Dealey, and Herbert Croly.

an officer of long standing and one of recent tenure"; whether there ought to be a trial before every dismissal; whether the reasons for dismissal should ever be suppressed, even in the supposed interest of the individual involved.[19] Plainly, one conference was not sufficient. What was needed was a continuous inter-disciplinary effort to clarify basic principles, and to build, out of case materials, a set of academic rules that would give to future thought some clear direction.

Finally, one striking incident drove home the need to perfect a machinery of investigation in academic-freedom cases.[20] In 1913, the high-handed orthodox Presbyterian president of Lafayette College forced the resignation of John M. Mecklin, an outspoken liberal philosopher.[21] Following the precedent established in the Ross case, Mecklin told his story (which he picturesquely entitled the victory of Calvin over Servetus [22]) to the two professional societies in which he was enrolled—the American Philosophical Association and the American Psychological Association. These associations appointed an investigating committee. Unfortunately, the precedent of the Ross case was followed all too closely: the attempt to elicit information from President Warfield met with the same evasive arrogance that President Jordan had displayed fourteen years before. The mild-mannered question, "May I express the hope that you will be good enough to let the committee have, from yourself personally, some more specific statement in regard to certain facts in the case," was answered by "I trust you will pardon me if I say that your committee has no relation to me personally which would justify my making a personal statement to you with regard to these matters." The committee roundly scored this official overbearance, which was all too common in the ruling echelons of academia:

[19] *Preliminary Report of the Committee on Academic Freedom and Academic Tenure* (December, 1914), pp. 1–6, 7.

[20] Cf. H. W. Tyler, "Comments on the Address by Dr. Capen," *Bulletin,* AAUP, XXIII (March, 1937), 204.

[21] Lafayette College in the period of Mecklin's tenure (1905–13) was facing in two directions: toward its early nonsectarian idealism and toward the orthodox high Calvinism of Princeton Seminary and its autocratic president. The desire to have the best of both worlds created great confusion as to what could be taught at the college. Mecklin's philosophical relativism, his interest in the philosophy of pragmatism, and his teaching of evolution led the president to demand his resignation. After his dismissal, Mecklin went to the University of Pittsburgh, where another kind of battle over economic philosophy was making academic freedom tenuous. In 1920, Mecklin took a chair at Dartmouth College. John M. Mecklin, *My Quest for Freedom* (New York, 1945), pp. 129 ff.

[22] *Ibid.,* p. 164.

The attitude thus assumed does not seem to this committee one which can with propriety be maintained by the officers of any college or university towards the inquiries of a representative national organization of college and university teachers and other scholars. We believe it to be the right of the general body of professors of philosophy and psychology to know definitely the conditions of the tenure of any professorship in their subject; and also their right, and that of the public to which colleges look for support, to understand unequivocally what measure of freedom of teaching is guaranteed in any college, and to be informed as to the essential details of any case in which credal restrictions, other than those to which the college officially stands committed, are publicly declared by responsible persons to have been imposed. No college does well to live unto itself to such a degree that it fails to recognize that in all such issues the university teaching profession at large has a legitimate concern.[23]

This was a lusty rebuke and well deserved, but it also underscored the inability of the learned society to muster enough power and prestige to persuade administrators to cooperate with it.

These, then, were some of the forces that worked toward professorial solidarity in the first decade and a half of the twentieth century. Yet, powerful as they were, it is doubtful that they would have produced a viable organization had the initiative not been taken by a few movers and shakers, by a few professors who, academically, had "arrived." The first call for a conference looking toward the formation of a national association was issued by eighteen full professors of Johns Hopkins University. It was addressed to the faculties of the nine leading institutions of the country, and seven of them—Clark, Columbia, Cornell, Harvard, Princeton, Wisconsin, and Yale—responded by sending delegates. The first meeting, at the Johns Hopkins Club, was an assemblage of academic notables. John Dewey and J. McKeen Cattell represented Columbia; Charles E. Bennett and E. L. Nichols, Cornell; Maurice Bloomfield and A. O. Lovejoy, Johns Hopkins; Edward Capps, E. M. Kammerer, and H. C. Warren, Princeton; C. S. Minot, Harvard.[24] These delegates, in turn, established a committee on organization, consisting of a select group of thirty-four, which included new stars, among them Roscoe Pound and W. B. Munro of Harvard, William E. Dodd of Chicago, Frank Thilly and

---

[23] Report of the Committee of Inquiry, "The Case of Professor Mecklin," *Journal of Philosophy, Psychology and Scientific Method*, XI (January, 1914), 70–81. Warfield was dismissed by the Lafayette trustees two weeks after the adoption of the Committee's report.

[24] *Science*, New Series, Vol. XXXIX (March 27, 1914), p. 459.

Alvin S. Johnson of Cornell.[25] Finally, when the organization had been mapped out, invitations were extended to "persons of full professorial rank whose names appeared on the lists of distinguished specialists prepared for the committee in each of the principal subjects." [26] This invitation was accepted by 867 professors in 60 institutions, who thus became charter members of the AAUP. The elitist inspiration and composition of the organization were reflected in the membership clause of the first constitution adopted, which provided that "any university or college teacher of recognized scholarship or scientific productivity who holds and for ten years has held a position of teaching or research" was eligible.[27] The membership base was only gradually broadened: in 1920, the required period of service in teaching or research was reduced to three years; in 1929, junior membership for graduate students was provided, with the right to attend the annual meetings but not to vote. The AAUP was not, as at first envisioned, "one big union for all," but a union of the aristocrats of academic labor.

It may be taken as a commentary on the prudence, the idealism, and the crochets of the American professoriate that, despite the eminence of the founders, quite a few prominent men had reservations about joining. J. E. Creighton of Cornell wrote to Lovejoy that

one or two of our most prominent men whose names we should especially like to get were anxious to know of what is involved in the proposal. They were impressed by the names of the J. H. U. signers; but wanted some assurance that the idea behind the movement was not that of attacking the existing condition of affairs in any destructive or antagonistic spirit.[28]

At the second meeting of the Association, Charles A. Beard, without his knowledge, was nominated for membership.[29] Two years later, when he was asked to remit his dues, Beard wrote to the secretary: "I beg to say that, to the best of my knowledge and belief, I have never joined the Association. I regarded it as a futile enterprise when it was begun, and the results have confirmed my suspicions." [30] Men of the caliber of

---

[25] Pearson, "Decisions of Committe A," p. 22.

[26] A. O. Lovejoy, "Organization of the American Association of University Professors," *Science,* New Series, Vol. XLI (January 29, 1915), p. 154.

[27] *Bulletin,* AAUP, I (March, 1916), 20.

[28] Letter of J. E. Creighton to A. O. Lovejoy, May 23, 1913, in Pearson, "Decisions of Committee A," p. 21.

[29] Letter of H. W. Tyler to Beard, June 21, 1917, in Seligman Papers.

[30] Letter of Charles A. Beard to H. W. Tyler, June 16, 1917, in Seligman Papers.

Barrett Wendell and Albert Bushnell Hart did not immediately join,[31] and W. T. Councilman of the Harvard Medical School justified his refractoriness with this comment:

The matter does not interest me. I am opposed to anything that savours of organization or the formation of societies of any sort. The modern habit of organization I regard as a pernicious form of activity. The present unfavorable conditions of university life will finally be remedied not by organization but by the refusal of capable men to enter into it.[32]

The academic bohemian, the conservative, and the radical all were wary. Still, the membership rolls showed continuous growth. Within six months, the Association had 1,362 members representing 75 institutions; by January, 1922, it had 4,046 members from 183 institutions.[33]

Because of the suspicion that the Association aroused in the profession it sought to serve and the hostility it incurred from the general public, the major effort of the leaders of the AAUP in the early years was to win respectability. A bellicose attitude toward trustees, a militant stand on academic freedom, any of the usual postures of the trade union, would have alarmed and repelled the great majority of American professors. Accordingly, the original conference call issued by the Johns Hopkins professors contained only a few references to academic freedom or to what might be called "unfair labor practices." The main goals of the association appealed to professors as professional men, not as employees.[34] Dewey, in his address to the committee on organization, scotched the idea that the investigation and punishment of infractions of academic freedom would preoccupy the attention of the Association:

I do not know of any college teacher who does not hold that such infringement, when it occurs, is an attack on the integrity of our calling. But such cases are too rare to even suggest the formation of an association like this. . . . In any case, I am confident that the topic cannot be more than an incident of the activities of the association in developing professional standards.[35]

But on this score the philosopher did not possess the gift of prophecy. The Association was astounded and disheartened by the calls that came from all over the country to lend its assistance to professors in their unequal

[31] Pearson, "Decisions of Committee A," p. 24. Hart was listed on the AAUP rolls in 1921.

[32] Letter of Councilman to Lovejoy, December 4, 1914, in Pearson, "Decisions of Committee A," p. 24. Councilman was listed on the AAUP rolls in 1921.

[33] *Bulletin*, AAUP, II (April, 1916), 3–4; *ibid.*, VIII (January, 1922), 51.

[34] *Ibid.*, II (March, 1916), 12.

[35] Thilly, "American Association of University Professors," p. 200.

struggles with administrators. Distress signals came from the University of Utah, where seventeen professors resigned in protest when four of their colleagues were unceremoniously removed; from the University of Colorado, where a law professor believed he had been fired for testimony given before a government commission; from Wesleyan University, where a professor believed he had been removed because of anti-Sabbatarian remarks delivered at a nearby club; from the University of Pennsylvania, where Scott Nearing, in a case that achieved great notoriety, was removed from the Wharton School; from the University of Washington, where three professors had been discharged.[36] However much the founders wished to devote themselves to long-run constructive tasks befitting a professional society, they could not evade the fact that professors in trouble looked to them as to a grievance committee, as their long-sought avenging arm. "To have failed to meet the demands," Dewey commented later, "would have been cowardly; it would have tended to destroy all confidence in the Association as anything more than a talking body. . . . The investigations of particular cases were literally thrust upon us." [37]

The pressure on the Association resulted in a bifurcation of its interests and activities. Even as Committee A on Academic Freedom and Academic Tenure was set to work to fashion general principles for the guidance of the profession, special investigative subcommittees were sent scurrying over the country, hearing professorial complaints, investigating actual conditions, writing up reports. Thus, on the one hand, the AAUP tried to function as an agency of codification, fixing its sights on the larger aspects of academic freedom and other professional problems. On the other hand, it had to function as an agency of group pressure, investigating cases and imposing penalties in response to immediate demands. To the historian of the AAUP and the profession, the long-term efforts of the Association may stand out as its greater contribution. But there

[36] "Report of the Committee of Inquiry on Conditions at the University of Utah," *Bulletin,* AAUP, I (July, 1915); "Reports of Committees concerning Charges of Violation of Academic Freedom at the University of Colorado and at Wesleyan University," *ibid.,* II (April, 1916); "Report of the Committee of Inquiry on the Case of Professor Scott Nearing of the University of Pennsylvania," *ibid.,* II (May, 1916); "Report of the Sub-Committee on the Case of Professor Joseph K. Hart of the University of Washington," *ibid.,* III (April, 1917).

[37] John Dewey, "Presidential Address," *Bulletin,* AAUP, I (December, 1915), 11–12. Such was the pressure on Committee A that three cases had to be referred to the learned societies: one, arising at Dartmouth College, to the American Philosophical Association; one, at Tulane University, to the American Physiological Society; one, at the University of Oklahoma, to the American Chemical Society. *Ibid.,* p. 18.

can be no doubt that, because of its immediate involvement in institutional conflicts, the Association became stamped, in lay and professional circles alike, as an organization of professorial defense. In the ensuing years, whatever else it accomplished, the reputation of the AAUP was to hinge on its successes and failures in recognizing and rectifying abuses.

ACHIEVEMENTS: THE AAUP AS AN AGENCY OF CODIFICATION

The first attempt of the AAUP to work out the scope and limits of academic freedom was Committee A's Report on Academic Freedom and Academic Tenure of 1915, the general philosophy of which we examined in a previous chapter. Briefly, its fundamental premises were that academic freedom was a necessary condition for a university's existence; that trustees occupied the position of public officials discharging a public trust; that the only exception to this was when they served private propagandistic purposes, in which case those purposes ought to be made explicit; that in the classroom professors were limited by the norms of neutrality and competence; that outside the university professors had the same right as any other citizens to freedom of utterance and action, limited only by the obligation to observe professional decorum. These ideas were not militant or extreme. The Report emphasized the unassailably respectable if somewhat bromidic point that there were no rights without corresponding obligations, that academic freedom was not academic license. It strained for balance in its judgments. In chiding those trustees who regarded professors as their employees and the university as their own private property, it also took account of the tradition that sanctioned this point of view, and of the restrictions imposed by the charters. Noting the malfeasance of certain wealthy donors and trustees, it also called attention to the danger of political pressure from popular movements of reform.

But the report contained more than generalities; it offered practical proposals as well. And it was over its specific demands, rather than its philosophical principles, that the major battles with academic trustees and administrators were to be fought. Its practical proposals had two main objectives. The first was to place some limitation on the trustees' prerogative to fire teachers. Quite tentatively, the Committee suggested that aberrant opinion should never be grounds for dismissal. It recognized however, that differences in traditions and local conditions made it difficult to apply uniform substantive limitations. But it held that the procedural limitations could and should be uniform. At this point, the Committee made one of its most controversial proposals: it suggested trials under faculty auspices.

> Every university or college teacher (at the rank of associate professor or above) should be entitled, before dismissal or demotion, to have the charges against him stated in writing in specific terms and to have a fair trial on those charges before a special or permanent judicial committee chosen by the faculty senate or council, or by the faculty at large.
> At such trial the teacher accused should have full opportunity to present evidence, and if the charge is one of professional incompetency, a formal report upon his work should be first made in writing by the teachers of his own department and of cognate departments in the university, and if the teacher concerned so desire, by a committee of his fellow specialists from other institutions appointed by some competent authority.[38]

The second objective of these practical proposals was to provide security and dignity in the academic job through definite rules of tenure:

> In every institution there should be an unequivocal understanding as to the term of each appointment. . . .
> In those state universities which are legally incapable of making contracts for more than a limited period, the governing boards should announce their policy with respect to the presumption of reappointment in the several classes of position, and such announcements, though not legally enforceable, should be regarded as morally binding.[39]

Academic freedom was the end: due process, tenure, and establishment of professional competence were regarded as necessary means.

These practical proposals were indicative not only of how much professors had come to rely on bureaucratic safeguards, but also of how much the views of these particular professors reflected their elite position. On every count, the proposals embodied a double standard to distinguish between academic men of high and low estate. Whereas teachers above the level of instructors were to be entitled to one year's notice of dismissal, instructors were only to be entitled to warning three months before the close of the academic year. Whereas those of the rank of associate and full professors were to be entitled to a judicial hearing, it was to be sufficient that the faculty approve the dismissal of anyone below that

---

[38] "Report," Committee on Academic Freedom and Academic Tenure, *Bulletin,* AAUP, I (December, 1915), 41–42.

[39] *Ibid.,* p. 41.

grade. Whereas all above the grade of instructor were to have permanent tenure after ten years' service, nothing was said about when trustees had to decide to promote or remove instructors. Tenure was identified with rank, but no length of service was specified to insure promotion to rank.[40] Perhaps these distinctions were not entirely the result of the oligarchic character of the Association. In 1915, the ratio of senior to junior officers in American institutions of higher learning was much larger than it subsequently became, particularly after the Great Depression, when cheap academic labor to serve in lower ranks was relatively easy to procure. But it was a weak architectural plan that embellished only the upper floors, and omitted provision for an orderly access to them.

The antagonism and misrepresentation that greeted the AAUP code were the best proofs that it was needed. An editorial writer for the New York *Times* wrote:

Academic freedom, that is, the inalienable right of every college instructor to make a fool of himself and of his college by . . . intemperate, sensational prattle about every subject under heaven, to his classes and to the public, and still keep on the payroll or be reft therefrom only by elaborate process, is cried to all the winds by the organized dons.[41]

Nor did certain academic governors show greater sapience than this journalist. Chancellor Day, who in 1895 had allegedly ejected John R. Commons from the University of Syracuse, observed:

If the professor has the right to give up his position because of his conscience and conviction, what about the right of the trustees to consult their consciences and convictions? Have they not as much right to act by their consciences as he has? Have they not the right to act according to their best judgment after securing all the facts?

This equation of the right to extinguish opinion with the right to express it drew an exasperated response from John Dewey:

It is bad enough when such insults to scholarship and scientific preparation come from a man in the street. It is literally appalling when they come from the head of a university, for, acted upon, they mean the death of American scholarship.[42]

One of the most significant reactions was that of the Committee on Academic Freedom and Tenure of Office of the Association of American

[40] *Ibid.,* pp. 40–41.
[41] "The Professors's Union," quoted in *School and Society,* III (January 29, 1916), 175.
[42] "Is the College Professor a 'Hired Man'?" *Literary Digest,* LI (July 10, 1915), 65.

Colleges, an organization of college presidents also founded in 1915. Without undertaking to debate the philosophical assumptions of the AAUP Report, the presidents' committee dismissed its practical proposals as presumptuous. "No way has yet been found," it asserted pontifically, "to play the 'cello or the harp and at the same time to direct the orchestra." The Committee seemed to feel that it had a better right to speak for professors than the AAUP, which, it observed, excluded from its membership the key men of the universities—the presidents—and a large number of academic teachers "who . . . may be doing work of as much importance as the members of the Association." The Committee was of the opinion that "a man who is truly dedicated to teaching is likely to recognize the importance of the division of functions and usually does not wish to participate, except in the most general way, in administration." Making the best of existing conditions is "more alluring to the right-minded man than a more general, more diffuse and more distracting distribution of privileges." [43] The Committe resorted to the argument perennially used by conservatives—the basic solidarity of all interests.

At the same time, the Committee was of the opinion that should this solidarity be endangered by a professor too obtuse to recognize it, the only appropriate course of action was for the professor to resign. It thought institutional harmony far more important to academic life than formal procedural protections. That, in order to preserve harmony, it would be just as appropriate for a trustee to resign, did not cross the minds of these executives:

A man who accepts a position in a college which he has reason to believe is a Christian institution and who, further, may properly infer that the canons of good taste forbid, perhaps, the asking when the contract is made, of intimate personal questions about his own religious belief, can scarcely assume that freedom of speech includes either the right privately to undermine or publicly to attack Christianity. The man called to the average college which believes in monogamy as essential in the upbuilding of student character can scarcely expect the college to submit to a long judicial process in tardily effecting his release if he openly states and on inquiry admits that he believes in free love.

Incompatability of temperament in an educational institution is as serious a problem as in marriage; and since no right-minded corporation will make a contract for life with a new teacher, divorce in a college would seem to be open to few objections provided it be done decently and in order.[44]

[43] "Report," Committee on Academic Freedom and Tenure of Office, *Bulletin*, Association of American Colleges, III (April, 1917), 49–50.
[44] *Ibid.*, p. 51.

The analogy of a marriage was vulnerable: it opened interesting possibilities of a suit for breach of promise or perhaps an award of something corresponding to alimony until the professor was able to rewed.

On the subject of tenure, the presidential committee had this to say:

[The Committee] would gladly leave to professors the determination of the professional standing of their fellows. But there is a bigger question and that is: Shall any association of university professors compel a corporation to retain in office for an indefinite time one who is manifestly unfit for that particular place . . . ?[45]

Of course, the AAUP had proposed no such thing. It had gone to pains to suggest a procedure by which the "manifestly" unfit could be discharged; it insisted only that this unfitness be made "manifest" to competent authorities. Nor did it propose that the AAUP should rate the qualifications of professors. The animus that produced such a gross distortion hardly needs underscoring.

If the claim that professors and administrators had identical interests needed any refutation, it was supplied by the following remarks with which the presidents embellished their report:

Since your Committee regard it as their duty to speak frankly, they would like to add that there are enough cases known to the educational world in which executives have saved institutions from scandal, graft and other grave perils by prompt action, even at great personal risk. . . .[46]

[Trustees] must do the best they can, giving a sense of security to teachers, but at the same time not unmindful that rarely does a teacher give the institution which he serves any sense of security or consider the larger interests of an institution if he has a chance to go to a wider field of usefulness at a greater salary. In fact, many an educational position is used—no one will deny—as a stepping stone to self-promotion, sometimes shamelessly.[47]

There are certain other cases which almost every institution has now and then to manage in which what a trustee of Cornell once called "vexels" or mischief-makers can break the continuity of an institution and set back for years its best interests. The very fact that "vexels" know that some excellent men in responsible positions sometimes advise that at any cost colleges get on with so-called impossible persons, is a distinct encouragement never given in a well-organized corporation to mischief-makers to retard administrative processes.[48]

The presidents' committee seemed to regard the AAUP Report as a revolutionary dictate rather than as a serious attempt to solve a profes-

---

[45] *Ibid.*, p. 54.   [46] *Ibid.*, p. 53.
[47] *Ibid.*, p. 55.   [48] *Ibid.*, p. 51.

sional problem. A document less distinguished for grammar or common sense than the presidents' report could hardly have been composed.

Interestingly enough, within six years the attitude of the AAC college presidents toward the AAUP Report took a complete turn. Perhaps the softening of animosities was the result of the cooperation between the two organizations during the country's involvement in the war. Another reason for the change may have been the reconstitution of the AAC's academic freedom committee, which, by 1922, had come under the able chairmanship of Dean Charles N. Cole of Oberlin, and had acquired C. F. Thwing, president of Western Reserve University, a noted historian of education, and William J. Hutchins, president of Berea College, the father of Robert Maynard Hutchins.[49] Certainly, credit must also be given to the merits of the AAUP Report, which loomed as a massive contribution compared with the efforts of its critics. At any rate, the leaders of American higher education proved to be educable. In its 1922 report, the AAC's Academic Freedom Commission referred graciously to the work of the AAUP as "significant and highly important." It went on to accept almost every argument that the AAUP Report had made. On the basic principles of academic freedom, it agreed that teaching should be free, and should be limited only by the requirements of neutrality and competence; that teachers acting or speaking outside the university had the right "to precisely the same freedom and the same responsibility as attach to all other persons, subject only to the necessity of protecting the good name and the welfare of the college against serious injury." [50] More remarkable was the wide area of agreement on faculty participation and tenure. The Commission agreed that all appointments and terminations of contracts should be made in conference with the departments concerned, and "might well" be approved by a faculty committee or the faculty itself. Reflecting the attitudes of the late war, the Commission declared that gross immorality or "disloyalty" were grounds for summary dismissal. But in all other cases, and

in all cases where the facts are in dispute, the accused teacher should always have the opportunity to be heard in his own defense by all bodies that pass

---

[49] The old committee was composed of Herbert Welch, President of Ohio Wesleyan; Lyman P. Powell, President of Hobart; William F. Slocum, President of Colorado; Robert J. Kelly, President of Earlham; and Alexander Meiklejohn, President of Amherst. Other members of the 1922 committee were H. M. Gage, President of Coe, and Roy C. Flickinger, President of Northwestern.

[50] "Report," Commission on Academic Freedom and Academic Tenure, *Bulletin, AAC*, VIII (March, 1922), 100.

judgment upon the case. In the trial of charges of professional incompetence, the testimony of scholars in the same field, either from his own or from other institutions, should always be taken.[51]

Tenure, after an unspecified period of probation, should be long-term, indefinite, or permanent; timely notice of dismissal should be given; the precise terms and expectations of every appointment should be stated in writing. The difference between the AAC and the AAUP had narrowed to details: the AAC added another reason for immediate dismissal without trial, namely financial exigency making drastic retrenchment necessary; and it omitted reference to some of the precise guarantees of due process that the AAUP Report had included.[52]

In its early years, the AAUP had been reluctant to join with the presidential organizations to formulate a code of academic freedom. "Standing alone and united," wrote Frank Thilly, the third president of the Association,

our influence is great; as one unit in a divided, perhaps hostile, group we are apt to lose our force. . . . At present we are slowly winning a battle here and there. . . . Might not an unsuccessful conference with the united representatives of our friend, the enemy, lead to a solid front against us? . . . Somehow I cannot help but feel that we shall be stronger if we do not entangle ourselves in foreign alliances, even though our progress may be slow.[53]

That this caution was justified at the time is amply supported by the first report of the AAC. But the concessions of the second AAC report disarmed the professors. After much preliminary negotiation, the American Council on Education called a conference in 1925 which was attended by representatives of the American Association of University Women, the American Association of University Professors, the Association of Governing Boards, the Association of Land Grant Colleges, the Association of Urban Universities, the National Association of State Universities, the Association of American Colleges, and the Association of American Universities. With only slight textual changes, the AAC's 1922 statement was adopted by the conference, though only the AAUP and the AAC endorsed it.[54] A great bridge had been crossed.

The colleges and universities did not incorporate the 1925 statement into their by-laws except in very rare instances. Cast in the form of

[51] *Ibid.,* p. 103.   [52] *Ibid.,* pp. 102–3.

[53] Letter of Frank Thilly to H. W. Tyler, March 21, 1917, in Seligman Papers.

[54] H. W. Tyler, "The Defense of Freedom by Educational Organizations," in *Educational Freedom and Democracy* (Second Yearbook of the John Dewey Society, New York, 1938), pp. 229–39.

mandatory rules, it was rejected by one board after another as a transgression of charter provisions. Giving equal weight to principles and procedures, it was rejected by presidents and trustees who balked at the formal machinery but accepted the spirit behind it. It was estimated in 1939 that only six or seven boards of trustees in the entire United States had adopted the statement formally.[55] The conviction that what was needed was a statement of policy that invited approval, not a set of rules that required adoption, led to a revision of the code by the AAUP and the AAC in 1938. The new conference at which this was done provided an opportunity to correct the long-standing discriminatory provisions against the lower-ranking members of the profession. A probationary period of six years was specified, after which the teacher, if he was retained, was to be entitled to permanent tenure. Notice of dismissal was to be given one year in advance for all teachers, even those on probation. Finally, the 1938 report declared that "during the probationary period a teacher should have the academic freedom that all other members of the faculty have." Another rift in the academic profession was closed.

The AAC endorsed the 1938 report with several amendments, which necessitated further consideration by the two associations. The new agreement, reached in 1940, changed the probationary period from six to seven years and eliminated the statement that the judgment of what constitutes fulfillment of the obligations of decorum should rest with the teacher.

As the fruit of a quarter-century of thought and labor, the 1940 statement deserves to be quoted in full:

The purpose of this statement is to promote public understanding and support of academic freedom and tenure and agreement upon procedures to assure them in colleges and universities. Institutions of higher education are conducted for the common good and not to further the interest of either the individual teacher or the institution as a whole. The common good depends upon the free search for truth and its free exposition.

Academic freedom is essential to these purposes and applies to both teaching and research. Freedom in research is fundamental to the advancement of truth. Academic freedom in its teaching aspect is fundamental for the protection of the rights of the teacher in teaching and of the student to freedom in learning. It carries with it duties correlative with rights.

Tenure is a means to certain ends; specifically: (1) Freedom of teaching and research and of extra-mural activities, and (2) A sufficient degree of

[55] See Henry M. Wriston, "Academic Freedom and Tenure," *Bulletin,* AAUP, XXV (June, 1939), 329.

economic security to make the profession attractive to men and women of ability. Freedom and economic security, hence tenure, are indispensable to the success of an institution in fulfilling its obligations to its students and to society.

ACADEMIC FREEDOM

(a) The teacher is entitled to full freedom in research and in the publication of the results, subject to the adequate performance of his other academic duties; but research for pecuniary return should be based upon an understanding with the authorities of the institution.

(b) The teacher is entitled to freedom in the classroom in discussing his subject, but he should be careful not to introduce into his teaching controversial matter which has no relation to his subject. Limitations of academic freedom because of religious or other aims of the institution should be clearly stated in writing at the time of the appointment.

(c) The college or university teacher is a citizen, a member of a learned profession, and an officer of an educational institution. When he speaks or writes as a citizen, he should be free from institutional censorship or discipline, but his special position in the community imposes special obligations. As a man of learning and an educational officer, he should remember that the public may judge his profession and his institution by his utterances. Hence he should at all times be accurate, should exercise appropriate restraint, should show respect for the opinions of others, and should make every effort to indicate that he is not an institutional spokesman.

ACADEMIC TENURE

(a) After the expiration of a probationary period teachers or investigators should have permanent or continuous tenure, and their services should be terminated only for adequate cause, except in the case of retirement for age, or under extraordinary circumstances because of financial exigencies.

In the interpretation of this principle it is understood that the following represents acceptable academic practice:

(1) The precise terms and conditions of every appointment should be stated in writing and be in the possession of both institution and teacher before the appointment is consummated.

(2) Beginning with appointment to the rank of full-time instructor or a higher rank, the probationary period should not exceed seven years, including within this period full-time service in all institutions of higher education; but subject to the proviso that when, after a term of probationary service of more than three years in one or more institutions, a teacher is called to another institution it may be agreed in writing that his new appointment is for a probationary period of not more than four years, even though thereby the person's total probationary period in the academic profession is extended beyond the normal maximum of seven years. Notice should be given at least one year prior to the

expiration of the probationary period if the teacher is not to be continued in service after the expiration of that period.

(3) During the probationary period a teacher should have the academic freedom that all other members of the faculty have.

(4) Termination for cause of a continuous appointment, or the dismissal for cause of a teacher previous to the expiration of a term appointment, should, if possible, be considered by both a faculty committee and the governing board of the institution. In all cases where the facts are in dispute, the accused teacher should be informed before the hearing in writing of the charges against him and should have the opportunity to be heard in his own defense by all bodies that pass judgment upon his case. He should be permitted to have with him an adviser of his own choosing who may act as counsel. There should be a full stenographic record of the hearing available to the parties concerned. In the hearing of charges of incompetence the testimony should include that of teachers and other scholars, either from his own or from other institutions. Teachers on continuous appointment who are dismissed for reasons not involving moral turpitude should receive their salaries for at least a year from the date of notification of dismissal whether or not they are continued in their duties at the institution.

(5) Termination of a continuous appointment because of financial exigency should be demonstrably bona fide.

The salutary influence of these written ordinances is unmistakable, though not precisely measurable.[56] Generally, they can be said to have conferred three benefits. First of all, they cut through the intellectual tangles in which thinking on the subject of academic freedom had become ensnarled. They indicated, for example, how professors could fight for academic freedom and yet accept the presence of denominational colleges in their midst. They demonstrated how greater faculty participation in choosing and retaining personnel could be reconciled with the unlimited prerogatives granted trustees by the charters. They showed how the need for a competent faculty could be adjusted to the equally strong need for a secure one. Though margins of vagueness remain, and new crises have demanded new formulations, the unending discussion over academic freedom has taken on a cogency and clarity that had been missing before 1915. For all this the AAUP deserves great credit. It was the pioneer, and its achievement inspired other agencies—the National Educational Association, the Progressive Education Association, the

---

[56] Evaluation of the work of the AAUP is difficult because the central files of the Association are inaccessible and in a very disorganized state. The inner story of the AAUP cannot be written until these files are opened to the historian.

American Civil Liberties Union, the American Federation of Teachers, and, as we have seen, the Association of American Colleges—to take part in the task of codification.[57]

Secondly, the *lex scripta* provided a standard for measuring publicized reforms. Thus, when in 1915 the University of Pennsylvania yielded to public criticism of its handling of the Scott Nearing case and undertook to revise its procedures, the AAUP had a yardstick with which to evaluate this reform. The provision for faculty-trustee cooperation in all dismissals won its approval, but the AAUP committee noted that there was no provision for a trial of scholars based on explicit charges, that there was no provision for judicial proceedings, and that no arrangement was made for eliciting the judgment of fellow specialists.[58] It was now possible to detect and indict the provisions for forms without substance, the variety of gestures without motion.

Finally, the AAUP was effective in getting academic administrators to accept its rules. Not all of its rules, not every administrator. The 1925 statement to the effect that doubtful extramural utterances of a teacher should be referred to a committee of the faculty was so little observed that it was dropped in the 1940 statement. Official recognition of the rules by statutory inclusion was, as we have seen, very rare. Nevertheless, the rules were useful as guides to administrative practice. To take one striking illustration: When the University of Minnesota rescinded in 1938 its action dismissing Professor Schaper during the First World War, it entered a statement upon its records that was a paraphrase of the words of the AAUP.[59] When an institution was ready to be enlightened, it had a formula and a text to draw upon.

ACHIEVEMENTS: THE AAUP AS AN AGENCY OF INVESTIGATION

In the second category of its activities, the AAUP was much less successful. Plunged into investigations from the very beginning, it excited ex-

[57] H. W. Tyler, "Defense of Freedom by Educational Organizations," pp. 243–48. It is interesting to note that the Association of American Universities has not established a committee on academic freedom, and that, aside from cooperating in the 1925 Washington Conference, it has not attempted to legislate on this question.

[58] "Report," Committee of Inquiry on the Case of Scott Nearing, *Bulletin, AAUP*, II (May, 1916), 42–57.

[59] See F. S. Deibler, "The Principles of Academic Freedom and Tenure of the American Association of University Professors," *The Annals of the American Academy of Political and Social Science*, CI (May, 1922), 136–37.

pectations among professors that it was unable and unwilling to fulfill. It neither would be nor could be a police department for ferreting out, a grand jury for sifting, or a trial court for testing all reports of academic injustice. That it *would not* be these things in all cases was assured by its temper and ideology. It did not wish to stiffen resistance by making frontal attacks upon administrators; it preferred to change underlying conditions rather than avenge the crimes which arose from them.[60] But even if it had wished to, it *could not* have served the academic world as policeman, judge, and jury. Finances and personnel had unavoidable limitations. Without an endowment or a subsidy from an outside source, entirely dependent upon a dues-paying membership which before 1940 was fewer than 15,000, the AAUP could not hope to support the battery of lawyers and field workers required for extensive operations. Except for the paid assistance it received from an executive secretary and a legal adviser, the latter appointed in 1926, the AAUP was dependent upon the voluntary help of its members. And there was the rub. To track down a case on a strange campus, the investigator needed the talents of a psychologist, a lawyer, and a philosopher—and an abundance of common sense. Those who were professional crusaders and those who could be easily cajoled were poor material for the job. Thus there were two groups of professors who could at once be eliminated—those who thought all administrators malevolent and those who were too susceptible to their charms. After these discriminations were made, the Association had to take regional factors into account. Since repeated visits to the campus might be necessary, the investigator could not be stationed far away; but since detachment and independence were required, a too close proximity might be undesirable. Finally, some of the most likely prospects for this difficult business eliminated themselves: it was not easy to dislodge a scholar from the peace and quiet of his study and prevail upon him to probe some remote external unpleasantness.

The AAUP had no alternative but to apportion its resources among the cases it received. Whenever possible, and not only out of necessity but out of policy, it tried to use its good offices to mediate between conflicting parties in a way agreeable to both sides. In 1934, it was estimated that for every case written up in the *Bulletin* of the Association, three were settled informally and quietly through mediation.[61] When this approach

---

[60] "Higher Learning in Time of Crisis," *Bulletin,* AAUP, XXVI (October, 1940), 542–46.

[61] Committee A, "Report for 1934," *Bulletin,* AAUP, XX (February, 1934), 99.

failed, the AAUP launched a full investigation into those cases that involved some fundamental question of general principle, or that involved more than one dismissal, or that exemplified a new abuse. In 1934, it was estimated that only half of the non-mediated cases received a full-dress investigation.[62] As a consequence, the AAUP investigations have served a limited purpose—to warn and to illustrate, rather than to avenge and redress.[63] As a consequence, too, the accounts of cases published in the *Bulletin* do not give an accurate picture of the state of academic affairs. On the one hand, they soften the outlines by presenting only a fraction of the abuses that come to the attention of the Association (mediated and non-pressed cases are presented only in statistical form). On the other hand, they make the picture too harsh by detailing only those cases that are not amenable to compromise or conciliation.[64]

Nevertheless, the cases reported in the *Bulletin*—there were 124 of them through 1953—can be categorized in such a way as to yield several interesting conclusions. It is significant that comparatively few of these cases involved a clear violation of the right to free expression. In only 20 of the 94 cases in which the AAUP held the administration to have been in the wrong was the existence of ideological pressure substantiated. In only 17 out of 94 cases was the extramural activity of the teacher one of the grounds for dismissal. On the other hand, in 57 cases, or in almost two thirds, the issues were intramural and largely personal, hinging on the jealousy between a president and a professor, or the conflict between strong personalities, or the petty vindictiveness of someone in high office, or—this was particularly true during the Depression—the decision to cut down the staff in an effort to economize. In 52 cases, the subcommittees found the president to have been autocratic and arbitrary. At one place, a professor and four colleagues were dismissed for having submitted a proposal recommending greater faculty participation in the governing of the college; the subcommittee found the president guilty of "serious ad-

[62] *Ibid.*

[63] A. M. Withers, "Professors and Their Association," *Journal of Higher Education,* XI (March, 1940), 126–28, 129; Walter W. Cook, "Address of the Retiring President," *Bulletin,* AAUP, XX (January, 1934), 85–87; Report of Committee A, "Academic Freedom and Tenure," *Bulletin,* AAUP, XX (February, 1934), 98–102; Ralph E. Himstead, "The Association: Its Place in Higher Education," pp. 463–65.

[64] Any teacher in a junior college, a four-year college or a university, of any rank, and regardless of whether he is a member of the Association, has the right to appeal to the AAUP to investigate his case.

ministrative incapacity." [65] At another place, a professor was dismissed for supporting a colleague who had been fired; the subcommittee found grave fault with the president and the trustees.[66] Elsewhere, a professor was dismissed because he refused to endorse a financial drive to build a business college, and because he charged that a disproportionate share of the funds was going to the managers of the campaign.[67] In certain places, presidential highhandedness and stupidity decimated faculty ranks. At DePauw University, during the five-year tenure of G. Bromley Oxnam as president, 60 persons on the faculty resigned, failed of reappointment, or were dismissed.[68] In investigating the Turner case at the University of Pittsburgh in 1934–35, the subcommittee found that 84 teachers of professorial rank had left the university during the last five years, and that administrative practices had "brought into the lives of the men and women of the faculty, and into the lives of those dependent upon them, acute anxiety, worry, and fear." [69] Were these cases not part of the police docket, one would assume that academic relations were utterly bereft of the ordinary decencies. This would not be true, any more than that reports of crime depict average patterns of behavior. But these cases do give color to the belief that administrative, not professorial, incompetence is the great unsolved problem of academic life.

The reported cases also justify the assumption that academic freedom is dependent upon academic tenure and due process. In fully 63 of the 94 cases in which the administration was held to blame, guarantees of tenure were absent and dismissal on short notice was permitted by the institution. Indeed, the absence of law and fixed procedure was the one element that these remiss institutions had in common. They were heterogeneous with respect to size, geographical location, and form of control. They even varied with respect to scholarly importance, though it is true that, with the exception of Pennsylvania, Yale, and Smith, none of the major private or state universities incurred the disgrace of appearing on

[65] "Report of the Committee of Inquiry on Conditions in Washburn College," *Bulletin,* AAUP, VII (January–February, 1921), 126.

[66] "Report on the University of Louisville," *Bulletin,* AAUP, XIII (October, 1927), 443–57.

[67] Report of Committee A, "Academic Freedom and Tenure," *Bulletin,* AAUP, XV (April, 1929), 270–76. The institution was Boston University.

[68] Report of Committee A, "Academic Freedom and Tenure," *Bulletin,* AAUP, XX (May, 1934), 295–302.

[69] Report of Committee A, "Academic Freedom and Tenure," *Bulletin,* AAUP, XXI (March, 1935), 248–56.

the Association's censure list. Clearly, there was a problem antecedent to and inclusive of the problem of protecting freedom, and that was the problem of establishing a government of law, not of whim.[70]

The question of how to penalize offending administrations was a nettling one. Methods of retaliation useful in other situations—the strike, the boycott, the picket line—were not available to the professors. It was therefore proposed that the publication of reports in the *Bulletin*—which had an uncertain punitive effect at best—should be supplemented by an AAUP "blacklist" of disapproved institutions. There was a long debate over this proposal. One side argued that the Association was incompetent to rate institutions, that there could not be just and complete classification, that the penalty would be visited on the innocent—the students and teachers—rather than on the guilty—the administrators—who were often prepared to brazen it out.[71] On the other side, the arguments were that the Association needed sharper weapons than those of moral suasion and publicity, and that the profession needed some device to warn academic candidates to keep away from contaminated places.[72] The tactic finally devised was a compromise between the two extremes. In 1931 the AAUP set up a list of "non-recommended" institutions (not a "blacklist," which carried trade union connotations, nor a list of institutions rated for degree of purity),[73] and it appended to that list the statement that no "censure is visited by the Association upon the whole institution or upon the faculty, but only upon its present administration." [74]

Only its most admiring devotees would claim that the AAUP has carried out its investigative function with a maximum of efficiency. The long time that elapses between the receipt of a complaint and the publication of a final report makes redress difficult and restitution all but impossible. The reports vary in fullness and relevance, and sometimes show the amateur's touch. The fact that institutions remain on the censured list

[70] Frank Thilly, "Presidential Address," *Bulletin*, AAUP, III (February, 1917), 8–9.

[71] See S. P. Capen, "Privileges and Immunities," in *The Management of Universities* (Buffalo, 1953), pp. 46–49.

[72] See L. L. Thurstone, "Academic Freedom," *Journal of Higher Education*, I (March, 1930), 136–38.

[73] In 1935, the word was changed to "ineligible." But since this made members of the faculty of listed institutions ineligible for membership in the Association at a time when they were most likely to join, in 1938 the heading was changed to "censured administrations" and members of those faculties were permitted to join.

[74] See H. W. Tyler, "Defense of Freedom of Educational Organizations," pp. 254–55.

for long periods of time is some indication that this is not as effective a device as it was hoped it would be (though it must also be remembered that the institutions placed on the list are among the more hardened offenders).[75] Frequently, the investigations stirred up so much resentment in administrative quarters that they evoked obstinacy, not remorse.[76] Still, in the balance sheet of forty years of continuous effort, positive contributions must also be entered. The AAUP introduced an apparatus for finding facts in a field that had been ruled heretofore by unevaluated testimony. It threw the light of publicity upon certain institutions wherein for years malpractices had gone undetected. The threat of an investigation was often all that was needed to give administrators second thoughts when they contemplated questionable actions. And in a sense, the very weakness of the AAUP was a healthy reminder that there was no substitute for courage on the part of each professor. Inadvertently, the AAUP gave strength to the maxim: If this shall be the land of the free, it must also be the home of the brave.

THE FIRST WORLD WAR, LOYALTY, AND THE AAUP

The crisis of 1917 plunged the academic profession into vast and unheralded new difficulties. A mob fanaticism arose that put every freedom in jeopardy. The American university, always vulnerable to the opinions of the community, could not escape its coercive spirit. Indeed, professors, being by trade and usually by disposition somewhat more detached from mass obsessions, became the particular targets of the country's enthusiasm and anxiety. All over the nation, patriotic zealots on boards of trustees, in the community, and on the faculties themselves, harassed those college teachers whose passion for fighting the war was somewhat less flaming

[75] Seven institutions were carried on the list for five years or fewer, five for from five to ten years, eight for from ten to fifteen years.

[76] As one example, there is the letter of J. T. Kingsbury, President of the University of Utah, to Nicholas Murray Butler, November 5, 1917: "The professors' committee headed by Professor Seligman of C. U. took for granted that it was treating me and the University of Utah very justly by publishing a blue book against the University of Utah and myself and so prejudicing the professors and institutions through the country as to prevent, if possible, the filling of the places made vacant. . . . Looking back now upon our disturbance I sometimes think that both the regents and myself probably made a mistake in showing Mr. Lovejoy the courtesy we did or in having anything whatever to do with him when he came to Utah to make an investigation." In Cattell Papers, Columbia University Library.

than their own. Suddenly, the gains for academic freedom that had painfully and gradually been won—the greater acceptance of the principle, the beginnings of a regime of academic law—were swept aside. With frightening quickness, the hard-to-learn manners of tolerance yielded to crude tribal instincts of taboo. The academic profession and its young Association confronted the almost total collapse of the moral and institutional safeguards that had been wrought in the slowness of time.

Nothing in the experience of the professors prepared them to deal with the problem of loyalty in a time of national emergency. No other orthodoxy commanded such allegiance; against no other orthodoxy was resistance so difficult to sustain. Unlike other heretics known to the republic, "the slacker," "the pro-German," "the pacifist" were liable to prosecution by the state. Unlike other hunts for heretics, the search for disloyal citizens was not confined to certain well-defined breeding grounds, but extended throughout the community. The new orthodoxy thus transcended every other in its power and its totality. It exceeded religious orthodoxy, for it was not limited by unchanging doctrine; it exceeded economic conventionalism, for it permitted no havens of dissent. Its pharisaical division of the saved and the damned was not only the concern of sectarians, but of every group in society.

In 1917, the cult of loyalty had a particular morbidness. It was widely feared that new Americans, whose loyalties were complicated by immigration, were not sufficiently patriotic. It was widely feared that many Americans, attracted to pacifistic ideals, were not sufficiently bellicose. Though deep and genuine loyalty does not seek or require advertisement, this country, in its insecurity, demanded public display. It encouraged oaths of loyalty—hollow rituals of affirmation; rallies for the sale of war bonds—unity via the spirit of the crowd; patriotic societies—censors of other people's public virtue. For all this, America was pathetically ill-equipped to define the loyalty it demanded. The country was not content to look for the overt forms of disloyalty in treasonable conduct; it sought subtler traces in ideas and ideologies. This was a dangerous course, rendered more so by our disparate traditions. What creed could define Americanism? What social or political stance was manifestly loyal or disloyal? The tendency was for loyalty to become that belief which the inquirer took for granted, disloyalty that belief which raised doubts in some beholder.

To survey only a few of the First World War academic-freedom cases is to reveal the vagueness of the new orthodoxy and the fervor with which it was enforced. In 1918, the Nebraska State Council of Defense submitted to the University of Nebraska Board of Regents a list of twelve professors who had, for one reason and another, "assumed an attitude calculated to encourage among those who come under their influence, within and without the university, a spirit of inactivity, indifference, and opposition towards this war and an undesirable view with respect to the several fundamental questions inseparable from the war." [77] After investigation, it was disclosed that three professors did variously believe in internationalism, impede the sale of liberty bonds, and criticize their more patriotic colleagues. For these transgressions, and after a trial by the board, the three professors were dismissed.[78] At the University of Virginia, Leon R. Whipple, director of the School of Journalism, was charged with disloyalty for a speech in which he declared that "we can win the war only by freeing the spirit of democracy in the Germans by good-will," that "war does not remove the menace of autocracy, [or] make the world safe for democracy," and that Russia will be the spiritual leader of the next generation. The president of the university, paying his respects to Whipple's energy, capacity, and attention to duty as a teacher, considered this speech "a document of disloyalty." After a trial by the Board of Visitors, Whipple was let go.[79] The University of Minnesota's Board of Regents had still another conception of what constituted disloyalty. It dismissed Professor William A. Schaper, chairman of the Department of Political Science, for having said that he did not wish to see "the Hohenzollerns . . . wiped out root and branch." [80] Schaper weighed on Minnesota's conscience: twenty years later the Board of Regents reinstated him, granted him the title of Professor Emeritus, and expunged the earlier verdict from the record. How another generation could regard the same problem and the same evidence is given in the statement written by the Board in 1938:

The Board of Regents sitting in 1938 recognizes with regret and not in a spirit of condemnation of its predecessors that periods of national crisis are characterized by widespread loss in social perspective and a strain upon the values that prevail when conditions are more nearly normal. It would also affirm in these calmer days and against another day of storm and stress that in

[77] *The Nation,* CVI (June 1, 1918), 639.
[78] Charles Angoff, "The Higher Learning Goes to War," *American Mercury,* XI (March, 1927), 188.
[79] Letter of Leon R. Whipple to *The Nation,* CV (December 20, 1917), 690–91.
[80] James Gray, *University of Minnesota* (Minneapolis, 1951), p. 247.

times of crisis the need for adherence to accepted values and traditions and procedures, especially by institutions of higher education, is most necessary.[81]

At Columbia University, an overzealous board of trustees, a dictatorial president, and a distinguished but personally offensive professor were the figures in a loyalty case that shook the academic world. To the Columbia Board of Trustees went the doubtful distinction of being the first private governing board to institute a general program of investigation in order to ascertain, as the minutes have it,

whether doctrines which are subversive of, or *tend to* the violation or disregard of, the Constitution or the laws of the United States or of the State of New York, or which *tend to encourage* a spirit of disloyalty to the government of the United States, or the principles upon which it is founded, are taught and disseminated by officers of the University.[82]

A Committee of Nine, consisting of five deans and four faculty members, was appointed to help the trustees inquire into the state and ultimate tendency of teaching in the university. The Columbia faculty was deeply affronted. The Faculty of Political Science thought the idea of a "general doctrinal inquisition" violated every principle of academic freedom.[83] A number of Columbia's luminaries, including Wesley C. Mitchell, Herbert L. Osgood, James T. Shotwell, and John Erskine, sent an angry rejoinder to the trustees:

The action taken by the Trustees . . . has in fact created . . . a general impression that disloyal doctrines are so extensively propagated by Columbia instructors that the authorities do not deem it sufficient to take action against individual offenders, but contemplate a regulation of instruction that will make such offenses rare if not impossible. Such an impression is both unjust and injurious. It is unjust, because Columbia is not a hot bed of disloyalty. . . . It is injurious because it discredits the loyalty of the University and seems to threaten its liberty.[84]

The Nation saw the absurdity of undertaking a limitless search to find felonious states of mind.

How is the investigating committee to go to work? Will it draw up a formidable questionnaire for all the professors . . . ? Perhaps it will be enough to station the clerk of the trustees near the lecturer's chair. How could there be

[81] "Higher Learning in Time of Crisis," *Bulletin,* AAUP, XXVI (October, 1940), 544.

[82] *Minutes of the Trustees of Columbia University,* XXXVII (March 5, 1917), 208. Italics supplied.

[83] Charles A. Beard, "A Statement," *New Republic,* XIII (December 29, 1917), 250.

[84] Petition to the trustees, undated, in Seligman Papers.

"disloyalty" in the awful presence of the clerk? . . . Should the trustees persist in their unexampled inquisition, however, they may expect the turn about which is fair play. The faculty might appoint a committee to investigate *them*. The instructions would be to "inquire and ascertain" whether the trustees were not suffering from a bad state of nerves.[85]

President Nicholas Murray Butler earned another dubious distinction for Columbia: he was one of the few university presidents who formally withdrew the privilege of academic freedom for the entire duration of the war. On June 6, 1917, at a Commencement Day gathering of the alumni, Butler declared that

so long as national policies were in debate, we gave complete freedom, as is our wont, and as becomes a university—freedom of assembly, freedom of speech, and freedom of publication to all members of the University who in lawful and decent ways might wish to inform and to guide public policy. Wrongheadedness and folly we might deplore, but we are bound to tolerate. So soon, however, as the nation spoke by the Congress and by the President, declaring that it would volunteer as one man for the protection and defense of civil liberty and self-government, conditions sharply changed. What had been tolerated before becomes intolerable now. What had been wrongheadedness was now sedition. What had been folly was now treason.

The president had an interesting conception of what was tolerable, and not seditious or treasonable:

This is the University's last and only warning to any among us, if such there be, who are not with whole heart and mind and strength committed to fight with us to make the world safe for democracy.[86]

Loyalty was defined in effect as the particular degree of indignation and bellicosity displayed by President Butler.[87]

Professor J. McKeen Cattell was one of the leading psychologists of his generation; but the psychology at which he was proficient was experimental, not applied. By all accounts he was brash, tactless, and offensive—

[85] "Trustees and College Teaching," *The Nation*, CIV (March 15, 1917), 305.

[86] Commencement Day Address, June 6, 1917, in Columbia University Archives.

[87] That Butler was suffering from war shock and not from any permanent disability is attested by his much-quoted statement on proprietary gifts which he made just after the war in one of his annual reports. An intimate of wealthy men and a political conservative, he was unequivocal in his condemnation of conditional gifts. "Under no circumstances should, or can, any self-respecting university accept a gift upon conditions which fix or hamper its complete freedom in the control of its own educational policies. . . . No university is so poor that it can afford to accept a gift which restricts its independence, and no university is so rich that it would not be impoverished by an addition to its resources which tied the hands of its governing boards." Nicholas Murray Butler, *Annual Report* (1919), pp. 7–8.

not only to the president, with whom he conducted a running battle for years, but to such kind and patient colleagues as E. R. A. Seligman and John Dewey. As early as 1910, President Butler, stung by Cattell's charge that he regularly acted as an autocrat, substantiated the charge by proposing to the trustees that Cattell be removed or that steps be taken to silence him.[88] The trustees did not then take action. In 1913 they moved to retire Cattell without his consent, but certain members of the faculty interceded and helped forestall final action.[89] Cattell was not made prudent by the precariousness of his position. In 1917, he wrote a letter to the faculty in which he referred to the president as "many talented and much climbing" and in which he suggested that the president's house should be expropriated and used for the benefit of the teachers.[90] Once more, the trustees, this time with much faculty assent, were ready to dismiss Cattell, but were headed off by his note of apology. Cattell remained unreconstructed, however: in a letter to Seligman, he criticized his colleagues for taking offense at his *lèse majesté*, and attributed their attitude to "the traditionalism and the conventionalism, the lack of perspective and the lack of humor, which deaden university life." [91] He evidently preferred exhibitionism and acrimony to enliven it.

The ineptness of the president and the trustees matched that of the professor. When they finally discharged him, it was not over the issue of his personality, but over the issue of his loyalty. One supposes that, in the shallow perspective of wartime, this seemed to be the stronger ground, the one most likely to appeal to a public excited by war and Wilsonian rhetoric. But if this was the motive, it was grievously at fault, for it converted a possibly valid case of dismissal for personal unfitness into an indefensible attack upon academic freedom. What Cattell did to precipitate his dismissal was to send a petition (on a Columbia University letterhead) to three Congressmen, urging them not to approve a bill then pending which would have sanctioned the use of American conscripts on European battlefields.[92] With appalling disrespect for the constitutional privi-

[88] Extract from the *Minutes of the Committee on Education* (trustees) (December 22, 1910), in Cattell Papers.

[89] Letter of Edmund B. Wilson to Butler, May 20, 1913; M. I. Pupin to Butler, May 19, 1913, in Cattell Papers.

[90] J. McKeen Cattell, "Confidential Memorandum to Resident Members of the Faculty Club," January 10, 1917, in Cattell Papers.

[91] Letter of Cattell to Seligman, March 8, 1917, in Cattell Papers.

[92] Letters of Cattell to Julius Kahn of California, S. Wallace Dempsey of New York, and E. R. Bathrick of Ohio, August 23, 1917, in Cattell Papers.

lege of petition, the three Congressmen told Butler about it, one of them complaining that Cattell was "sowing the seeds of sedition and treason with the sanction of the institution." [93] That was the final straw. "We have got the rascal this time!" the clerk of the trustees exulted.[94] So eager was the board to make disloyalty the gravamen of their charge against Cattell that they overrode the faculty recommendation that he be retired without any mention of the grounds. They publicly bracketed his dismissal with that of Henry Wadsworth Longfellow Dana, an assistant professor of comparative literature, who was condemned for having encouraged student agitation against the Conscription Act while it too was pending.[95] To cap it all, the trustees issued a statement to the press which erroneously declared that the university's faculties had seconded their action.[96] Incompetence was often a miry ground on which to justify dismissal, but compared to the charge of disloyalty, it was as a high plateau to a swamp.

The swamp was soon to ensnare less offensive Columbia professors. In 1916, Dr. Leon Fraser, instructor in politics at Columbia College, made some critical remarks about the military camp in Plattsburg. For this he was haled before a committee of the trustees, and, in the following year, was discharged. Ironically, Fraser had been engaged to work for the Association for International Conciliation, a pacifist organization, by none other than President Butler—but this had been before pacifism became unacceptable, and the young instructor was not sufficiently resilient to change his mind with the times.[97] Soon afterwards, the eminent historian Charles A. Beard was summoned before the trustees' star chamber. A sensationalistic newspaper had accused Beard of condoning a speaker

[93] Letter of Julius Kahn to Butler, August 27, 1917, in Cattell Papers.

[94] Letter of John B. Pine, Clerk of the Trustees, to Butler, September 21, 1917, in Cattell Papers.

[95] The Committee of Nine asked the trustees to give no publicity to Dana's dismissal, and to grant him a leave of absence without salary for the remainder of the year. In this, as well as in the Cattell case, the trustees overruled the committee of faculty members and deans. *Report of the Committee of Nine* (October 9, 1917), p. 5.

[96] New York *Times*, October 2, 1917. The only support that the trustees received officially from the faculty was a statement from eight members of the Committee on Instruction of the Schools of Mines, Engineering, and Chemistry. Letter to Butler, September 19, 1917, in Cattell Papers. The Committee of Nine, though it recommended the retirement of Cattell, did so without referring to his patriotism. Letter of Seligman to George L. Ingraham, Chairman of the joint committee of the trustees, September 24, 1917, in Seligman Papers.

[97] *Minutes of the Trustees of Columbia University*, XXXVI (May 1, 1916), 292–93; Beard, "A Statement," p. 250.

who was alleged to have said "To Hell with the Flag." Despite his public denial, Beard had to convince the board that he had never condoned that statement. Evidently he did so convince it. But the board did not let him go without casting further aspersions upon his colleagues. Demanding its ounce of prevention, it ordered Beard to warn the other Columbia historians that teachings "likely to inculcate disrespect for American institutions" would not be tolerated. "I repeated my order to my colleagues," wrote Beard, "who received it with a shout of derision, one of them asking me whether Tammany Hall and the pork barrel were not American institutions!" [98] A week after Dana and Cattell fell, Beard handed his resignation to President Butler:

Having observed closely the inner life of Columbia for many years, I have been driven to the conclusion that the University is really under the control of a small and active group of trustees who have no standing in the world of education, who are reactionary and visionless in politics, narrow and medieval in religion. . . . I have, from the beginning, believed that a victory for the German Imperial Government would plunge all of us into the black night of military barbarism. . . . But thousands of my countrymen do not share this view. Their opinions cannot be changed by curses or bludgeons. Arguments addressed to their reason and understanding are our best hope.[99]

Before the loyalty craze had run its course at Columbia, two other professors, Henry R. Mussey, assistant professor of economics, and Ellery C. Stowell, associate professor of international law, also resigned.[100]

The grim story of academic freedom during the First World War is relieved by at least one president's moral courage and one board's emotional calm. In 1916, a story was circulated in the press that a Harvard alumnus was threatening to annul a bequest of $10,000,000 to Harvard unless the openly pro-German professor, Hugo Münsterberg, was deprived of his chair. The Harvard Corporation stated officially that the "University cannot tolerate any suggestion that it would be willing to accept money to abridge free speech, to remove a professor or to accept his resignation." [101] And President Lowell, in the next year's annual report, stood four-square for academic freedom in wartime:

[98] Beard, "A Statement," p. 249.

[99] Letter of Beard to Butler, *Minutes of the Trustees*, XXXVIII (October 8, 1917), 89–90.

[100] Letter of Mussey to Seligman, November 6, 1917, in Cattell Papers; *Minutes of the Trustees*, XXXVIII, 145–46, 299.

[101] Henry Aaron Yeomans, *Abbott Lawrence Lowell, 1856–1943* (Cambridge, Mass., 1948), p. 316.

If a university or college censors what its professors may say, if it restrains them from uttering something it does not approve, it thereby assumes responsibility for that which it permits them to say. This is logical and inevitable, but it is a responsibility which an institution of learning would be very unwise in assuming. It is sometimes suggested that the principles are different in time of war; that the governing boards are then justified in restraining unpatriotic expression injurious to the country. But the same problem is presented in war time as in time of peace. If the university is right in restraining its professors, it has a duty to do so, and it is responsible for whatever it permits. There is no middle ground. Either the university assumes full responsibility for permitting its professors to express certain opinions in public, or it assumes no responsibility whatever, and leaves them to be dealt with like other citizens by the public authorities according to the laws of the land.[102]

It had taken centuries for Henry Dunster's college to achieve such a high degree of balance and sanity.

For the AAUP, the potion of war produced intense internal conflicts. The Association could not, lest it betray all that it stood for, consider freedom a peacetime luxury. Its docket of academic-freedom cases was filling up with sordid evidences of the censorship that called itself patriotism and the malice expressed in the name of loyalty. At the same time, it had given itself without compunction to those martial symbols and apocalyptic hopes with which America goes to battle. Its historians had given up research to write propaganda tracts for the Committee on Public Information; its scientists were devoting their skills to the multifarious problems of war.[103] Most of its leaders—Arthur Lovejoy, John Dewey, Franklin Giddings, to name only a few—had gladly enrolled in the campaign to sell the war to Americans. In 1918, the AAUP sent an official message to the President of the United States, expressing its "hearty and grateful approval of the course you have pursued in calling the nation to arms against a foe who has ruthlessly violated the rights of law-abiding and peaceful peoples." [104] For this group, loyalty had not one focus but two, and the problem that had to be decided was which would be given precedence.

The report of the AAUP Committee on Academic Freedom in Wartime presented the Association's decision. "There are two sides," it said, "to the duty of the citizen in time of war." The more urgent duty was to help

[102] *Ibid.*, pp. 311–12.

[103] Merle Curti, "The American Scholar in Three Wars," *Journal of the History of Ideas*, III (June, 1942), 241; Guy Stanton Ford, *On and Off the Campus* (Minneapolis, 1938), pp. 73–100; F. P. Keppel, "American Scholarship in the War," *Columbia University Quarterly*, XXI (July, 1919), 171.

[104] *Bulletin*, AAUP, IV (January, 1918), 8.

win it. The other—less obvious and perhaps less appealing—was to preserve democratic institutions. But, it declared, and with this declaration it took its stand on the problem of loyalty, all the processes of democracy cannot go on in time of war.

When . . . a democracy finds itself forced into war in defense of its rights, of the integrity of the law of nations, and of the safety of democracy throughout the world, it will, if it has any practical wisdom, temporarily adapt its methods of political action and of governmental procedure to the necessities of the grave and perilous business immediately in hand.

What this gospel of expediency portended for academic freedom was soon made apparent. The Committee cited four grounds on which academic authorities might legitimately dismiss professors, and only one of them presupposed prior punitive action by the government. These were: (1) "conviction of disobedience to any statute or lawful executive order relating to the war"; (2) "propaganda designed, or unmistakably tending, to cause others to resist or evade the compulsory service law or the regulations of the military authorities"; (3) action designated "to dissuade others from rendering voluntary assistance to the efforts of the Government"; (4) in the case of professors of Teutonic extraction and sympathy, violating the obligation "to refrain from public discussion of the war; and in their private intercourse with neighbors, colleagues and students, to avoid all hostile or offensive expressions concerning the United States or its government." [105] The various qualifications that the Committee introduced—that trustees should exercise magnanimity in dealing with pacifists, that teachers should be spared the extreme penalty of dismissal on their first offense, that the proceedings should be strictly judicial in character—were of comparatively small importance. The Committee, as the *Nation* put it, "hands over the keys of the castle to the enemy." [106] It assumed that the war had fundamentally changed the conditions of academic freedom. It assumed what Lowell denied, that the university should be responsible for its professors' outside utterances. It accepted the premise that the university might impose greater restrictions of speech upon its members than the state imposed upon its citizens. The unnerved professors of the Committee bear witness that not all the casualties of war are to be found upon the battlefield.

[105] "Report," Committee on Academic Freedom in Wartime, *Bulletin*, AAUP, IV (February–March, 1918), 30. The Committee was composed of A. O. Lovejoy, Edward Capps, and A. A. Young.

[106] "The Professors in Battle Array," *The Nation*, CVI (March 7, 1918), 255.

Though civil liberties were under attack for years after the war, academic freedom suffered most during the period of the war itself. In this respect, the pattern of inquisition in that day differs from the one existing today: academic freedom, relatively little affected during the Second World War, has been severely tried in the post-war, cold-war atmosphere. There are other differences and some similarities between that day and this, which we set down by way of linking the present work to its companion volume.[107] After the First World War, as at the time of writing, disloyalty in a time of national danger was the central problem. At both times "loyalty" was defined with a woolly vagueness. At both times, as suspicion began to fray the social fabric, certain pathological types rose to national prominence: the informer, whose repeated purgations of guilt acquired the public's sanction; the defamer, whose aggressions against his fellows took socially acceptable forms; the investigator, who was allowed to pry and accuse without the customary judicial restraints. Finally, at both times, the public, called upon to judge difficult problems of individual guilt or innocence, took refuge in the passive and naive assumption that where there is smoke there must be fire, neglecting to inform itself as to whether there might not in fact be a smokescreen. These are some of the constants, some of the similarities in tone.

But the differences are more important. Academic freedom faces in some ways a more ponderable threat today. For one thing, the present generation has inherited the burden of the infatuation with Communism in the 1930s, an involvement wider and more compromising than, say, the involvement of the professors of an earlier day in Wobblyism, or Socialism, or pan-Germanism. There are now just enough skeletons in professorial closets—not many, to be sure—to give investigators into "disloyalty" some return for their labors. Moreover, the greater danger in the present situation stems from the nature of the Communists' operations. When Cattell was fired from Columbia in 1917, there was no question about what he had done—he had petitioned Congress not to send our troops abroad; everyone knew where he stood, and the issue for the faculty and for professional opinion was whether this behavior merited that punishment. But the secretive character of Communist activities—in part the result of their repression, in part the result of their masked language and tactics of infiltration—argues for an apparatus of investigation, not to discover the propriety of a professor's act, but to discover

[107] Robert M. MacIver, *Academic Freedom in Our Time* (New York, 1955).

whether the act was ever committed. The alleged act in addition, is rarely as overt as indiscreet speech, rarely as apparent as open indoctrination, but is usually a pattern of association from which subversive intentions are inferred. This makes, or threatens to make, investigation—by trustees, by state legislative committees, by filiopietistic groups—a built-in characteristic of academic life, an organ of administration, interminable because it is nonspecific, incalculable in effect because it rarely relates to professional behavior. And, of course, most important in any comparison is the fact that peace has not yet come after the Second World War to give the tension of superpatriotism a chance to relax, to permit the usual libertarian reaction.

But if these are the ways in which the present crisis seems worse than the previous one, there are other ways in which it seems decidedly better. A more sympathetic and profound understanding of academic freedom is more widespread among teachers, administrators, and trustees today than in 1917. The institutional mechanisms for the defense of academic freedom are far better developed. The prevalence of rules of tenure, the technique developed by the AAUP for investigating cases, are important modern protections. The AAUP, today an organization of 42,000, is a power of some significance in the academic world. In the present climate of opinion, these factors are not sufficient to give courage to the circumspect or timid, but they provide a considerable measure of security for professors who have the hardihood to assert themselves.

No one can follow the history of academic freedom in this country without wondering at the fact that any society, interested in the immediate goals of solidarity and self-preservation, should possess the vision to subsidize free criticism and inquiry, and without feeling that the academic freedom we still possess is one of the remarkable achievements of man. At the same time, one cannot but be appalled at the slender thread by which it hangs, at the wide discrepancies that exist among institutions with respect to its honoring and preservation; and one cannot but be disheartened by the cowardice and self-deception that frail men use who want to be both safe and free. With such conflicting evidence, perhaps individual temperament alone tips the balance toward confidence or despair.

GPSR Authorized Representative: Easy Access System Europe, Mustamäe tee
50, 10621 Tallinn, Estonia, gpsr.requests@easproject.com